OECD Thematic Review
of Early Childhood Education and
Care Policy in Ireland

BAILE ÁTHA CLIATH
ARNA FHOILSIÚ AG OIFIC AN TSOLÁTHAIR
Le ceannach díreach ón
OIFIG DHÍOLTA FOILSEACHÁN RIALTAIS,
TEACH SUN ALLIANCE, SRÁID THEACH LAIGHEAN, BAILE ÁTHA CLIATH 2,
nó tríd an bpost ó
FOILSEACHÁIN REALTAIS, AN RANNÓG POST-TRÁCHTA,
51 FAICHE STIABHNA, BAILE ÁTHA CLIATH 2,
(Teil: 01 - 6476834/35/36/37; Fax: 01 - 6476843)
nó trí aon díoltóir leabhar.

DUBLIN
PUBLISHED BY THE STATIONERY OFFICE
To be purchased directly from the
GOVERNMENT PUBLICATIONS SALES OFFICE,
SUN ALLIANCE HOUSE, MOLESWORTH STREET, DUBLIN 2,
or by mail order from
GOVERNMENT PUBLICATIONS, POSTAL TRADE SECTION,
51 ST. STEPHEN'S GREEN, DUBLIN 2,
(Tel: 01 - 6476834/35/36/37; Fax: 01 - 6476843)
or through any bookseller.

Price: €10.00

The views expressed in the document are those of the authors and do not necessarily reflect the opinions of the Irish authorities, the OECD or the OECD Directorate for Education.

Design > Q design/print@4908 201

FOREWORD

Minster for Education and Science

The OECD's Thematic Review of Early Childhood Education and Care Policy in Ireland represents a wide-ranging examination of the area in the Irish context. I welcome this report as both an assessment of the current situation and as a stimulus to debate and reflection on the future of early childhood education and care provision.

In Ireland and elsewhere there has been growing recognition of early years education and care as key factors in combating disadvantage and promoting equality of opportunity at every level of life experience. Research has shown that access to quality pre-school services plays a vital role in preparing children for entry into primary education. It also has potentially significant long-term benefits both to the individual and society.

In preparation for the Review, a detailed *Background Report* was commissioned by my Department. This sets out the context of current early childhood services in Ireland and analyses recent developments in policy and practice. The Report was prepared in consultation with relevant Departments, agencies and stakeholders and was presented to the OECD Directorate for Education's review team prior to their visit here.

In compiling their *Country Note,* the team were able to draw upon their considerable international experience and expertise in the field of early childhood education and care. Their recommendations focus on the key aspects of quality, access and co-ordination of provision in Ireland and will no doubt provoke much interesting discussion amongst policy-makers, agencies, parents and those practicing in the field.

I am happy that both documents, the *OECD Country Note* and the Irish *Background Report,* are published together in the present volume. In order to gain a holistic overview of this complex and evolving sector, it makes logical sense that the two reports should be read in tandem.

I would like to extend my sincere thanks to the OECD Directorate for Education for facilitating us in our request for this review. I would like to acknowledge the professionalism and dedication of the team headed up by John Bennett, who carried out such an insightful analysis of the area during their visit. I would also like to express my appreciation to the Editorial Committee who assisted Carmel Corrigan with the preparation of her excellent *Background Report* and who provided assistance to the OECD authors during the drafting process.

I congratulate and thank all those who were involved in this work.

Noel Dempsey

Noel Dempsey, T.D.,
Minister for Education and Science.

RÉAMHFHOCAL

An tAire Oideachais agus Eolaíochta

Tugann Athbhreithniú Téamach an ECFE ar Pholasaí Oideachais agus Cúraim don Luath-Óige in Éirinn léargas fairsing ar an earnáil sin i gcomhthéacs na hÉireann. Fáiltím roimh an tuarascáil seo mar mheasúnú ar an scéal faoi láthair agus mar ábhar díospóireachta agus ábhar machnaimh ar sholáthar oideachais agus cúraim don luath-óige amach anseo.

In Éirinn agus in áiteanna eile tá sé aitheanta níos fearr ná mar a bhíodh cé chomh bunúsach agus atá oideachas agus cúram luath-óige chun an ceann is fearr a fháil ar mhíbhuntáiste agus chun comhionannas deiseanna a chur chun cinn ag gach leibhéal de shaol an duine. Tá sé léirithe ag taighdeoirí go mbíonn páirt ollmhór ag an rochtain ar dhea-sheirbhísí réamhscoile in ullmhú leanaí don bhunoideachas. Bíonn buntáistí fadtéarmacha aige chomh maith don indibhidiúil agus don chomhluadar.

Mar ullmhúchán don Athbhreithniú choimisiúnaigh mo Roinnse *Tuarascáil Chúlra* mionsonraithe. Déantar cur síos ann ar chomhthéacs na seirbhísí luath-óige mar atá in Éirinn faoi láthair agus déantar mionscagadh ann ar an méid atá tarlaithe le blianta beaga anuas maidir le polasaí agus cleachtas. Réitíodh an Tuarascáil i gcomhchomhairle le Ranna, gníomhaireachtaí agus páirtithe leasmhara agus cuireadh faoi bhráid fhoireann athbhreithnithe Stiúrthóireacht Oideachais an ECFE é sular tháinig siad ar cuairt anseo.

Agus iad ag cur an *Nóta Tíre* le chéile, níor bheag an cúnamh don fhoireann a dtaithí agus a saineolas idirnáisiúnta i réimse an oideachais agus an chúraim luath-óige. Díríonn a moltaí ar na príomhghnéithe, caighdeán, rochtain ar, agus comhordú an tsoláthair in Éirinn agus gan amhras spreagfaidh sé mórán phlé i measc lucht déanta pholasaí, i measc gníomhaireachta agus tuismitheoirí, agus ina measc siúd atá ag cleachtadh sa réimse sin.

Is maith liom go bhfuil an dá cháipéis, *Nóta Tíre an ECFE* agus *Tuarascáil Chúlra* na hÉireann, dá bhfoilsiú le chéile san imleabhar seo. Má táthar chun forbhreathnú iomlán a fháil ar an earnáil chasta seo, luíonn sé le ciall go léifí an dá thuarscáil i ndiaidh a chéile.

Ba mhaith liom buíochas ó chroí a ghlacadh le Stiúrthóireacht Oideachais an ECFE as géilleadh d'ár n-iarratas go ndéanfaí an t-athbhreithniú seo. Ba mhian liom a admháil chomh maith chomh gairmiúil agus chomh tiomanta agus a bhí an fhoireann a stiúir an tUasal John Bennett, a rinne anailís ghrinn ar an réimse le linn a gcuairte. Ba mhian liom buíochas a ghlacadh freisin leis an gCoiste Eagarthóireachta a chuidigh leis an Uasal Carmel Corrigan agus í ag ullmhú na Tuarascála Cúlra, atá go sár-mhaith, agus a thug cúnamh d'údair an ECFE le linn an phróisis dhréachtaithe.

Tréaslaím le gach duine a raibh baint acu leis an obair seo agus glacaim buíochas leo.

Noel Dempsey

Nollaig Ó Díomasaigh, T.D.,
Aire Oideachais agus Eolaíochta.

FOREWORD

OECD Directorate for Education

Interest in early childhood education and care has surged in OECD countries over the past decade. Policy makers have recognised that access to quality early childhood education and care strengthens the foundations of lifelong learning for all children, contributes to equality of opportunity for women, and supports the broad educational and social needs of families. Research shows too that families operate best in a framework of security supported by services, and that young children develop well within quality early childhood services.

Recognising that cross-national information and analysis can contribute to the improvement of policy development, the OECD Education Committee launched the Thematic Review of Early Childhood Education and Care Policy in 1998. To date, twenty countries have volunteered to participate in the review: Australia, Austria, Belgium, Canada, Czech Republic, Denmark, Germany, Finland, France, Hungary, Ireland, Italy, Korea, Mexico, the Netherlands, Norway, Portugal, Sweden, the United Kingdom and the United States.

In interventions at Education Committee meetings at OECD headquarters, delegates from the Irish Department of Education and Science have strongly supported the project. They have assigned a high priority to the goal of improving access to and quality in early childhood education and care in Ireland, with the aim of strengthening the foundations of lifelong learning. In the context of the rapidly expanding Irish economy and of unprecedented labour force participation by women, the Department invited in 2002 a review of early childhood education and care services in Ireland. The present volume, combining the Irish Background Report and the OECD Country Note, provides an analysis of the situation in Ireland at that time.

Throughout this Country Note, the suggestions offered by the OECD review team are tentative, in recognition of the difficulty facing a visiting team—no matter how well briefed—in fully grasping the variety and complexity of a country-wide system. For this reason, our recommendations are offered to the ministries involved in early childhood education and care in Ireland not as hard and fast conclusions, but in a spirit of professional dialogue for the consideration of Irish policy makers and specialists. We trust, however, that our external perspective, based on comparisons with other OECD countries, will prove to be a useful basis for discussion and progress.

In particular, I wish to thank personally Minister Noel Dempsey and the Department of Education for their support to the OECD reviews and for the publication and dissemination of this report. Their conduct of the review was exemplary throughout, guided by the desire to allow the OECD team to interview as wide a range of stakeholders in the early childhood field in Ireland as was possible in a weeklong visit. It gives me pleasure also to acknowledge the key contribution to this work made by John Bennett from the Education and Training Policy Division of OECD's Directorate for Education.

Barry McGaw, Ph.D.
Director
Directorate for Education, OECD

RÉAMHFHOCAL

Stiúrthóireacht Oideachais ECFE

Tá an-bhorradh tagtha ar spéis an phobail in oideachas agus cúram luath-óige i dtíortha ECFE le deich mbliana anuas. Aithníonn lucht déanta polasaí go láidríonn rochtain ar luath-oideachas agus cúram atá ar ardchaighdeán bunús na foghlama fadsaoil do chuile leanbh, go gcuireann sé le comhionnanas deiseanna do mhná, agus go dtacaíonn sé tríd is tríd le teaghlaigh ina gcuid riachtanas oideachasúla agus sóisialta. Léiríonn taighde freisin gur i gcúlra sábháilteachta a bhfuil seirbhísí mar thaca leis is fearr a fheidhmíonn teaghlaigh, agus go bhforbraíonn leanaí óga go maith laistigh de sheirbhísí luath-óige atá ar ardchaighdeán.

Ag aithint dóibh gur féidir le heolas agus anailís trasnáisiúnta cur le forbairt pholasaí, lainseáil Coiste Oideachais an ECFE an tAthbhreithniú Téamach ar Pholasaí Oideachais agus Cúraim don Luath-Óige i 1998. Go nuige seo, ghlac fiche tír orthu féin a bheith rannpháirteach san athbhreithniú: An Astráil, An Ostair, An Bheilg, Ceanada, Poblacht na Seicslóvaice, An Danmhairg, An Ghearmáin, An Fhionlainn, An Fhrainc, Éire, An Iodáil, An Chóiré, Meicsiceo, An Ísiltir, An Ioruaidh, An Phortaingéil, An tSualainn, An Ríocht Aontaithe agus Stáit Aontaithe Mheiriceá.

Agus iad ag déanamh idirghabhálacha ag cruinnithe den Choiste Oideachais i gceanncheathrú ECFE, thug toscairí ó Roinn Oideachais agus Eolaíochta na hÉireann tacaíocht láidir don tionscadal. Tá tosaíocht ard tugtha acu do rochtain agus caighdeán feabhsaithe sa luath-oideachas agus cúram in Éirinn, agus é mar aidhm acu bunús na foghlama fadsaoil a láidriú. I gcomhthéacs an leathnaithe tapaidh atá ag teacht ar eacnamaíocht na hÉireann agus líon na mban i measc an lucht oibre a bheith níos airde ná mar a bhí riamh, d'iarr an Roinn i 2002 athbhreithniú ar sheirbhísí oideachais agus cúraim luath-óige in Éirinn. Tugann an t-imleabhar seo, ina bhfuil an *Tuarascáil Chúlra* Éireannach agus *Nóta Tíre* an ECFE le chéile, cur síos ar an scéal in Éirinn ag an am sin.

Tríd an *Nóta Tíre* seo ar fad, is moltaí trialacha iad moltaí fhoireann athbhreithithe an ECFE, mar go n-aithníonn siad na deacrachtaí roimh fhoireann a thagann isteach – is cuma cén mionteagasc a tugadh dóibh – tuiscint imleor a fháil ar éagsúlacht agus castacht córais tíre ina iomláine. Mar gheall air sin, ní mar thuairimí daingne atá ár moltaí dá dtairiscint againn do na hAireachtaí atá rannpháirteach in oideachas agus cúram luath-óige in Éirinn, ach ar mhaithe le hagallamh gairmiúil agus mar ábhar machnaimh do lucht déanta polasaí agus speisialtóirí. Táimid ag súil, áfach, go mbeidh an léargas atá againn ón taobh amuigh, bunaithe mar atá sé ar chomparáidí le tíortha eile an ECFE, ina bhunús úsáideach do phlé agus do dhul chun cinn.

Ba mhaith liom buíochas ar leith a ghlacadh go pearsanta leis an Aire Noel Dempsey agus leis an Roinn Oideachais as an tacaíocht a thug siad d'athbhreithnithe an ECFE agus as an tuarascáil seo a fhoilsiú agus a scaipeadh. Ba mhaith an eiseamláir é i rith an ama an chaoi a stiúir siad an t-athbhreithniú, agus an fonn a bhí orthu deis a thabhairt d'fhoireann ECFE agallamh a chur ar an réimse is leithne páirtithe leasmhara san earnáil luath-óige in Éirinn agus ab fhéidir le linn na cuairte seachtaine. Cuireann sé áthas orm chomh maith a admháil go raibh páirt lárnach san obair seo ag John Bennett ón Rannóg Polasaí Oideachais agus Oiliúna i Stiúrthóireacht Oideachais an ECFE.

Barry McGaw, Ph.D.
Stiúrthóir
Stiúrthóireacht Oideachais, ECFE

Early Childhood Education and Care Policy

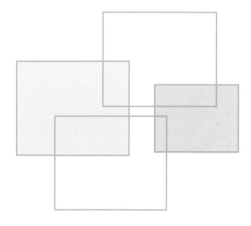

COUNTRY NOTE

for

IRELAND

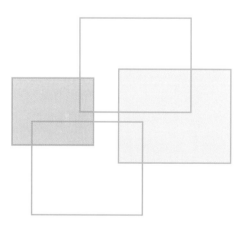

OECD Directorate for Education
July 2004

TABLE OF CONTENTS

EXECUTIVE SUMMARY

The *Country Note for Ireland* is the outcome of an intensive review of early childhood policies and services in Ireland by an OECD review team, which took place over five days in November 2002. The review was initiated by an invitation to the OECD Directorate for Education from the Irish Department of Education and Science.

Chapter 1 of the report outlines the framework of OECD early childhood education and care (ECEC) reviews. A premise of the OECD approach is that the development of young children in a country depends greatly on equitable social structures, on family support for early development and learning; and on the informed practice of qualified professionals who provide - in a caring environment - structured yet open frame-work programmes appropriate for young children. The chapter concludes with definitions of ECEC terminology as used in Ireland.

Chapter 2 presents an overview of the early childhood education and care system in Ireland. It is descriptive in emphasis, outlining the political, administrative, social and economic contexts, recent policy initiatives in the field and key features of the current system. These include policy responsibility, types of provision and coverage, funding, regulatory procedures, staffing and staff training, programme regulation, and parental engagement.

Chapter 3, entitled *Policy Issues Arising from the Visit,* is analytic and discursive in emphasis. In addition to the central issues of access, quality, staff training and co-ordination, more contextual issues such as the impact of ECEC services on the Irish economy, the new roles of Irish women, parental engagement, early childhood education and care models, research / evaluation / information systems are explored. The question of funding new initiatives for young children in Ireland is also discussed, particularly in the context of the challenge presented by the Barcelona European Council, 16-17 March 2002.[1]

Chapter 4 puts forward for consideration by the Irish authorities a number of suggestions and recommendations. They are offered in a spirit of professional dialogue, basing our proposals on experience of other countries and on our discussions with the ministries and the major stakeholders in the field whom we interviewed in Ireland. In summary, these conclusions are as follows:

---

[1] The Barcelona conclusions state that Member States should remove disincentives to female participation in the labour force and strive, in line with national patterns of provision, *to provide childcare by 2010 to at least 90% of children between 3 years and mandatory school age and at least 33% of children under 3 years of age.*

A Summary of Conclusions

General remarks

From the perspective of the OECD review team, significant strengths exist in Ireland:

A well-established early education network within the primary school system for children aged between 4 and 6. Early education in Ireland benefits from stable funding, trained teachers, structured programming and regular monitoring and evaluation. Though insufficiently adapted to the learning patterns of young children and to the needs of contemporary parents, the network exists all over the country and is well-respected;

The presence of an active voluntary and community sector, which, although poorly funded, is closely in touch with the needs of working and disadvantaged parents, and acts to improve the quality of the services it offers;

A strong spirit of partnership at local level: Organised partnerships at county level are beginning to support the local communities, the voluntary sector and the business/local development sector to resolve the childcare needs of parents;

However, it is clear that a national policy for the early education and care of young children in Ireland is still in its initial stages. Care and education are still treated separately and coverage is low compared to other European countries. Over the coming years, significant energies and funding will need to be invested in the field to create a system in tune with the needs of a full employment economy and with new understandings of how young children develop and learn.

Co-ordination of ministries, agencies and resources

In light of the urgent need to improve the present population/employment ratio in Ireland and establish a coherent and affordable system for the early education and care of children outside the home – in a context where there is a dispersion of responsibilities across many ministries and agencies - the OECD team proposes for consideration:

- The integration of all early education and care policy and funding under one ministry or under a designated funding and policy agency. Ireland has much to gain – in terms of effective policy-making, accountability and economies of scale - by taking an integrated approach to early education and care for children from one to six years, conducted by one ministry or agency, as has become the practice in many OECD countries.

- The urgent formulation of a *National Plan for Early Childhood Services Development,* rolled over on a three-year basis, with clearly spelt out goals, targets, time-lines, responsibilities and accountability measures from co-operating Departments. While universal in intent, the plan should include annual targets and specific funding for the important subsystems, such as disadvantaged children, children from Traveller communities and children with special needs.

- Decentralisation of the planning and management of all early childhood education and care services to integrated agencies or committees at the county/city level. Decentralisation to the local level needs to be backed by adequate regulatory powers and state funding.

Improving general access

Children aged 0-3 years

Access to accredited developmental programmes for Irish children in this age group is very weak. Yet, research suggests that the development of quality childcare is self-financing through increased tax returns from women's work and less dependency on social security. To meet the needs of younger children, the authorities may wish to consider:

- Extending funded parental leave to one year after the birth of a child. Many countries – most recently Canada - take the view that the individualised care of infants and the planned return of women to the labour force can be achieved most effectively through this policy[2] (see Table 4). A measure in this sense from government would almost certainly be more attractive to Irish parents than large-scale investment in collective infant care or than the present reliance on informal care during the critical first year of the child's life;

- Increasing the supply of childcare places for young children one year and older through accrediting and subsidising the quality childminders, encouraging them to form at county level accredited family daycare networks that can look after children more professionally, and can handle on behalf of their members administrative issues such as qualifications, training, funding, salaries, insurance, social security, holidays, etc.;

- Removing barriers to affordability for low- and modest-income families through capping parental fees and providing operational subsidies to accredited centre-based or networked providers for each eligible child present in their services.

- Increasing parent support and education through professional planning and management of local services from the county level; through building model child-and family centres in each county or large centre of population; through information; and where demand exists, through the provision of professionally managed drop-in services for at-home mothers with young children.

Children aged 3-6 years

By European standards, access to early education and care for children in this age group is also comparatively weak and inequality at the starting gates of school is clearly evident for specific groups of children. The OECD team recommends for consideration:

- The entitlement to a place in a free, accredited early education service for all children who have reached their 4th birthday. Where the infant school is concerned, the measure could be made acceptable to both parents and teachers by the provision of a trained Child Assistant to all infant classes, thus effectively reducing child-staff ratios for this age group to a maximum of 15:1;

- The development, based on the local school or accredited provider, of a publicly-funded morning education session for all children from the age of 3 years;

- The extension of the infant school (or accredited pre-school) day in areas where there is sufficient demand, and in all areas of disadvantage. In consultation with the local providers, the County/City Committees may wish to encourage and manage the extension of the infant school day – if possible on-site - through the provision of fee-paying, pre-school/educare in the afternoon ensured by local providers;

- DES accreditation and financial support to the voluntary, community and private organisations that are capable of delivering high quality developmental programmes to the age group, and which are willing to follow the basic requirements of public services, including agreed fee levels and an equitable and appropriate intake of special needs and disadvantaged children;

Improving access for special groups

Children with disabilities

---

[2] Parental leave schemes are financed by different mechanisms in different countries, but in general are linked to employment status. In common, they provide family care for infants, ensure the working status of women, replace lost income to some degree, and avoid the heavy costs of infant care, which because of the age of the child requires ideally one-to-one attention.

According to information received, services for children with disabilities and their families are very insufficient. With the exception of children with visual or hearing impairment, children with disabilities under 4 years have no entitlement to education provision. These children remain at home with their parents and/or are placed with the support of the Health Boards, in a variety of settings. In general, parents lack the sustained supports that are necessary. From the age of four years, some children with milder disabilities may be enrolled in the infant school where they receive periodic attention from resource teachers, who may not be qualified to support a particular type of disability or who may lack essential support services. As there is significant evidence of the positive effects of intensive early intervention from birth and during the critical early years, the OECD team proposes:

- The urgent consideration and implementation of the recommendations in favour of Irish children with special needs made in the course of the National Forum of Early Childhood Education, 1998. This would include specific legislation (as in the USA and other countries) and the creation of a comprehensive national system of early years services for these children and their families that can lead to each child achieving "the fullest possible social integration and individual development" (Article 23, Convention on the Rights of the Child). In practice, these children should receive structured and regular educational support from birth, or at least from the time of the first identification of disability. Crucial time is lost if educational intervention starts only at the beginning of infant or primary schooling. When children with disabilities are enrolled in mainstream schools, we encourage DES, communities and school principals to ensure that they receive appropriate care, individualised learning programmes and adequate support services.

Children from disadvantaged backgrounds:

The OECD team proposes for consideration:

- *Intensive quality programming for disadvantaged children from as early an age as possible.* As with children with special needs, appropriate early intervention is the key. The team recommends the continuation and improvement of the *Early Start Project* on a full-day basis. Improvements would include enhanced outreach to parents, more appropriate programming and better integration of school and community services. Renewed contact between DES, the county committees and the community/voluntary sector is also recommended to explore how to extend this programme on a basis acceptable to all. An improved *Early Start* programme would include a morning session conducted by the school or other accredited body, with an afternoon pre-school session taken in charge by an accredited community, voluntary or private provider, supported by adequate funding and qualified personnel.

Children from the Traveller community

In the context of this report, the level of educational achievement of Traveller children is a matter of deep concern. The low enrolment rates of Traveller children in pre-schools and the infant school suggest that most Traveller children are entering primary school already at a great disadvantage – a hypothesis which seems to be confirmed by the massive drop-out of Traveller children before entry to secondary school.[3] It suggests also that a distrust of public institutions may be present, which requires, as in other countries, an active partnership approach between agencies and Traveller parents to bring appropriate education to young children on-site and in the public schools.

The OECD team recommends:

- The urgent implementation of the recent DES report, *Pre-School for Travellers,* taking into account the responses of Traveller agencies and parents to the report. We would suggest also the publication by an independent agency of an annual evaluation of actual outcomes for Traveller children, covering, in particular, indicators of health, educational enrolment and achievement. A special mentoring and

---

[3] The drop from 5,500 child enrolments in primary school to only 1,600 in secondary school needs urgent investigation.

documentation service to support Traveller children through their studies in schools and transitions to work should also be considered. Within the infant schools used by Traveller children, a contributory element to their successful inclusion would be anti-bias teacher training, and attention to issues of diversity and identity (Derman-Sparks, 1989).

■ As participation is a catalyst for change, the government may also wish to consider the appointment of representatives from the Traveller community to the relevant policy bodies concerned with early childhood, primary and secondary education. In addition, within each Traveller pre-school, and in the infant classes that receive significant numbers of Traveller children, it would seem necessary – as is the custom in other countries - to ensure that a growing number of Traveller teachers and child assistants are trained and recruited. In line with the 1999 *White Paper* sections on *Qualifications and Training*, the DES may wish to begin consultations on the most appropriate means of assisting professionals "to obtain qualifications which would enable them to hold mainstream posts in national schools".

Improving the quality of early childhood education and care

Of concern to the OECD review team was the great shortage of quality services for young children under four years, and the observation of a predominantly didactic approach in *Early Start* and the primary school infant classes.[4] In keeping with the proposal to integrate early education and care, the OECD team suggests:

■ The formulation of a common *Quality Framework* for centre-based programmes for young children, focussing on agreed standards for services. A *Quality Framework* would include a description of what families can expect from centres, whether public or private: that is, licensed accreditation, qualified management, adequate facility requirements, appropriate child-staff ratios with a sufficient number of highly qualified staff, validated programmes, quality targets with regular team-evaluation procedures and external monitoring of outcomes, appropriate modalities of parent participation and community outreach...;

■ A voluntary accreditation and quality improvement scheme for service providers in line with the Quality Framework and public sector requirements. Adherence to the scheme would be indemnified by guaranteed operational grants from the Ministry having responsibility for young children;

■ A re-structuring of the infant school favouring autonomy, quality and accountability. The OECD review team encourages DES to consider the provision of a separate budget for the infant school, and specific management responsibilities given to its senior teacher. These proposed responsibilities are outlined in Chapter 4.

■ A thorough re-assessment of initial training for early childhood services at all levels, including profiling, training, career ladders and issues of compensation. As a change of pre-service training takes five to ten years to be felt on the ground, regular professional development (in-service training) opportunities need to be developed in the interim for early childhood professionals and infant school teachers.

Financing new measures

With the exception of current EOCP budgets, funding for early childhood services in Ireland has been low by international standards. In recent decades, education funding has been directed predominantly toward expanding university provision (see Table 8).[5] At the present stage of development in Irish education,

---

[4] Some direct instruction is helpful for young children, in particular, direct instruction to individual children on specific issues. It is the predominance of the model that is of concern. Research indicates that didactic programmes are less effective than child-centred programmes in producing cognitive results, and compare poorly with regard to socialisation (see Bauman et al., 2001 for a fuller discussion).

[5] At present, a student at tertiary level receives three-times greater public funding than the child (often from a low-income background or with special learning needs) at the foundation stage of learning. American and British research suggests that as many as 25% of children now entering schools have special needs or behavioural characteristics that can seriously impede their learning achievement.

some of this funding may be considered as deadweight loss. Countries such as Australia have proven that student loans, generous repayment conditions and tax breaks more than suffice to maintain tertiary enrolments. We are confident that cost-benefit analyses can show that adequate public funding of early childhood services in Ireland will be amply compensated by enhanced social cohesion, improved educational levels and productivity in the next generation, greater gender equality, increased tax returns from women's work and by savings in health and social security expenditure. The OECD team recommends for consideration:

■ A significant increase in ministry budgets for all early childhood services, so as to quickly reach the average rate of public expenditure for OECD countries (see Table 8 in Appendix 1). This expenditure can be paralleled by improved employment policies for women and increased support for families. Budgetary increases should also be envisaged to meet the extra costs of *appropriate* inclusion of children with special needs into mainstream education;[6]

■ A pooling of resources and sharing of costs across ministries, social partners, local communities and users, whenever common objectives are being attained for young children and their families, e.g. if wrap-around education and care for young children improves in turn social inclusion and labour market expansion, there is little reason why the capital and operational costs should not be shared across a range of ministries and other interest groups.[7]

■ A shifting of educational financing toward quality early childhood education and care, where research indicates that the human and social capital returns on investment are greatest. Equality of opportunity in education needs to be ensured from the earliest age possible.

■ Cost-effective coordination of early childhood policies at central level and concentration of services at local level, in particular for the 3-6 year olds. For example, rather than investments in rented and other premises, it would seem more rational in many instances to invest significantly in school infrastructure, and to bring early education, full-day and out-of-school care together in one location. This presupposes that the school as a public building can be developed to receive early childhood services, conducted also by accredited non-governmental providers. Concentration of centre-based services helps to reduce costs considerably, improves quality and facilitates working parents;[8]

■ A sharing of tasks with the voluntary, community and private sector, and the incorporation – whenever possible - of non-public providers into a publicly funded and professionally managed system. The contribution made by non-governmental organisations and local private providers to the state network is often significant, even essential. Other countries accredit providers that maintain high quality standards and reward them with operational subsidies. Subsidies are particularly efficient when voluntary early education bodies accept children from disadvantaged or special needs backgrounds, and keep fees within the range defined by the public authorities.

■ Enlisting support from the corporate and business sectors. In many countries, employers are among the main supporters of early childhood services. In the Netherlands, for example, employers are expected to provide a crèche or purchase childcare places in accredited centres for the young children

---

[6] Additional costs for special needs children in early education are more than recuperated through downstream savings on special education units, remedial teaching and social security.

[7] In many countries, for example, builders are expected to include in their costs for housing estates, the construction of appropriately-designed crèches and schools. Local communities and industry can also be expected to contribute.

[8] Respect for the rhythms and interests of young children needs to be ensured in services attached to schools. In addition, the ministry, county or other body responsible for managing early childhood services at local level will need to consult and involve the community and voluntary sector in provision linked to the school.

of their employees. (see also   the *American Business Round Table* statement in Appendix 3). In yet other countries, e.g. Korea and Mexico, firms employing a certain quota of young women are required by law to establish an on-site day care centre or subsidise child care expenses for their employees.

- A comparitive study of funding mechanisms in the early childhood field across OECD countries. In the Nordic countries, local authorities have powers to raise taxes, which are devoted to supplementing the State allocation for health, social welfare and early education services. In Belgium and Italy, a significant part (about 1%) of social security and/or corporate tax is channelled toward childcare. In Finland, the alcohol tax has been used for many years to subvention early childhood services, in particular, out-of-school care. In the USA, grants from the large corporations toward early childhood services are common, as tax concessions can be granted by the public authorities for large donations. State lottery proceeds are also used to fund early childhood services and to provide subventions to needy third-level students wishing to enter college.

Chapter 1

INTRODUCTION

The OECD Thematic Review

1. The *Country Note for Ireland* is an output of the *Thematic Review of Early Childhood Education and Care Policy*, a project launched by the OECD's Education Committee in March 1998. The impetus for the project came from the 1996 Ministerial meeting on *Making Lifelong Learning a Reality for All.* In their communiqué, the Education Ministers assigned a high priority to the goal of improving access to and quality in early childhood education and care, with the aim of strengthening the foundations of lifelong learning (OECD, 1996). A detailed description of the review's objectives, analytical framework, and methodology is provided in OECD (1998a).

2. In March 1998, twelve countries volunteered to participate in the review: Australia, Belgium, Czech Republic, Denmark, Finland, Italy, the Netherlands, Norway, Portugal, Sweden, the United Kingdom and the United States. Early in the review process, these countries reached agreement concerning the framework, scope and process of the review, and identified the major policy issues for investigation. Between 1998 and 2000, OECD review teams conducted visits to the 12 participating countries. Information on the visits and several reports from the review may be viewed on the project web site: <http://www.oecd.org/els /education/reviews>. A Comparative Report entitled *Starting Strong: Early Childhood Education and Care,* was released at an international conference held in Stockholm, 13-15 June 2001.

3. At its meeting in November 2001, the OECD Education Committee authorised a second round of early childhood reviews. Countries were offered the choice of inviting either a *full review* of their policies and services over a ten-day period, or a *short review* of five days focussing on two or three challenges important for a country at a particular moment. To date, nine further countries have joined the second round: Austria, Canada, Germany, Hungary, Korea, Mexico and Spain for full reviews; France, and Ireland, for shorter reviews. These countries provide a diverse range of social, economic and political contexts, as well as varied policy approaches toward the education and care of young children.

4. In scope, the reviews seek to cover children from birth to compulsory school age, as well as the transition to primary schooling. In order to examine thoroughly what children experience in the first years of life a broad, holistic approach is adopted. To that end, consideration is given to social policies and various environmental influences on children's early development and learning. More specifically, the reviews investigate concerns about *quality, access* and *equity,* with an emphasis on policy development in the following areas: regulations; staffing; programme content and implementation; family engagement and support; funding and financing. A premise of our approach is that the educational success of young children depends greatly on their well-being and involvement; on family support for early learning; on the informed practice of highly qualified professionals who provide - in

a caring environment - structured yet open frame-work programmes appropriate for young children. With respect to at-risk children, particular attention by early childhood professionals to family outreach, social integration and support is critical.

The review process

5. In preparation for the visit of the OECD review team, the national, sponsoring ministry commissions a *Background Report* on ECEC policy and services in the country. Guided by a common framework that has been accepted by all participating countries, *Background Reports* are intended to provide a concise overview of the country context, major issues and concerns, distinctive ECEC policies and provision, innovative approaches, and available quantitative and evaluation data. Preparation is a participative exercise at country level, and normally should provide a forum of debate for the different stakeholders in early childhood in each country. After the country visit, the OECD produces a short *Country Note* that draws together the national background materials and the review team's observations.

6. After analysis of the *Background Report* and other documents, review teams composed of OECD Secretariat members and experts with diverse analytic and policy backgrounds (see Appendix 1) visit each participating country. The visit is co-ordinated by the sponsoring ministry. In the course of the visit, the team interviews the major actors involved in ECEC policy and practice, and are invited to observe a number of examples of early childhood programmes. The selection of particular sites reflects in general not only a concern for geographical diversity but also the desire to show the review team a representative selection of both typical and innovative services.

Features of the review specific to Ireland

7. Ireland was the first country to be visited in the course of the second round of reviews, from 18th - - 22nd November, 2002. It was also the first country to invite a short review, focussing on *access, quality* and *co-ordination.* The issue of co-ordination proved particularly challenging for the team, as the early childhood system in Ireland remains fragmented, in terms both of policy responsibility and service delivery. In the course of the visit, the team met with many government departments, agencies and stakeholders in the early childhood field, and made site visits covering a range of services for young children from four months to six years.

Structure of the Irish Country Note

8. The *Country Note* presents the review team's analyses of key policy issues in the early childhood field related to *access, quality* and *co-ordination.* Following the terms proposed by the Department of Education and Science, it seeks a) to place the issues around early childhood provision firmly within the Irish context; b) to review early care and educational policies and practices as they currently meet the needs of Irish children and their families; c) to consider ongoing developments with a critical eye for sustainability and the capacity to go to scale; d) to make tentative recommendations that would render success more likely, as well as to indicate areas for future effort and emphasis.

9. In addition to the present introduction, which forms *Chapter 1*, the structure of the Country Note is as follows: *Chapter 2* provides an overview of governance, administration, current policies and provision in Ireland, outlining also approaches to funding, regulation, staffing, programme regulation and parental engagement. In *Chapter 3*, some of the main issues related to policy and practice in ECEC in Ireland are explored. Seven areas are chosen for comment: new roles for Irish women; access; quality; co-ordination; parental engagement; research/evaluation and funding. The conclusions, in *Chapter 4*, offer some orientations and policy recommendations for future thought and action.

Acknowledgements

10. The OECD wishes to thank the Department of Education and Science for making this review possible and, in particular, for the comprehensive programme organised for the team review visit. The

reviewers also wish to place on record their appreciation of the open and informative meetings that were held in the other ministries and agencies with responsibility for children. Our visits to the various early childhood services, and our talks with managers, providers, and early childhood professionals were also most informative, and we thank them for responding to our questions so graciously. Finally, we should like to thank warmly John Fanning and his team at the Department of Education who organised the review with efficiency and courtesy, Carmel Corrigan, author of the Irish *Background Report*, and the inter-agency Steering Committee team who helped to produce a comprehensive report of Irish efforts in the early childhood field.

11. Throughout the *Country Note*, the suggestions offered by the review team are tentative, in recognition of the difficulty facing a visiting team—no matter how well briefed—in fully grasping the variety and complexity of a country-wide system and the range of issues that need to be taken into account. In the case of Ireland, the challenge was more difficult than usual as the team had only a five-day field visit to make an in-depth case study. Even when multiplied by the number of members of a team, a five-day review is extremely limiting in terms of the amount of data that can be collected and verified. Moreover, as this report will make clear, the clustering of so many parallel initiatives on behalf of children at central level presents a challenge even for very experienced policy analysts.

12. The facts and opinions expressed in the *Country Note* are the sole responsibility of the review team. While acknowledging with gratitude the valuable help received from ministry officials, researchers and practitioners in Ireland, we wish to underline that they have no part in any shortcomings or opinions which this document may present. To lessen the potential for misunderstanding or error, it is assumed that the *Country Note* will be read in conjunction with the *Background Report* contracted by the Department of Education and Science, as the two documents are intended to complement one another.

Terminology

13. The terminology used throughout the report follows in general the usage of *Starting Strong* (OECD, 2001). Children aged 0-4 years covers children from birth up to their fourth birthday, but does not include 4 year olds. Children aged 4-6 years covers children from 48 months to their sixth birthday, but does not include six year olds. *Infants* are children from birth to 12 months; *toddlers* from 12 months to 30 months; and *pre-school* children from about two-and a half years to obligatory school age. *Early childhood education and care* is often abbreviated throughout the text as ECEC.

14. Among the Irish definitions used throughout this report are the following (see Hayes, 2000; Irish Background Report, 2002).

> *Childcare and Education sectors.[9] In Ireland, the Childcare sector caters for children from three months to 5 years. The labour market participation of parents has been the driving force for establishing grant-aided provision in the sector, although today, the part of the sector guided by the Department of Justice, Equality and Law Reform (DJELR)[10] places a strong emphasis also on quality and the development of children. The Education sector in Ireland organises and supports provision for 4 and 5 year olds in primary schools. The curriculum focuses on child development and learning. In addition, some early intervention programmes have been initiated for 3- and 4-year old children from disadvantaged backgrounds.*

[9] For early childhood specialists, this division is arbitrary and unsatisfactory: education and care/childcare are inextricably intertwined. For this reason, a number of OECD countries have moved towards eliminating structural policy divisions in this area and creating an integrated and co-ordinated approach to early childhood services from birth up to compulsory school age, e.g. in New Zealand, Sweden, Spain and the UK under the auspices of the Education ministry; Finland and Denmark under the auspices of the Social Affairs ministry; Norway under the Ministry of Children and Family Affairs.

[10] Most of the sector is private and informal.

Regulated care. The adjective "regulated" normally includes not only compliance to broad legislation, but also the conformity of a service to policy goals, protocols, pedagogical standards, outcome goals and good practice. Readers should note that the term is used in Ireland in a very limited sense (see paragraph 162). Regulation occurs by virtue of the Child Care Act, 1991 and the Child Care (Pre-School Services) Regulations 1996 which impose an obligation on childcare providers who care for more than 3 children to notify their local Health Board.

Parental Care – refers to children being looked after at home, almost always by the mother or by a female, live-in relative. This is the most common arrangement, particularly for children under two years (ESRI, 1998). Parental care may be supplemented by baby-sitting arrangements for short periods.

Informal Care – is present when parent(s) use other family members, friends, neighbours baby-sitters to look after their children for sessional periods or longer, generally in the child's own home. The term may also include childminding in the child's own home, on terms negotiated freely between the childminder and the child's parent(s). There is no legislation or regulation of this practice, and no requirement to notify the local Health Board.

Childminding (family day care) – In this arrangement, children are looked after on a sessional, half-day or long-day basis by a self-employed childminder in the home of the carer, on freely negotiated market terms. This sector takes in charge the majority of children in need of childcare outside the home. Under the Child Care Act, 1991 and the Child Care (Pre-school Services) Regulations 1996, childminders caring for more than 3 children, who are not relatives or of the same family, are required to notify their local health board. The majority of childminders do not come within the remit of the Regulations. Such childminders are encouraged to avail of a voluntary notification and support system.

Workplace crèches: These are crèches established in the workplaces of parents, and are generally subsidised by employers. In Ireland, they are few in number.

Drop-in crèches – Again, few in number, they provide irregular and very short sessional care in shopping centres, leisure centres, etc.

Community nurseries - These are non-profit, community-owned nurseries created through government capital grants, and generally situated in urban disadvantaged areas. They receive operational grants both from the Health Boards and the Department of Justice, Equality and Law Reform. Many of their staff are trainees from Community Employment Schemes.

Nurseries and crèches – These private nurseries, often in receipt of government capital grants, cater for children from 0-6 years, on a fee-paying basis. They are generally full-day, although some offer part-time places. Most are registered with the National Children's Nursery Association.

Parent/Toddler groups – These informal groups are generally attached to other childcare services, and offer play and social interaction to young children, with a degree of informal support to parents.

Playgroups – Playgroups offer a care and education programme, mainly on a sessional basis, to children aged 3-5 years. Fees are modest. Some 80 % are privately run, and most are affiliated to the IPPA (Irish Pre-school Playgroups Association) – the Early Childhood Organisation.

Naíonraí – These are Irish-language playgroups, offering services to children aged 3-5 years.

Pre-school programmes – There are a number of Montessori, High/Scope and Steiner groups operating in Ireland, generally privately owned. They provide a fee-paying, mainly sessional service to children aged 3-5 years.

Early Start – This is a pilot pre-school project, within the primary school system, for 3- and 4-year old children from some designated urban areas of disadvantage. It is fully funded by the Department of Education and Science, and caters for 1680 children.

Traveller Pre-schools – Usually founded by voluntary bodies and/or Traveller support groups, Pre-schools for Traveller Children are funded to 98% of teaching and transport costs by the Department of Education and Science. 52 such pre-schools exist, catering for 530 Traveller children aged 3-5 years. Traveller Pre-schools are not considered part of the primary school system.

Early Primary Education (junior infant classes, senior infant classes) – This is a free, universal service (four hours and forty minutes daily) provided in primary schools by the Department of Education and Science. Over half of the 4-year olds and almost all 5-year olds avail of the service.

Special Schools – Special schools are schools catering exclusively for children with learning and/or physical disabilities.

Out-of-school care (OSC) – that is, provision for children aged 3-12 years before or after infant/primary school hours, organised either on school premises or outside. Though some community and private providers are entering the field, OSC is in general underdeveloped and unregulated in Ireland.

The Irish Background Report is referenced throughout the text as the *Background Report* and cited as *Irish Background Report (2002).*

Chapter 2

CURRENT ECEC POLICIES AND PROVISION IN IRELAND

Chapter 2 presents an overview of the early childhood education and care (ECEC) system in Ireland. It is descriptive in emphasis, outlining the political and administrative contexts, recent policy initiatives in the field and key features of the current system. These include policy responsibility, types of provision and coverage, funding, regulatory procedures, staffing and staff training, programme regulation, and parental engagement.

1. Governance and political context

15. Ireland is a parliamentary democracy with a population of fewer than four million people. Legislation is proposed and voted by the elected representatives in the lower chamber or *Dáil*. Policy decisions are made by the Cabinet of chief ministers, presided by the *Taoiseach* or prime minister. Departmental ministers can promulgate statutory instruments, that is, rules and regulations with the force of law, e.g. road traffic rules, or the curriculum for schools.

16. Policy implementation in Ireland is the responsibility of three main groups: the central administration or civil service consisting of government departments and officials; second, autonomous state agencies;[11] and finally, an elected local government system based primarily at county and borough levels. There is no directly elected tier of government at regional level in Ireland, but because of European regional policies and structural funding, some Regional Operational programmes exist covering diverse groups of counties along the Border, the West and the South. Several ministries have also established non-coterminous,[12] regional authorities to decentralise the delivery of services in a manner more responsive to local needs.

17. Ireland has been governed in the last fifteen or so years by centrist coalition governments, aiming primarily to achieve economic stability and growth. The economy is mixed, with low direct taxation rates, and is bolstered by significant inward investment from abroad. Public-private partnerships, entrepreneurship, and job creation are seen as key elements in future development. *The National Development Plan* (2000 – 2006) includes an important chapter on social inclusion, in which both childcare and early education are given a place.

---

[11] These agencies carry out a wide range of advisory (e.g. the National Economic and Social Council), developmental (e.g. Enterprise Ireland; the Tourist Board); social (e.g. health boards); training (FAS); and commercial (e.g. public utilities) functions, which are often statutory. They report annually to their "parent" ministries.

[12] That is, covering different groups of counties.

The European dimension

18. Ireland's engagement with the European Union is complex and spans a wide array of issues. European Community law is superior to and takes precedence over all forms of national law, and the Irish authorities, like other national authorities, are required to implement and give effect to it. The country has been and still remains a substantial net beneficiary from EU funding. Due to increased prosperity, it is likely to become a net contributor to the European Union towards the end of this decade.

19. Since accession to the Union in 1973, Ireland has been generally supportive of EU initiatives and strategies even when these do not have the force of law, e.g. within the framework of Employment Strategy, Ireland is seeking to achieve the target of an overall employment rate of 70% by 2010, with a rate of 60% for women (Government of Ireland, 2002). Likewise, Ireland supports European Union measures in favour of equal opportunities, with a focus on gender mainstreaming and increased participation of people with disabilities. It has committed also to developing indicators on the provision of care facilities for children and other dependants. According to the ministries which the OECD interviewed, Ireland intends to respond positively to the conclusions of the Barcelona European Council (16-17 March 2002). These conclusions state that Member States should remove disincentives to female labour and strive, in line with national patterns of provision, *to provide childcare by 2010 to at least 90% of children between 3 years and mandatory school age and at least 33% of children under 3 years of age.*

20. Education, social protection and health care remain a matter for the member States. Yet, in these domains, Ireland has been and will continue to be much influenced by EU norms and programmes. A significant part of European funds has been used for a variety of educational and social purposes, e.g. the increase in third-level graduations and Post-Leaving Certificates that Ireland achieved in the 1990s was assisted by European funding of the regional Institutes of Technology established at that time. At the present moment, the development of the childcare sector is being resourced under the EU Supported National Development Plan. Both EU and Exchequer funding are being made available to the childcare sector through the Department of Justice, Equality and Law Reform's Equal Opportunities Childcare Programme (EOCP) 2000 – 2006.

The Irish economic context

21. Signs of the growing importance of early childhood education and care can be found in the current *National Development Plan,* 2000-2006 (Government of Ireland, 1999), in the *Social Partnership Agreements* (including the most recent *Sustaining Progress,* published February, 2003) and in the various programmes for government that have been published in recent years. In these documents, the development of childcare is treated at different times as an instrument to support social inclusion and gender equality, but above all, to facilitate "people with family responsibilities to avail of employment and training opportunities" (National Development Plan, p.23)

> The lack of adequate childcare facilities has been identified as a significant contributor to exclusion from education, training and employment opportunities. This impacts most severely on women, and in particular on disadvantaged women and single-parent families. The objectives of the childcare measures include reconciling work and family life and facilitating access for women to education, training and employment. It will have both an equal opportunities and a social inclusion focus. It will also address the needs of men and women generally in reconciling their childcare needs with their participation in the labour force (National Development Plan, p.192).

22. Early education receives less attention. It is mentioned in the National Plan and other documents, but its expansion has not been foreseen, except as a measure targeted at disadvantaged children. A section (4.1 of Framework IV) is devoted to early childhood education in the *Programme for Prosperity*

and Fairness (PPF), but the section heading is misleading since the text refers predominantly to primary schooling. In fact, the PPF simply reiterates three of the recommendations of the *White Paper on Early Childhood Education* (1999a), viz., the creation of an Early Childhood Education Agency, the promotion of a Quality in Education Mark, and the provision of targeted interventions for children from disadvantaged backgrounds. In parallel, *the Agreed Programme for Government* devotes two sentences to early education:

> *To ensure that early education services deliver the maximum benefits for all children, we will introduce a national early education training, support and certification system, and expand funded early education places. Priority will be given to a new national system of funded early education for children with intellectual disabilities in areas of concentrated disadvantage. (Agreed Programme for Government, p.23)*

The present social partnership agreement, Sustaining Progress 2003-2005, foresees also "Priority to early education and childcare facilities for disadvantaged families in the context of a joint approach between the Departments of Education and Science and Justice, Equality and Law Reform."

23. Although well-informed discussions of the fundamental early childhood policy issues are found in departmental documents, such as the *White Paper on Early Childhood Education* (Government of Ireland, 1999a) or the *National Childcare Strategy,* (Government of Ireland, 1999b), a public debate about the nature and necessity of early childhood care and education has still to be engaged in Ireland, e.g. Why should a country invest public funds in early childhood services? Do these services actually harm or benefit young children? What is their status vis-à-vis parental care? What is the optimal length of time for an infant to receive full-time care from his/her parent(s)? How should the state act to ensure real choice for working mothers with infants? Are early years services different from primary education? Are childcare and education different functions, or should they be considered in an integrated way as educare or early years services, with strong links to family and social policy? What should take place in early childhood services for acceptable quality to exist? Is a fair investment being made in young children compared to other groups in society?

2. Policy

24. Compared to most other countries in Europe, policy-making in Ireland for young children outside the home environment has had a relatively short history. The care and education of the youngest children was considered until recently to be the private responsibility of the family (Hayes, 2000, p.3). Government-supported, centre-based childcare facilities were minimal in number, and these were seen as catering for children designated 'at risk' and in need of protection. Small grants were allocated to these services through the local Health Boards. The growing demand for childcare places was met primarily by non-accredited private providers.

25. A somewhat similar situation pertains in the early education sector in Ireland. Little development of the infant school has taken place in recent decades. As far as the OECD team could judge, teacher training has remained predominantly geared to primary schooling, while classroom practice has remained didactic, targeting primarily cognitive skills and school outcomes (see section on Quality in the next Chapter). In the 70s and 80s, while other countries were broadening access to 4-year olds, and then progressively to 3-year old children, access levels in Ireland remained virtually at a standstill. Today, as can be seen from Figures 5 and 6 in Appendix 1, coverage rates for children in these age groups are low by European standards, leaving an enormous challenge for government and the present generation to reach the targets set by the European Union (see para. 19 above).

26. Since the mid-1990s, renewed attention has been given to the education and care of young children in Ireland, and today, an unprecedented surge of policy interest in the field can be seen, particularly in the childcare sector. In the context of a buoyant economy, the increasing participation of women in the labour market, and slowly changing societal beliefs about the importance of early educational experience in group settings, a number of significant policy documents and implementation strategies have been introduced. Since these initiatives are far-reaching in their current and potential impact on the ECEC landscape in Ireland, they are now presented in overview as the current backdrop for a system undergoing considerable change.

Recent policy initiatives

Childcare

27. In 1996, the Child Care (Pre-School Services) Regulations were introduced, followed in 1997 by the (Amendment) Regulations 1997. These Regulations are currently under review. The *National Childcare Strategy* was launched in 1999 as an outcome of the 1997 National Agreement. For the first time in the history of children's services in Ireland, an *Expert Working Group on Childcare* convened by the Department of Justice, Equality and Law Reform (DJELR) and comprising 70 stakeholders in the field formulated 27 recommendations encompassing registration, staffing, training and pay, supply and demand strategies, and examined the organisational structures and procedures needed to implement the overall strategy. In terms of reference, the *National Childcare Strategy* is inextricably linked to employment policy. It emphasises the needs and rights of children whose parent/s are active in the labour market. It was not conceptualised as a general move towards universal provision of early childhood education and care.

28. The *National Childcare Strategy* is being implemented through the Equal Opportunities Childcare Programme (EOCP) 2000 - 2006. The main body of funding is channelled through the two Regional Operational Programmes of the NDP which together make €328 million available (including €170 million of EU funding), while the Exchequer has supplemented this funding with a further €109 million making a total of €436.7 million available to develop childcare over the life of the Programme. Within this framework, one measure provides capital grant assistance to create new and quality-enhanced childcare places while two sub-measures support staffing grants where there is a focus on disadvantage and quality enhancement initiatives through the national voluntary childcare organizations.

29. The Department of Justice, Equality and Law Reform is the Implementing Department for the EOCP and the day to day administration is undertaken by ADM Ltd.[13] on behalf of the Department. Other support structures put in place to implement the *National Childcare Strategy* include the Childcare Directorate of the Department of Justice, Equality and Law Reform, the National Childcare Co-ordinating Committee, an Inter-Departmental Childcare Synergies Committee and the thirty-three County and City Childcare Committees.

Early education

30. In the early education field, a decisive breakthrough in terms of policy *recommendations* was the publication of a *White Paper* by the Department of Education and Science in 1999, entitled *Ready to Learn: White Paper on Early Childhood Education.* Building on proposals made by the National Forum on Early Childhood Education, which convened and produced a report in 1998, the *White Paper* represents "one of the most comprehensive documents ever produced on early education in Ireland" *(Irish Background Report 2002,* p.23). The stated objective of the *White Paper* is to "support the

---

[13] Area Development Management is a private company established in 1992 by the Irish Government in agreement with the European Commission. ADM's mission is to support integrated local economic and social development through managing programmes targeted at countering disadvantage and exclusion, and promoting reconciliation and equality.

development and educational achievement of children through high quality early education, with particular focus on the target groups of the disadvantaged and those with special needs." (Government of Ireland, 1999b, p.14). The National Development Plan 2000 -2006 allocated €93.98 million toward the implementation of the *White Paper's* recommendations.

31. The *White Paper* made a number of far-reaching proposals, both action-oriented and structural. Actions to be undertaken included general activities to address present weaknesses and improve quality, e.g. the Quality in Education Mark, expansion of research, use of external expertise... and specific activities addressed to particular groups, such as, disadvantaged children, children with special needs, Traveller children, parents, children 3 to 4 years cared for in the home, children under 3 years, etc.

32. Structural proposals envisaged, in particular, the creation of:
    - A specialist *Early Years Development Unit* within the Department of Education and Science responsible for policy formulation and co-ordination with other ministries;
    - An *Early Childhood Education Agency* (ECEA) that would be responsible for administrative and executive tasks, such as the management of the Department's early childhood education provision, the development of a Quality in Education (QE) Mark, the production of materials and curriculum development...

33. To date, few of these recommendations have been implemented, but a start has been made to prepare the grounds to establish an Early Childhood Education Agency, and to begin the task of addressing the quality issue in early education. To this end, a *Centre for Early Childhood Development and Education (CECDE)* was established by the Department in 2001 and officially opened in October 2002. The CECDE is jointly managed by two training establishments, one in the Education sector (St. Patrick's College, Drumcondra, which trains primary school teachers), the other in the Childcare sector (Dublin Institute of Technology, which offers courses of study to degree level for those working in early childhood care and education). The defined objectives of the CECDE are:
    - To develop a quality framework for all aspects of early education, including the development of a Quality in Education (QE) Mark for providers,
    - To develop targeted interventions on a pilot basis for children up to 6 years of age classified as educationally disadvantaged or with special needs,
    - To prepare the groundwork for the establishment of an Early Childhood Education Agency as recommended in the *White Paper.*

3. Administrative responsibility

Ministerial responsibility

34. Seven different government departments have responsibility for various parts of early childhood and family policy. In practice, however, the ministries responsible for early childhood provision in Ireland are mainly three: the Department of Health and Children (DHC); the Department of Justice, Equality and Law Reform (DJELR); and the Department of Education and Science (DES). The Department of Social and Family Affairs has also important policy responsibilities for families, parents and young children, but in principle, it does not engage in early childhood provision.[14] The contribution of the three central ministries to early childhood provision is summarised in Table 5 in Annex 1. Although provision is handled *de facto* by DJELR, DES and DHC, no clear responsibility has been given to any one Department or agency to lead integrated policy or to provide coherence across the various early childhood bodies and services.

---

[14] Some Family Centres do actually provide or support childcare, but surprisingly, there is no formal co-operation between family centres and the care and education network. In other countries, Family Centres are often the preferred choice of parents for daycare, particularly in rural areas and small towns.

> **Box. 1 Integrating early childhood services**
>
> In England (Scotland and Wales have separate education jurisdictions), the Government is working to develop a more coherent approach to the delivery of integrated early childhood services, and to bring together various policies and funding streams into an integrated whole. Services had already been formed into three recognisable groups: childcare, early years education (with a wider range than in Ireland), and Sure Start (the cornerstone of government policy to tackle child poverty and social exclusion). In July 2002, the Government brought together these units into a single inter-departmental division called the Sure Start Unit, based in the Department for Education and Skills (DfES) but responsible to both the DfES and the Department for Work and Pensions. About 300 people work in this Unit. The new unit will be responsible for delivering integrated early years education, childcare and family support at both national and local levels. One of the key objectives will be the delivery of 800 new Children's Centres. These centres will bring together good quality childcare, early years education, family support and health services in disadvantaged areas. The government also announced a combined budget for the Unit of €2.4 billion Euros. The funding will be used to provide a free nursery education place for all 3-year olds by 2004, and the creation of 250,000 extra childcare places by 2006.

35. Part of the reason for the dispersion of responsibilities in Ireland is that early childhood policy has traditionally been subsumed under larger issues, such as family policy, primary schooling, general health or other policy. The age group 0-6 years has not been considered as a defined age group with its own specific health, developmental and cognitive traits. Many small, specialised agencies and sub-structures attached to all the above ministries do exist, some important at national level, such as the National Children's Office, the Centre for Early Childhood Development and Education, the Family Support Agency, or the National Framework Committee on Family Friendly Policies. As these bodies are not major ministries and do not control major funding, they are not in a position to take in charge the large-scale policy renewal and integration that the early childhood and the family policy field in Ireland will require in the coming years.

The role of local government in early education and care

36. Local government in Ireland is complex, and in recent years has undergone change and reform. During the late 1980s and 1990s, growing recognition of the limitations of councils or of central government to respond satisfactorily to local needs[15] led to the creation of new agencies, planning groups and partnerships to meet the challenge of social and economic problems concentrated at local level. In response to the increasingly complex policy environment, the government established in 1998 a *Task Force on the Integration of Local Government and Local Development Systems.* While preserving the autonomy of the various bodies and agencies, the report of the Task Force proposed a common framework of strategic planning at *county level* to enhance co-ordination and deliver policies effectively. The newly created City/County Development Boards (CDBs) will increasingly provide administrative and management structures, financial resources and evaluation mechanisms. Composed of local representation, the state agencies and the social partners (employers, unions, farming organisations and the voluntary sector), the Boards are delegated to formulate and implement polices relating to the economic, social and cultural development of each county (see Box 2 below).

37. Because of the relevance of childcare to local employment and human resource development, the *City and County Childcare Committees (CCCs)* have been given the responsibility of implementing the childcare policy of the Department of Justice, Equality and Law Reform. Each city and county area (thirty-three in all), has now established a Childcare Committee, with a board, management and a

---

[15] The experience of the OECD reviews also points to the need for local solutions to early education and care, but would also underline the irreplaceable contribution of government to policy steering, regulation, funding, training, certification and quality standards.

Table 1. Composition of City/County Development Boards

Sector	Members	Number
Local Government	SPC Chairs; Council Chair or Mayor; County/City Manager; Urban representative	7
Local Development	2 each from: County/City Enterprise Board; LEADER II groups; ADM supported Partnership Companies and ADM supported Community Groups	6
State Agencies	As appropriate: Health Board; FÁS; Teagasc; VEC; Enterprise Ireland; IDA; Regional Tourism organisations; D/CSFA regional officer; SFADCo/Údaräs	7
Social Partners	Employers and Business organisations (1); Trade Unions (1); Farming organisations (1); Community and Voluntary organisations (2)	5
Total		c. 25

carefully drawn up plan. The City and County Childcare Committees relationship with the CDBs was put on a more formal footing in spring 2003 when the CCCs became working groups of the CDBs and the chairpersons of the CCCs become Board members of the CDBs. According to the proposals set out in the new social partnership agreement, *Sustaining Progress 2003-2005,* in its section on childcare: "Each County Childcare Committee will identify local needs for childcare, establish annual targets and assist in the development of childcare services in each county, to meet identified need." The CCs are assisted by the Department of Justice, Equality and Law Reform and by a professional agency, the ADM, (Area Development Management Ltd.), which takes in charge the financial management of DJELR grants. The ADM plays, on behalf of DJELR, an important role in the managing and monitoring of the grant applications at the local level. It has also carried out the National Childcare Census on behalf of DJELR, providing figures on the number of children being served at the county level and information on providers.

The role of the community in ECEC

38. Because of the shortness of the visit, the team was not able to research how the county level interfaces with the local communities, and how education and care are integrated at that level. From what was reported, it seems that there is growing dynamism, and greater sensitivity to local needs. However, early education, as part of the primary school system, is still outside the remit of the local authorities and County Childcare Committees. Although many teachers in Ireland are actively involved in local affairs, primary education (in which early education is included) is administered directly and independently by the Department of Education and Science through school Boards of Management. It seems that there is no statute or written framework to direct the education, childcare, health, family and social welfare actors to work together at community level around the issue of child and family development.

4. Co-ordination

39. A defining characteristic of the ECEC system in Ireland is the involvement of a several government ministries in the development and implementation of policies regarding support systems for families and the education and care of young children. The situation raises the issue of effective co-ordination between Departments and across sectors.

Childcare

40. Through the *National Childcare Strategy,* the Department of Justice, Equality and Law Reform (DJELR) has achieved in a short period a good level of co-ordination across the tiers and between the various

stakeholders within the Childcare sector. A central networking forum is the *National Co-ordinating Childcare Committee* (NCCC). The NCCC brings together, on a bi-monthly basis, representatives of key government Departments as well as members of the non-statutory sector, including the Social Partners and the National Voluntary Childcare Organisations (NVCOs). Sub-committees focus on specific issues (currently: certification /qualifications; after school provision; equality and diversity). The NCCC clearly plays a central role in improving co-ordination across services and professionals and contributing to coherency and partnership in aims and delivery of services.

41. Although the recent NDP evaluation was critical about the actual monitoring of quality outputs from the NVCOs, NCCC sponsorship of the voluntary organisations deserves special mention. In line with social partnership values, the NCCC has given the voluntary organisations a place at the table, and provides them with funding in recognition of the services that they continue to provide to Irish parents and their children. Their special strengths and sensitivity to the needs of particular groups of parents are most useful for the system. Moreover, if EU benchmarks are to be met by the year 2010, these organisations will need to be included in the official network providing accredited education, care and after-school care for Irish children.

Box 2. IPPA (Irish Pre-school Playgroups Association), the Early Childhood Organisation

IPPA has been in operation for over thirty years, and is the largest voluntary supplier of early years services in Ireland. Founded by parents to provide playgroups for young children on a sessional basis, it has evolved into an organisation of 1900 services serving 37,000 children. It seeks to engage parents not only in the education and welfare of their children, but also in their own personal development and further education. A non-profit body, its services depend on a mix of parental fees, government funding sources and voluntary labour. In the absence of statutory input, IPPA has been an important actor in organising the pre-school sector in Ireland and in promoting values, standards and guidelines. It has long offered both training and professional advice to its members.

---

42. Potentially, the NCCC also provides a framework for cross-Departmental consultation. However, the remit of the Committee is advisory, and decisions made as a result of consultations are - in accordance with the Committee's terms of reference - the responsibility of DJELR and located within the Childcare sector. While the DES is formally a member of the National Co-ordinating Childcare Committee, the review team was unsure about the nature of its role on that Committee.

43. A further co-ordinating structure which is variously mentioned in relation to the National Childcare Strategy is the Inter-Departmental and Inter-Agency Synergies Childcare Group, chaired by DJELR. Through it, high-level representatives of a number of Government Departments which formerly managed individual strands of childcare funding met regularly to ensure co-ordination of approach to the funding of childcare services. However the transfer of all State funding resources for childcare to the Department of Justice, Equality and Law Reform diminished the role of that Group. It is understood that the Department of Justice, Equality and Law Reform is considering the establishment in the near future of a new cross-Departmental, Inter-Agency Group to discuss cross cutting childcare policy issues. The NDP evaluation of childcare also proposes that a newly constituted Inter-Departmental committee "should focus on the co-ordination of policy and interventions towards childcare and children generally across government departments." The OECD supports the recommendation but would substitute for "childcare" "early education and care" to take into account the common tasks of DES and DJELR.

Education

44. The DES has responsibility for national education policies for young children. In accordance with the recommendations of the *White Paper,* it established the Centre for Early Childhood Development and

Education (CECDE) in 2002. The Centre will focus on professional issues, e.g. developing a Quality in Education Mark, conceptualising targeted interventions for disadvantaged children, encouraging parental involvement, standard-setting and play a facilitating role in relation to the field (practitioners, training, support agencies, etc.)

45. From what the review team understood, the statutes of the CECDE do not perceive direct links with DJELR as a constitutive part of its co-ordinating role, and no mention is made, for example, of the *National Childcare Strategy* in the Centre's Programme of Work (2001). While having a key contributory role to play in developing co-ordination in early childhood education policy at national and local level, the CECDE remains ex-departmental, and has limited official responsibility with respect to co-ordination of policy-making, regulation and financing.

46. The *White Paper* 1999 (p.132) envisaged that an *Early Years Development Unit* should be set up within the Department to co-ordinate the formulation, development and implementation of early childhood education policies. It was underlined that co-ordination "will be the key role of the new Unit" (p.133). However, this new Unit has not been established, and the review team members were informed that its creation is not foreseen for the immediate future. Officials explained that target groups as such were not a priority, but that it was preferable to treat thematic goals, such as social inclusion, across the whole primary sector, including early education.

47. However, the view would seem to overlook the specific goals of early childhood systems, and contrasts clearly with practice in other OECD countries. Early years policy units exist in most European countries (See Box 1: *Integrating Early Childhood Services*), and sometimes even enjoy particular political sponsorship in government, e.g. Belgium, Sweden, the United Kingdom. These units are seen to be responsible for the first, foundation stage of lifelong learning. They formulate policy and regulations for government approval, ensure the collection of relevant data, provide guidelines for pre-service and in-service training of early childhood professionals, supervise quality, monitor infra-structure (early childhood rooms and outdoors are specific in design and layout), ensure that delivery targets are met, accredit institutions, and interface with other government ministries. It is difficult to see how these tasks can be assumed by more generalised units, particularly at a moment in Ireland when much effort will be needed to expand access, and lay the foundations of a national system.

48. *Vertical co-ordination from DES to the schools* – another aspect of co-ordination is the vertical relationship between the Department and the local schools. The relationship has traditionally been intense, with ongoing inputs from the Department in all relevant areas, such as funding, school-buildings, curriculum, inspection, etc. However, these inputs have been made almost strictly from the perspective of primary school requirements, a perspective which does not always pay sufficient attention to the particular needs and specific learning patterns of the younger children. An example is the allocation of teachers to schools, calculated on staffing ratios for primary school children. In consequence, 37% of junior infants in Ireland find themselves in classes of 25-29 children, cared for by one teacher. There is no regulation requiring School Boards to respect the principle: *the younger the child, the lower the child:staff ratio.* In contrast, the childcare regulations require for children aged 3-6 years, one care staff for 8 children (full-time), or one to 10 children (sessional). Likewise, in the education sector, there are no specific regulations for the training of teachers of the younger children, or for classroom design, classroom organisation and equipment – elements that ought to be differentiated when dealing with the younger children.

Co-ordination and policy implementation at the regional / local level

49. At a regional / local level, the major co-ordinating bodies in the Childcare sector - set up within the National Childcare Strategy - are the County Childcare Committees. To date these Committees - which operate as working groups of the County and City Development Boards and liaise with DJELR and the

NCCC - have been established in all 33 counties or cities. Within the remit of the EOCP 2000 - 2006, their task is to develop and implement co-ordinated strategic plans for childcare provision within the region. Proposed implementation strategies on a yearly basis are laid down in annual Action Plans.

Box 3. Galway City & County Childcare Committee

The Galway City and County Childcare Committee was originally set up as the Galway City and County Childcare Strategy Group in response to a crisis in childcare provision following the implementation of the Child Care (Preschool Services) Regulations 1996. Its members are 26 individuals representing the Statutory Sector, Partnership Boards, the Social Partners, the Childcare Sector; and Parent Representatives.

The *Galway Childcare Development Plan 2001 - 2006* was published in December 2001. The development of childcare services is reviewed and monitored on an on-going basis and an evaluation system is being established. The role of the Committee is:

- to implement the strategies outlined in the Development Plan;
- to assist the development of new and existing childcare services;
- to assist communities in: identifying needs and gaps in service provision; developing new services to meet these needs; planning future development; developing childcare services that address cultural and linguistic diversity;
- to provide information on: existing childcare services; establishing new services; training, resources and funding;
- to support local networks of childcare providers, childminders, parents and parent and toddler groups;
- to assist in the development and implementation of a Quality Assurance system for childcare services.

Since the establishment of the Committee in 2000, 97 new childcare services and a total of 1,535 new childcare places have been established. 90 services at pre-development stage are currently being assisted which will provide a total of 1,851 new places. More than 50 % of all new services developed are community based services managed by voluntary committees and it is these not-for-profit services which are given the main input of assistance, support, staff time and resources. Special initiatives include a resource library and outreach service, 2 mobile play-bus services, 2 childminding initiatives, various information packs, and training initiatives.

---

50. The terms of reference of the County Childcare Committees include: developing information strategies on childcare for parents and providers, identifying gaps in childcare provision, promoting the establishment of new childcare facilities, formulating priority objectives for the region, and supporting networking initiatives of childcare providers at a local and county level. The advantages of this co-ordinated approach include: the pooling of agencies' resources for the expansion of services; avoiding duplication of services; sharing information; strategic planning with a view to identifying needs and gaps and prioritising resources; and improving service quality through a partnership approach. The Committees appear to be dynamic and purposeful bodies.

51. In general, the Education sector (e.g. the inspectorate, schools or training colleges) is not represented on these Committees. The review team was informed that because the DES is not regionalised, it is unable to nominate representatives to locally-based committees, without significant resource implications. This appears to be hindering the establishment of effective co-ordination structures across sectors at the local level. The notion of care and education as a continuum – both horizontally and vertically – is emphasised often enough in the relevant policy documents. However, in practical implementation terms, this does not seem to be happening.

> ### Box 4. A Dutch example of co-ordination to deliver programmes for disadvantaged children, aged 2-4 years old
>
> As in Ireland, primary schooling in the Netherlands begins at 4 years, and play groups have traditionally been the dominant form of provision outside this service. Significant investment is now being poured into early education for the 2-4 year olds from disadvantaged backgrounds both by the Ministry of Education and the Ministry of Social Affairs. This investment is co-ordinated and administered at local level by municipal authorities. A Local Authority Disadvantage Policy Act was passed in 1998, to enable the educational and local authorities to create socio-educational programmes for disadvantaged children and families in designated areas.[16]
>
> The new funding goes predominantly to municipal play groups and pre-school programmes for the 2-4 year olds established in primary schools or other premises. In addition, the local municipality prescribes the number of at-risk children that groups should enrol in their programmes, and provides matching funding. In parallel, the ministries offer the local boards funding and direct help, in particular to establish collaboration with local services, to improve their planning and management capacity, and to enhance quality through staff training.
>
> All primary schools in designated areas are now expected to engage not only in the education of children, but also in community service and outreach to families. Collaboration between playgroups, pre-school and primary education has been made mandatory. At the same time, regular evaluations are carried out on the learning achievement of young children in both pre-school and play groups. Each must follow a special curriculum tested by the Dutch education authorities.
>
> Although they sometimes criticise the quality criteria and accountancy levels required by the ministries, all the major municipalities in the Netherlands now implement the new programmes. The number of disadvantaged and bi-lingual children participating in pre-school programmes of three hours daily from the age of two years has greatly increased.

52. In summary:

   - *Co-ordination at a horizontal level within the childcare sector* seems to be strong and well-led. The *National Co-ordinating Childcare Committee* (NCCC) brings together the key government Departments as well as the non-statutory sector, including the Social Partners and the National Voluntary Childcare Organisations. In addition, the sector is guided by well-defined goals in the *National Childcare Strategy* (1999) and is supported both by the Childcare Directorate of the DJELR and ADM for field administration.

   - *Vertical co-ordination* toward the County Childcare Committees has been initiated and is growing in strength. If devolved powers and funding can be allocated to these Committees, they may in turn be able to provide vertical co-ordination within each county, and encourage horizontal co-ordination across schools, childcare providers and community agencies. *Vertical co-ordination by the DES toward schools* in the education sector is also effective, but often overlooks the specific needs and learning patterns of the younger children. Regulations for child:staff ratios, the training of teachers of the younger children, or classroom design and organisation are rarely differentiated from those applicable to children in obligatory education.

   - *Horizontal co-ordination across early education and childcare* is weak. County Childcare Committee members spoke to the team of the need for new services bridging the education/childcare divide, for the use of school premises for play groups and after-school care. It was suggested that co-ordination could be helped by more regular specialist ECEC representation from the DES in the inter-departmental committee, and at county level. Whatever the reason, no effective, cross-sectoral structure exists at decision-making level that is able to provide a clear policy and action framework agreed by the major Departments.

---

[16] Designated areas are those neighbourhoods having one or more primary schools at which more than 50% of the children have a weighted assessment of 1.25 or over. The concept of "weighting" is as follows: schools, receive for each child; of Dutch parents, the per capita grant x 1; of Dutch unskilled parents, the per capita grant x 1.25 grant; of Traveller parents, the per capita grant x 1.7 grant; of unskilled, immigrant parents, the per capita grant x 1.9 grant. Special needs children receive a higher weighting.

5. Provision

Types of provision and coverage

The overall picture of ECEC provision in Ireland is as follows:

53. Provision in the Childcare sector is diverse and fragmented. A survey carried out by the Economic and Social Research Institute (1998) revealed that 38 % of all parents with children aged 4 years and under rely on some form of paid childcare arrangement. 21 % of mothers with children aged less than 5 years used childminders. Centre-based care services were the second most commonly used form, taken up by 14 % of parents. "However, over one-fifth (22 %) of mothers with full-time jobs and 47 % of those with part-time jobs used no paid childcare at all, indicating a reliance on informal provision provided either by partners, family, friends or neighbours." (*Irish Background Report* 2002, p.29).

54. Apart from childminders (who, in general, remain outside any regulation), services are unequally spread across the country, are diverse in type and are funded from different sources. The *Health Boards* subsidise some 7000 places, while the Department of Justice, Equality and Law Reform has already made available grant assistance of over €180 million to develop new and enhanced childcare facilities and to support childcare places in disadvantaged areas. It is expected that when fully drawn down, this assistance will support over 42,000 childcare places. The remaining funding will be allocated over the period 2003 to 2006 and should lead to the creation and support of a significant number of additional places. These services use widely different programmes and cater for different group sizes and age ranges. Few outstanding models of quality or design yet exist at national level. However, since the taking in charge of the sector by the Childcare Directorate at DJELR, significant progress has been made, and no doubt, streamlining and adequate models will gradually emerge.

55. Provision within the Education sector is dominated by Ministry of Education public provision, which is centre-based, universal and free. The Department of Education and Science underwrites three main types of service: (1) Morning infant classes in primary schools catering for 56 % of 4 year olds and almost all 5 year olds; (2) Special needs facilities within a small number of schools; (3) Specific pre-school pilot programmes targeting 3 and 4 year old children from disadvantaged backgrounds (e.g. the *Early Start* Pre-School Pilot Project, Pre-Schools for Traveller Children). In its coverage, DES departs from the European norm, in which education ministries generally provide for all children from 3 years. Other than DES services, the care and education of young children from 3-6 years and beyond, is low in coverage, private and located outside the education sector. Most providers will claim to have an educational component in their programme, but support to them comes currently from DJELR/EOCP funding rather than from the Department of Education and Science.

Extent of coverage

56. Table 6 in Appendix 1, taken from the 2001 edition of OECD *Employment Outlook*, provides an idea of the comparative coverage of young children aged 0-3 and from 3-6 years in OECD countries. Where 3-6 year old children are concerned, Ireland's coverage is among the lowest in the European Union (just above Greece). The coverage rates for other countries are appreciably higher, as they have progressively expanded access over the past twenty years. Today, universal, free pre-school coverage in most European countries begins at the age of three years.

57. Where under-3s are concerned, the third column of the Table places Ireland toward the top of OECD countries in terms of coverage. This figure needs interpretation.[17] The ESRI survey of 1998, carried out for the Commission on the Family, gives a similar figure for all use of childcare outside the home. As we know that at least two thirds of Irish children, cared for outside the home, are looked after by private childminders, the figure of 38% for children in publicly accredited provision cannot be correct. In fact, from the raw data supplied in this table, it is not possible to know whether the childcare in

---

[17] In contrast, the enrolment figures provided in the Table for the Netherlands and the UK are too low...

question is public, grant-aided or private, whether the rate recorded refers to sessional, half-day or full-day usage, or whether programmes are monitored or completely escape inspection.

58. From the EOCP and other figures available, the percentage of 0-3 year old children in half-day or full-day, publicly subsidised services in Ireland seemed to the review team to be more probably in the range of 10% to 15%. It is estimated that grants already disbursed to childcare providers and community groups under the Equal Opportunities Childcare Programme (EOCP) will create 19,448 new childcare places (48% of childcare places receiving support) and will also support 21,429 existing places (DJELR, 2002). However, uncertainty about basic coverage points to another challenge, namely, to develop reliable statistics and data on young children. Young children have been traditionally a hidden group in Irish society. Today, their emergence as a specific group, with their own potential, needs and rights, requires public auditing of their status, including an analysis of financial flows toward them as a group (see Chapter 3).

Features of provision in the Childcare sector

59. Childcare in Ireland has traditionally been dominated by private childminder arrangements. In parallel, some education-oriented services such as the Montessori schools existed, catering typically for a small number of mainly privileged children from 3-6 years. From the 1970s also, some private and voluntary services began to be established, in particular Playgroups and Irish-language medium Pre-schools *(naíonraí)*. It was not until very recently – in the context of the *National Childcare Strategy* – that expansion of grant-aided provision to support and develop the community based/not-for-profit and private childcare sectors gathered any significant momentum.

60. Both the old and the new services within the Childcare sector are offered on a predominantly sessional basis, i.e. for less than 3.5 hours per day per child. Of a total of 3,496 services, only 1,124 (approx. 32 %) offer full-day provision (see Table 7 in Appendix 1). The most widespread forms of centre-based provision, catering mainly for 3 and 4 year old children, are the predominantly privately owned *Play Groups* and *Pre-schools.* Approximately 80% of these services are sessional. *Montessori schools* are privately owned and managed and provide for children aged 3 to 6 years. Just over half the places offered are full-day places. *Nurseries* (crèches, daycare) offer mainly full-day services for infants and toddlers from 2 to 3 months up to school-going age and may also cater for school-age children. They are either privately owned and operated or community-based and run. *Naíonraí* are Irish language pre-schools providing for 3 to 6 year olds. They are privately owned and part-funded by the Department of Community, Rural and Gaeltacht Affairs. Other services for children up to school-going age include *Parent and Toddler Groups* (mainly for children up to 3 years of age), *Workplace Crèches* and *Drop-in Crèches* (irregular and very short-term care in shopping centres, leisure centres, etc.).

61. *Organised daily, out-of-school services for infant school and school-age children* (e.g. childcare, breakfast clubs, after-school clubs, recreation, art and music education, sports and physical education…) are virtually non-existent. Exchequer funding has been specifically identified for the development of after-school services under the EOCP but demand for grant assistance to date has been slow. It is hoped that the publication of the Ad Hoc Working Group Report on School Age Childcare later this year will stimulate provision. This Working Group is a Sub-Group of the National Childcare Co-ordinating Committee.

62. *Childminding services* provide for children up to compulsory school age and also for school children before and after school hours and during school holidays. Childminding is typically an all-year service arranged on an individual basis to suit both the parent's and the childminder's needs. The Child Care (Pre-school Services) Regulations (1996) and (Amendment) Regulations (1997) requires childcare providers caring for three or more children (excluding their own offspring, offspring of their partner/spouse, other relatives or three children from the same family) to notify the local Health Board. Although strong efforts are being made to reduce the number of non-notified childminders,

the great majority of family day care provision is unregulated and informally paid. Consequently, there are data gaps regarding the actual number of childminders and of children in their care, and serious concerns about quality.

Box 5. Childminding in Ireland

In this arrangement children are looked after on a sessional, half-day or long-day basis by self-employed childminders on freely negotiated market terms. The Pre-school Services Regulations require that when a childminder cares for more than three children under the age of 6 years in her home, she should notify to the local Health Board, and become subject to certain regulations. According to figures provided by the National Childminding Association, 95 % of childminders operate outside this framework, resulting in a lack of accurate figures for childminding in Ireland. It is estimated, however, that 70 % of long-day care places in Ireland are provided through private childminding. The arrangements are generally unsupervised and escape health, safety, developmental and programmatic regulations. According to research on similar arrangement in the USA, informal arrangements – although reported by parents to be good – are generally of low quality (NICHD, 1997).

The DJELR, Health Boards and Childminding Ireland are at present actively encouraging those childminders who are not required to notify to the health boards to opt for voluntary notification as a measure to enhance their overall quality. A further task will be to transform childminding in general into the grant aided, supervised and trained service that the Nordic and other countries provide. In these family daycare networks, families choose their childminder (family daycare), but contracts (including rate of remuneration) and quality control are the responsibility of the local childcare board.

Features of provision in the Education sector

63. In most OECD countries, education ministries have responsibility for children aged 3-6 years, and in the majority of these countries, coverage for the age group ranges from 80-99%. Currently in Ireland, all 5 year olds and just over half of 4 year olds attend *infant classes* located in primary schools (OECD, 2002). Few children of 3-years of age are enrolled, giving an overall coverage rate for the age group 3-6 years of 56%, which is among the lowest in Europe.

64. Children in the infant classes are organised into two same-age classes: the junior infant class (for 4 year olds) and the senior infant class (for 5 year olds). Statutory schooling begins at age 6. Classes run approximately from 9:00 a.m. to 1:40 p.m. Official adult/child ratios are 1 teacher to a maximum of 29 pupils. However, recent figures from the Department of Education and Science (DES) reveal that 24 % of infant class pupils are in groups of 30 pupils or above (*Irish Background Report* 2002, p.62) – a child-staff ratio that would be unacceptable for young children in most European countries. Infant classes are staffed by a trained primary teacher and in some cases, have an additional assistant for children with special learning needs. Attendance is free of charge, but meals are provided to only a small proportion of children.[18]

65. The *Early Start Programme* was launched by the DES in 1994 as a targeted intervention for children considered 'at risk' of not reaching their potential within the education system. Since that date, *Early Start* units have been set up in 40 primary schools in designated disadvantaged areas, reaching 1,680 children throughout the country.[19] 15 children are grouped together in a class staffed by a primary school teacher and a qualified childcare worker. The curriculum emphasises the development of cognitive and linguistic skills.

---

[18] Many countries offering a half-day programme provide, in addition, a nutritious snack or full meal for young children. Preparing food and eating together is seen as an essential part of education and the socialisation process.

[18] There are 310 areas in Ireland designated as areas of educational disadvantage.

> **Box 6. Early Start in a suburban Dublin school**
>
> The intervention format of *Early Start* programmes is generally one of a 2¹/₂ hour session over one school year in a designated unit in a primary school, backed up by liaising visits to families by trained primary teachers. Within this National School of 15 classes, four *Early Start* units were established in 1995. The units function on a parallel, sessional basis, with 60 children aged 3 and 4 years attending for either from 9:00 a.m. to 11:30 a.m. or from 12:00 to 2:30 p.m. The groups of 15 children are staffed by one primary school teacher and one childcare worker.
>
> The demand for places far exceeds supply. At present there are 30 children on the waiting list. Selection is the responsibility of the principal teacher, who admits children according to self-defined criteria in consultation with the District Nurse, *Early Start* staff and Home-School Community Link scheme teachers regarding the "most marginalised" and "most disadvantaged" families. In order to avoid social stigmatisation, admissions criteria are not made public. Following the *Early Start* year, the children are spread out across the Junior infants in classes of 20 staffed by one teacher and one special needs assistant.
>
> The self-defined curricular focus within the *Early Start* unit is on literacy development. Co-ordination with other community agencies is an integral part of the programme. The unit also has links with a local vocational college offering course in adult literacy and a school completion programme. A crèche has been established for parents attending adult learning classes in the school building.
>
> The principal considers the *Early Start* experience to be a positive one for both children and parents. The programme helps to break down barriers generally and to ease the transition into formal schooling. Parents like to see their children as part of the school system, which for them represents a certain status (in contrast with prevailing views about childcare facilities). The principal would consider it a "huge loss" if the unit were to close. She sees Early Start as a focal point for building trusting parent-school relationships and strengthening community identity.

66. Children from the Traveller community often experience multiple effects of disadvantage, including inadequate accommodation, poor living standards, restricted opportunities and discrimination. To allow these children to have a fair start in life, grant-aided *Pre-Schools for children from the Traveller community* were introduced in 1984. In 2001, 48 Pre-Schools for children from the Traveller community were launched by the DES. These services cater for up to 624 children and are usually established by voluntary groups or Traveller support groups, with the DES providing 98 % of staffing and transport costs plus an annual grant for equipment and materials.

67. Most units are staffed by a teacher and a childcare assistant, many of whom are untrained. A Visiting Teacher Scheme ensures links with families and the various levels of education. There is usually one visiting teacher per 150 families. Unlike the *Early Start* units, the Traveller Pre-schools are not part of the primary school system. Each year the staff of these pre-schools may attend two days in-career development organised by the National Education Officer for Travellers and funded by the Department of Education and Science. A recently published evaluation study of 25 of these pre-schools was carried out in 2001 by the Inspectorate of the Department of Education and Science.

6. Funding

The Childcare sector

68. Public funding provision in the Childcare sector comes through different funding streams, but principally through the EU-supported Equal Opportunities Childcare Programme 2000 - 2006. The EOCP is being implemented by the Department of Justice, Equality and Law Reform and is assisting an increasing number of both new and existing childcare services. About €180 million of EU funding

(from the European Regional Development Fund and the European Social Fund) is being supplemented by an investment of €257 million from the Irish Exchequer. Funding measures include: capital grant assistance for childcare service providers; staff grant assistance for community-based, not-for-profit organisations in areas of significant disadvantage; grant assistance to national voluntary organisations and to county childcare committees to improve the quality of childcare provision; quality improvement measures for local childcare networks and national voluntary childcare organisations; a national childminding initiative and innovative projects (DJELR, 2002). By mid-2002, 1,533 grant applications had been approved for funding under the EOCP.

69. As provision in the Childcare sector is predominantly private, parental fees remain the major source of funding. A recent (2002) survey conducted by the National Children's Nurseries Association (NCNA) revealed that parents pay between €94 to €137 per week for toddlers and between €107 and €145 per week for infants less than 1 year of age, depending on the location of the facilities. More recently, the National Children's Nurseries Association reports weekly fees in excess of €170 being charged for full day care in Dublin. Such costs to parents, averaging over 30% of disposable income for the Average Production Employee, are unsustainable even in the medium term. Through an Anti-Inflationary Package, the DJELR has made funding available for the development of childminding services. This will probably be administered through the County Childcare Committees. DJELR is at present reviewing different options around the training, networking and information for childminders, and plans a comprehensive country-wide development initiative from mid-2003.

70. The hope was expressed to the OECD team on several occasions that the current funding via EOCP – welcome as it is - should not be simply a pump-priming exercise with a commitment to 2006 only. It was alleged that uncertainty about the future funding of the sector breeds insecurity and amateurism, and may undermine current efforts to expand provision and improve quality. Assumptions that childcare provision could be self financing and sustainable after three years of EOCP funding are unrealistic, particularly in relation to the community sector.

71. In sum, as the analysis in this Note will bring out, ECEC in Ireland is now approaching a decisive moment where funding is concerned. Affordability, widening access and improving quality are major issues to be resolved in the Childcare sector. Government-led funding at the level of EOCP, prolonged over the decade, may well bring in the necessary number of providers for children aged 1-3 years, and in parallel, improve the quality and affordability of the system. Without this direct funding and the leverage that can be exercised through it, it is difficult to see how quality (in particular, the status and training of staff) and fair access (in particular, childcare for low-income and special needs children) can be effectively addressed. (see discussion in Chapter 3).

The Education sector

72. The infant classes in primary schools are the only form of reasonably funded state provision for young children to be found all over Ireland. These classes currently provide for nearly all 5 year olds and just over half of all 4 year olds, on the basis of a four hour and forty minute session. From the perspective of families in employment, they are limited in terms of opening hours, both daily and round the year. For children from disadvantaged areas, the session would gain greatly if backed by afternoon educare programmes and wrap-around services (see discussion in Chapter 3). Core funding from DES now covers current and capital costs, teachers' salaries and capitation grants. Higher capitation grants are paid for children in schools with designated disadvantaged status or where a resource teacher for Traveller children has been appointed. Additional grants are awarded to schools with pupils encountering learning difficulties or at risk of educational disadvantage.

73. The Department of Education and Science also funds the targeted intervention programmes mentioned in the above section on provision (e.g. *Early Start,* Pre-Schools for Traveller Children). Again, funding covers the current and capital costs and teachers' salaries. The minimum per capita cost

for the *Early Start* Programme has been estimated at €2,330 in the school year 2000/2001 (*Irish Background Report* 2002, p.54), but in general, funding for young children in the education system compares poorly to European standards, or to per capita government investment in tertiary education (see Figure 4 and Table 8 in Appendix 1). In addition, access rates in early education are much lower than other European countries, except Greece. Education sectors in other countries have been building up enrolment rates in the past decades to cover all 4-year old children and most 3-year olds.

74. In sum, a number of funding challenges for early education are now emerging: How to address the significant Irish deficit with regard to the enrolment of 3-6 year old children? How to deliver quality services to disadvantaged areas and to Traveller children? How to prolong the ECEC day, especially in disadvantaged areas, so that young children can draw the maximum benefit from the free morning education session? In Chapter 3, we shall discuss these issues in some detail, outlining some of the funding solutions adopted in other countries.

7. The regulatory framework

75. The regulation of early childhood education and care services in Ireland reflects the divided nature of governmental responsibility for education and childcare as described above.

76. Services in the Childcare sector (and also the DES-funded Pre-Schools for children from the Traveller community) are officially regulated by the regional Health Boards under the Child Care Act 1991. Current regulatory policy – drawn up by the Department of Health and Children - is set down in the Child Care (Pre-School Services) Regulations 1996 and (Amendment) Regulations 1997. Assessment criteria include: appropriate child development supports (activities, materials, equipment, premises); health, safety and welfare aspects; adult/child ratios and child/space ratios; record keeping; inspection; insurance; fees. The main purpose of the Regulations is to ensure the health, safety and welfare of the pre-school child, but they do not cover quality-related issues such as staff qualifications and training, curriculum and pedagogy. The first inspection generally takes place within three months of notification of service provision and after that on an annual basis.

77. However, inspection is dependent on the staff available and the number of notifications received. According to certain sources, these inspections may take place at five-yearly intervals, but more official sources claim that many services are on their fourth or fifth consecutive annual inspection. As in the Education sector, Department of Health inspectors are not required to undergo a specific training for the inspection of early years services. The team was informed that most have a background in public health nursing or environmental health. Again, not all childcare provision is covered by the Regulations, and that the majority of childcare providers need not notify the Health Boards, e.g. those looking after fewer than 3 children or providing care for children after school.

78. However, the Child Care (Pre-School Services) Regulations 1996 and (Amendment) Regulations 1997 are at present being examined by a cross-sector Review Group. A grant of €1.5 million was allocated to the Department of Health and Children in order to improve the situation by introducing a voluntary notification and support system for childminders. The Health Boards also run an advisory service on service improvement issues for prospective providers and for present providers, but the great majority of childminders remain outside this system and have no formal professional qualification.

79. Regulatory procedures for the Education sector are laid down in the Education Act 1998, the Education (Welfare) Act 2000 and the Equal Status Act 2000 (section 7) as well as existing health and safety legislation. They cover all aspects of a school's functioning, including patronage and management, staffing, and material resources. School inspectors, reporting to the Department of Education and Science, assess the quality of schooling, advise on educational policy implementation, and generally

provide support for teachers (particularly for probationary teachers) and school management bodies. Approximately every six years an evaluation report is drawn up on the basis of a detailed on-site inspection. These inspections cover all age-groups in the primary school, including the *Early Start* units. There are no inspectors specifically designated or trained for early childhood education. However, the Evaluation and Support Unit of the Inspectorate carries out targeted programme evaluations, some which may focus on the early years. One such study was the 2001 evaluation of 25 Pre-Schools for Children from the Traveller community mentioned above. Currently, Education Welfare Officers are being appointed to work in close co-operation with schools, teachers, parents and community/voluntary bodies.

80. Beyond these two official systems of regulation and inspection, a number of the umbrella organisations for early education and childcare have issued their own quality standards to which members subscribe on a voluntary basis. These include the IPPA – the Early Childhood Organisation (formerly the Irish Pre-school Play Group Association), the National Children's Nurseries Association, An Comhchoiste Reamhscoliochta for the Irish medium Pre-schools, Montessori organisations, and Childminding Ireland.

8. The staffing of ECEC services

81. As with the policies governing regulation, staffing policies for the Childcare and Education sectors are also markedly different. Initial training, access to in-service education, working conditions, remuneration, and recruitment, retention and status are key issues. There is no agreed framework system for staff qualifications across the two sectors.

Initial training

82. Staff in the Childcare sector may have one of a variety of qualifications of variable quality and length or – particularly in the case of childminders - no formal professional qualification at all. Until very recently there has been virtually no state involvement in this sector, which has meant that the training of childcare workers has developed in an ad hoc manner. The courses offered by the Dublin Institute of Technology – originally a two-year certificate course, now a three-year degree level course – have been an exception. In general, courses have developed either in response to the needs of service providers, or in line with particular educational philosophies (e.g. Montessori training of one to three years' duration).

83. One of the key outputs of the National Co-ordinating Childcare Committee has been a recent policy document published in September 2002 entitled *Model Framework for Education, Training and Professional Development in the Early Childhood Care and Education Sector* (Government of Ireland, 2002). This framework document was developed, under the direction of the Department of Justice, Equality and Law Reform and the DIT/OMNA team, through extensive consultation with practitioners, childcare providers, training organisations and certifying bodies. For the first time in the history of children's services in Ireland, it provides a co-ordinated vision for training and professional development in the Childcare sector. The document sets down core values, occupational profiles and professional standards.

84. In contrast, staff with group/class responsibility in the Education sector are trained primary school teachers, i.e. they gain their qualifications through state-supported and approved training courses. Five third level colleges offer three-year degree courses. An extension to four years has been recommended recently (2002) by the main teachers' union, the Irish National Teachers' Association (INTO). Degrees (B.Ed. or B.Ed. (Hons)) are conferred by one of three universities (University of Limerick, Dublin City University, Trinity College). The National University of Ireland, Cork, offers a three-year BA in Early Childhood Studies.

Content of training

85. The content of training in the Childcare sector has been as varied as the courses offered. The new *Model Framework for Education, Training and Professional Development* (2002) outlines 6 core areas of skill and knowledge for work in ECEC services: (1) child development, 2) education and play, (3) social environment, (4) health, hygiene, nutrition and safety, (5) personal / professional development, (6) communication, management and administration.

86. In the Education sector, specific course content for the training of primary school teachers varies from college to college. However, all courses include academic subjects (e.g. English, French, Irish, geography, history, mathematics, biosciences, philosophy, and music), professional studies (e.g. philosophy / history / sociology of education, developmental and educational psychology, curriculum studies), subject methodology, and classroom modules of 18 weeks. There is no early childhood specialisation within the training curriculum.

87. Primary school teachers are required to be able to teach all age levels within the primary school, i.e. children aged 4 to 12 years. In the current three-year B.Ed. course at St. Patrick's College, Drumcondra, for example, within the Education component of the course of study (other components are: Academic Subjects, Professional Irish, Professional English, Certificate in Religious Studies, Teaching Practice, Gaeltacht) the focus on early childhood education is limited to 4 units (46 hours) within the first year of study. By way of comparison, the subject-areas physical education, religious education or maths are each allotted the same number of units, as are the foundation studies components sociology of education and philosophy of education (St. Patrick's College, undated). This particular training format with its very restricted attention to early childhood education differs from the approaches adopted in many other European countries (see Oberhuemer & Ulich, 1997; OECD, 2001a).

Remuneration

88. One of the most striking differences between the Education and the Childcare sector centres on the issue of remuneration. The pay scale for primary school teachers starts at €23,096 per annum and progresses to a highest point of €44,891. Extra allowances are allocated for the posts of principal and deputy principal and may also be awarded for additional qualifications. This contrasts starkly with the wage situation of staff in private childcare facilities, who – according to a survey of NCNA members – earn roughly from €8,900 as a junior practitioner and up to €11,900 as a senior practitioner (Government of Ireland, 1999a). It has been estimated that practitioners in public sector nurseries earn between €12,700 and €17,000 per annum.

In-service training and professional development

89. In-service training has been a major route for practitioners in the Childcare sector for gaining qualifications. However, access to the restricted offers of in-service courses has been very patchy, and very often practitioners have had to personally fund their participation during their own time. The *Model Framework 2002* offers for the first time a clear vision of professional development and articulation of professional roles on five levels: Basic, Intermediate, Experienced, Advanced and Expert. Value is placed on recognising and accrediting learning acquired through experience and developing forms of access, transfer and progression within the articulated framework. The *Model Framework 2002* represents the main submission of the Childcare sector to the recently (2000) established National Qualifications Authority of Ireland (NQAI), the government agency responsible for creating a national qualifications framework.

90. The In-career Development Unit of the DES provides for a range of in-service courses based on specific curriculum areas and targeted programmes. At present, each teacher is undergoing six days in-service training per year on the new primary curriculum, which is being phased in at two subjects per year.

The Irish National Teachers' Organisation has identified a desire among teachers in infant classes for a more extensive initial training focus on early years and for more in-service training geared to a comprehensive view of supporting young children's development and learning rather than the subjects focus of the current curriculum. It also informed the review team that because some School Boards do not consider in-service training a priority, supplementary training for teachers is often voluntary and takes place during evenings or school holidays.

9. Programme regulation

Childcare

91. There is no agreed pedagogical framework across the wide range of philosophical orientations and practices within the Childcare sector. However, the new training framework for the field can be seen as a step towards consensus on core principles. These include valuing:
    - *Diversity by acknowledging and promoting each child's and each adult's individual, personal and cultural identity;*
    - *Experiences and activities that support learning and allow children to actively explore, to experience, to make choices and decisions and to share in the learning process;*
    - *Play as the natural, constructive mode of children's interactions with their peers, adults and environment.* (Government of Ireland, 2002, p.17)

Early education

92. Programme content and implementation in the Education sector are highly regulated through national curricula, guidelines, and inspection practices. The 1971 Primary School Curriculum was superseded by a revised curriculum in 1999. The new curriculum emphasises individual learning paths and teaching approaches, children's developmental needs, guided activity learning, interdisciplinary approaches, a balance between knowledge, concept and skills acquisition, and the importance of assessment and planning as analytical and evaluative tools. Six curriculum areas encompass eleven subjects. These areas are (1) Language (English, Irish), (2) Mathematics, (3) Social, Environmental and Scientific Education (History, Geography, Science), (4) Arts Education (Visual Arts, Music, Drama), (5) Physical Education, and (6) Social, Personal and Health Education. Curriculum content is very detailed according to each subject and each level within the school. At the same time the need for flexibility in delivery according to individual and local needs is officially emphasised.

93. There is no formal curriculum for the *Early Start Programme*. However, curricular guidelines were developed in co-operation with the teachers and childcare workers employed in the units as part of their ongoing in-service training. These were introduced in 1998 and are to be continuously updated. The guidelines identify four central elements: (1) cognitive development, (2) language development, (3) personal, emotional and social development, and (4) creative and aesthetic development. Developmental profiles are provided for the first three elements.

94. As one of the outcomes of the White Paper on Early Education (1999) - and noted again in the Education Act - the *National Council for Curriculum and Assessment,* a government agency reporting to the DES, has been asked to develop an early childhood curriculum for the age-group birth to 6 years. The objective is to develop a specimen pedagogical framework which will serve as an orientation for the field without being mandatory. Work on this "Framework for Early Childhood Learning" is ongoing. A formal consultation process with key stakeholders in the field is planned for 2003. The curriculum is to be completed by mid-2004.

10. Parental engagement

95. Under the Education Act 1998, parents are represented on primary school Boards of Management and - in co-operation with the Board - may establish a parents' association to promote pupils' interests. A nationwide organisation of parents in primary schools – *the National Parents Council – Primary* – represents parents' views on school-related issues and also provides a number of services to parents (e.g. advocacy service, help-line, training/workshops funded by the DES and the European Social Fund). The Council is represented on the *National Childcare Co-ordinating Committee.* The *Home/School/Community Liaison Scheme* established as part of the DES targeted initiative promotes active co-operation between home, school and relevant community services.

96. Although the *White Paper on Early Childhood Education,* 1999, emphasises the need to stimulate and support parental participation in the educational process, a National Parents' Association does not exist in the Childcare sector, nor is there a branch for parents with pre-school children within the Education sector. The recently established *Centre for Early Childhood Development and Education* (CECDE) is expected to facilitate strategies for enhancing parental involvement, which traditionally has not been strong in the Education sector in Ireland.

97. In the Childcare sector, there is at least one parent representative on each County Childcare Committee. Parental involvement in the management of community-based services (particularly Play Groups) is fairly common. Generally, however, evidence gathered from the National Childcare Census would suggest that the concept of active parental involvement is not firmly anchored in this sector. Only 40% of facilities reported having a policy on parental engagement, and only 19% a written policy statement (*Irish Background Report* 2002, p.52).

Chapter 3

POLICY ISSUES ARISING FROM THE REVIEW VISIT

Chapter 3 is analytic and discursive in emphasis. It focuses on early childhood policy issues arising from the review visit, and seeks to place them in the context of international practice. In addition to the central issues of access, quality, and co-ordination that the Department of Education and Science invited the OECD team to address, we discuss also the new roles of Irish women, parental engagement, ECEC models, research/evaluation/information systems; and the question of funding.

1. New roles and issues for Irish women

98. Compared to a participation rate of 43.8% in 1990, 56.2% of Irish women between the ages of 15 and 64 participated in the labour force in Ireland in 2000. This is a considerable achievement. Although still significantly lower than the EU average, not to mention North America or northern Europe, the participation rate for younger women in the 25-34 age group is now well over 60%. According to a 1996 Labour Force Survey, 29.3% of mothers with a youngest child aged 2 – 4 years and 34% with a youngest child aged 0 – 24 months were in full-time work outside the home (Government of Ireland, 1999c).

99. A research survey carried out by the Economic and Social Research Institute (1998) revealed that 38% of all parents with children aged 4 years and under, rely on some form of paid childcare arrangement. 21% of mothers with children aged less than 5 years used childminders. Centre-based care services were the second most commonly used form, taken up by 14%. "However, over one-fifth (22%) of mothers with full-time jobs and 47% of those with part-time jobs used no paid childcare at all, indicating a reliance on informal provision provided either by partners, family, friends or neighbours." (*Irish Background Report* 2002, p.29).

100. In the decades to come, greatly increased working rates for women can be expected, as the older cohorts who traditionally did not join the labour force advance beyond 64 years. Already the tendency can be discerned: 54% of women with a child under 5 years are employed, compared to only 38% of women with children over 15 years of age.[20] In fact, among older women in Ireland, more than half are economically inactive, a weight that few modern economies can afford to carry. Where part-time work is concerned, the employment situation of women compares unfavourably with that of men, that is, a far greater proportion of women are in part-time work: 32.2% of women

---

[20] The tendency is confirmed by the employment/population (15-64 years) ratio, which has evolved in Ireland from 52.1% in 1990 to 65% in 2001, a little over the EU average of 64.1%. It is still well below the UK and USA figures of over 70%.

work less than 35 hours a week, compared to 7.7% of men. However, for the younger age-group, gains in full-time employment in Ireland in recent years have been made more by female workers than by males (see CSO, 2002).

Box 7. New child and family measures in France, 2003

The new centre-right government in France has recently strengthened the family/childcare policy of the previous socialist government. Under certain conditions, the following basic measures become valid in 2004:

- *A pregnancy payment:* A single payment of €800 to all mothers in the 7th month of pregnancy;
- *A child benefit:* A monthly payment of €160 for each child until the age of 3 years (90% of families benefit);
- *A home care benefit:* A monthly payment of €334 will be made to mothers who choose to leave work in order to care for their child/children at home. This payment ceases after three years. For mothers from the richer 10% of families who do not receive the basic child allowance of €160, the monthly payment becomes €493 per month. The measure is not intended to take women out of the workforce permanently: if mothers care for their child while maintaining a half-time job, more than 50% of the benefit will be granted.
- *A childcare subsidy:* Depending on revenue, a monthly subsidy of approximately €600 is accorded per month to families with at least one parent working, per child up to the age of 6 years, who is cared for in a crèche or by an accredited child-minder or by a declared employee in their home. In general, this payment will cover full costs. It is reduced by 50%, once the child is enrolled in the *école maternelle* (almost 100% of French children are enrolled in this free service from the age of 3 years).
- *Tax benefits:* Parents with children in their care will still receive (up to the 18th year and beyond) significant tax reductions, in particular, from the third child onwards. Reduced transport costs, back to school subsidies and other advantages are also offered to "familles nombreuses" (three children or more) by both the government and municipalities;
- *Workplace measures:* The costs of measures taken by firms to reconcile work and family responsibilities (including the provision of a crèche, part-time work, distance work, re-training of mothers…) will be reimbursed through remission of company tax to the level of 60%.
- *Provision of new childcare places:* A commitment has been made to invest 200 million Euros annually from 2004 to create 20,000 new crèche places – either public, public-private or in companies. (In 2000 and 2001, 46,000 new public crèche places had already been created);
- *Support to private initiatives,* especially to family and non-profit associations, who will be able to access public funding equally, especially if they can provide services to suit the working hours of parents;
- *Increasing the number of accredited child-minders:* The salaries, training and social security coverage for accredited child minders will be upgraded, so as to encourage more women to enter this profession.

The significant increase in public expenditure on families and young children is justified by the government from a number of different angles: to reconcile work and family responsibilities and to allow women to maintain without undue difficulty their participation in the labour market. The government also wishes to provide greater choice to parents. In future, parents will be subsidised: to remain at home with their children; or to enrol them in the publicly funded local or workplace crèche; or to place them with accredited childminders; or to employ a home help to look after children in their own home. The government also speaks openly of encouraging French families to have children, as the viability of the state pension regime[21] into the future depends, according to the government, on maintaining the present fertility rate, which at 1.9 per woman is just under the Irish figure of 1.98.

---

[21] Where pensions are concerned, France, like Ireland, also has the challenge of improving its employment/population ratio. The recent introduction of a home-carer's benefit in Norway has resulted in the withdrawal of a significant number of women – especially with some education - from the labour force.

101. From a labour market perspective, the trend therefore is favourable, with the employment /population ratio showing a marked improvement on previous generations. With more women remaining in the labour market, income tax returns, social security contributions and savings are greatly increased, and higher productivity is ensured due to maintaining trained employees in work. At the same time, there is less dependency on social assistance during both the productive and retirement ages (without a woman's work, many families fall below the poverty line). This positive trend can be maintained in Ireland through intelligent tax policies and energetic child care policies, although one should not underestimate the impact of the economic conjuncture, education, training, and general labour market conditions. The preferences and cultural attitudes of a society are also important. Higher female participation may also have some costs, in particular, public childcare spending has to be increased. However, this policy is to some extent self-financing insofar as it increases both labour supply and flexibility.

102. From a family perspective, the situation is also promising as increased employment improves family budgets and the material conditions of children. However, supports for Irish working women with young children are few and inadequately funded. Parental leave is short and unpaid, and as yet, a clear commitment to creating a publicly subsidised, early education and care system for the children and families who need such services has not been made. Although the home carers' allowance can be seen as positive in so far as it subsidises the family budget - and at the moment eases the demand for childcare spaces - it may detract in the long run from women's status in the economy and Irish society. A careful balance needs to be struck in societies between the time and care that children need from their parents(s) and the advantages - at personal, familial and societal levels – that parental employment brings. Without good services, this balance is difficult to maintain.

The gender perspective

103. In Ireland, the gender assumption that women will leave aside career for a few years to care for young children is still widely held. It is a valid assumption for many families, but is unfounded for a growing number of young couples who wish to combine career with rearing their children. Increasingly, young men are part of this change, and see themselves as equally responsible for day-to-day child-rearing tasks (Ryan, 2001). In terms of equity, it may be argued that a share of parental taxes should be channelled toward financing quality early childhood services, which would allow women choice, enable them to maintain throughout the life-cycle both salaries and pensions, and bring a better life-work balance to families.[22]

104. Women gain greatly, both at a personal and a professional level from being able to return to work after appropriate parental leave. Returning to work enables mothers to avoid long-term poverty damaging for themselves and for their children, an important consideration in situations of lone motherhood, separation and divorce, when children are normally left in the mother's custody.[23] Yet, the OECD team was informed on several occasions that a return to work when a second child is born is often not an option. According to our interlocutors – and borne out by government data - many working parents cannot afford two childcare places unless they have access to a subsidised public crèche. This means, for the vast majority of parents, recourse to the private market where ability to pay determines accessibility. If this fails, they must rely on informal arrangements with family, friends, and neighbours. Such arrangements and the resulting stress can influence work practices negatively, leading in turn to reluctance to hire women with children.

105. At the economic level, other research indicates that the lifelong effects of a woman's dropping out of work - or of downgrading to part-time work - for a number of years to care for young children,

---

[22] In over 90% of instances, women are given custody of children in case of separation or divorce. Such situations affect over 40% of couples in some urban milieus.

[23] American research indicates that such care arrangements are generally of quite poor quality (NICHD, 1997).

has considerable negative effects on professional development, lifelong earnings, pensions and career progression (Harkness and Waldfogel, 2002). According to Gunderson (1986), lessened professional activity among women may be a root cause of the differentials between male and female earnings, which today in Europe stand at an average ratio of 100:84. The drop-out of women from the work force is also a significant loss to the economy, because it reduces the tax base and deskills a large and better educated part of the labour force.

Parental leave

106.   Parental leave and benefits are variously referred to as family policies that protect maternal and infant health; or as employment policies that promote gender equity and respect the rights of workers to combine work and family responsibilities. The growing practice in Europe (see Table 4 in Appendix 1) is for governments to guarantee a remunerated maternity and parental leave for a period of about a year, financed by the contributions of the parents through their previous years of work. Thereafter, affordable early childhood services, regulated and partly financed by the state, are in place to supplement parental care. These services are generally open to all children, as the services are valued not just as a labour market or social inclusion support but also as a developmental opportunity for the children.

107.   Although the EU Directive allowed countries to introduce more favourable conditions than the minimum laid down, Ireland's response has not matched those of other countries, many of which are now well on the way toward providing a year or more of subsidised parental leave. The lack of subsidisation in Ireland after the 18th week after birth makes it extremely difficult for parents on modest incomes to prolong parental leave, unless a decision is taken that one of them, generally the mother, should leave the labour market.

2. Co-ordination issues

108. Across countries, as policy makers seek to improve the continuity of children's early childhood experiences and make the most efficient use of resources, a systemic and integrated approach to early childhood services is gaining ground. The advantages are considerable. Adopting a more integrated approach to the field allows governments to organise common policies, and combine resources for early childhood services. Regulatory, funding and staffing regimes, costs to parents, and opening hours can be made more consistent. Variations in access and quality can be lessened, and links at the services level – across age groups and settings – are more easily created. In integrated systems, a common vision of education and care can be forged, with agreed social and pedagogical objectives.

109. *The integrated model* - In the present Irish context, the integrated model would require a radical rethinking by the ministries and chief stakeholders not only of the developmental needs of young children but also of labour market requirements, equality of opportunity, and family policy. In the Nordic countries or in the municipality of Reggio Emilia in Italy, these considerations have led to sustained public expenditure on young children, with the state/municipality becoming the main direct provider of services. Both access and quality tend to be excellent, and a seamless and clear public service is offered to families with young children from 1 to 6 years. Financing is through government subsidy to the local authorities, local authority grants and parental fees. In this vision, a single framework covers the responsibilities of the various actors, and in the Nordic countries a core worker profile – the pedagogue - has emerged, with training level and salary conditions similar to that of teachers. Work status and conditions are such that many well-educated young women continue to be attracted to the profession, unlike in profit-driven systems where pay is poor for staff, with ensuing recruitment and turnover problems. Early childhood services provided by the Nordic integrated model are among the best in the world, with a strong emphasis on the health care, socialisation, well-being and active learning of children.

Box 8 - New Zealand: a community/private provider system financed by government

In New Zealand, the organisation of ECEC services at the national level has been a matter of discussion over the past three decades. ECEC services for young children are predominantly established by the voluntary/community and private sectors, with some developed and managed by employers or local bodies. The service programme may be 'teacher-led' or 'parent/whanau led'. [25] The government's role is financial and regulatory. In 1986, the whole sphere came under the responsibility of the Ministry of Education.

In its financing role, Government decided that funding (capitation grant) follows the child (not the family) to whichever ECEC service the parent chooses to use. There is no differentiation by age of children, except that children under two receive higher grants as child/staff ratios for this age of child must be lower than for older children. Government now covers over 50% of the operational costs of services. It also provides capital grants to develop not-for-profit services, and facilitates low-cost loans for caregivers or teachers who want to train as ECEC teachers. Fee subsidies are also provided by the Ministry of Social Welfare to assist low income families to pay for ECEC services.

In its regulatory role, the Ministry of Education sets standards, accredits and monitors services, and provides the curriculum (Te Whariki - a socio-cultural curriculum for infants, toddlers and pre-school children) and supporting materials. The Education Review Office, a government agency, carries out a programme of regular reviews of services. Most children in the ECEC sector are in Education and Care Centres (0-6 years) but there are also kindergartens (predominantly attended by 3 and 4 year olds), play centres, kohanga reo (Maori immersion centres), Pacific language(s) ECEC centres and a flourishing family day care system (called "home based care" in NZ). Over 30% of 0-3 year olds and 85 % of the 3-5 year olds are in regulated, publicly funded services.

In recent months, the government has agreed a quantified and time-referenced strategic plan for the development of the sector for the next ten years. It hopes to increase participation from disadvantaged groups, improve quality and promote collaborative relationships with other sectors. To achieve these aims, it is engaged in a complete revision of the funding and regulatory system; in the professional registration of co-ordinators of family day care and of contact personnel in teacher-led centres; and in better support for community-led initiatives.

Source: *A 10-Year Strategic Plan for Early Childhood Education,* Ministry of Education, Wellington (2002)

---

110. New Zealand provides a variation on the integrated model, where although integration of policy under one ministry has existed since 1986, the system is a *mixed* one, combining private providers, voluntary providers and some services managed by employers or communities:

111. *The split system model with a publicly managed childcare section* – The split system model is widespread across the OECD countries: "care" from birth to 3 years being taken in charge by a social services, health, family or gender equity ministry, with the "education" of children from 3-6 years being taken in charge by the education ministry. The weakness of the conceptual basis for this model can be inferred from the opening lines of *Eager To Learn* (Bowman et al, 2000), published by the American National Research Council:

> *Children come into the world eager to learn. The first five years of life are a time of enormous growth of linguistic, conceptual, social, emotional and motor competence. Right from birth, a healthy child is an active participant in that growth, exploring the environment, learning to communicate and, in relatively short order, beginning to construct ideas and theories about how things work in the surrounding world. The pace of learning, however, will depend on whether and to what extent the child's inclinations to learn encounter and engage supporting environments.*

---

[25] Kindergartens are an example of teacher led services; play centres and kohanga reo are parent/whanau led services.

112. At its worst, the model perpetuates the division between care and education, with low quality care being provided for the younger children, while children aged 3-6 years undergo a primary-type education in crowded classrooms. The salaries and employment conditions of childcare personnel remain low, resulting in great instability of employment in the care sector, with negative consequences for young children. Because of the low educational level of staff, active learning programmes are not a feature of many care contexts in the split system. In parallel, the socialisation and care of children in the school is often far from ideal.

113. At its best, the split system model may have a well-managed childcare sector and an education sector investing adequately in young children, with quality standards and approaches to young children in constant improvement. Flanders in Belgium is an example. In the childcare system, managed by a semi-state institution *Kind en Gezin* (Children and Parents), a comprehensive system of childcare centres and family daycare networks has been established, influenced strongly by quality standards and in-service training. In parallel, the "children's school", which caters for all children from 30 months to 6 years, has reduced child-teacher ratios to 18:1. Child-staff ratios are often much better, often reaching 9:1 in those schools that hire trained children's nurses to help teachers look after the youngest children. Pedagogical approaches are being progressively influenced by *Experiential Education,* an approach that emphasises active learning, guided by the principles of well-being and involvement of children.

114. *The split system with a market model of childcare* – In addition to splitting education and care, the market model generally assumes that childcare is a family responsibility, and that childcare should be purchased from private providers in an open market. At the same time, there is the parallel assumption that early education is a public good and a responsibility of government. Where childcare is concerned, the government's chief role is considered to be regulation, or to intervene if there is market failure.[26] Thus, government subsidises community or voluntary bodies to provided services in disadvantaged areas, where market conditions deter the investment of private capital. In addition, government will generally subsidise the childcare costs of poorer families to enable parents to stay in work.

115. The results from this model are generally disappointing. Without public management and sustained public funding, market-led childcare provision remains fragmented and inequitable. For this reason, governments in the English-speaking countries are obliged to intervene constantly by increasing childcare allowances, reviewing quality supervision and even directly funding parts of the system, such as Head Start (USA) or Sure Start (U.K.), that are aimed at targeted groups. Although competition can lead to some good programmes, these are often confined to parents who can pay high fees. When dominated by private, for-profit interests, profits are often derived from high fees, increased numbers of children per staff and/or low staff wages. There is a tendency to employ untrained staff at the bottom end of the market, where modest and disadvantaged families are the clients. In sum, the children who need the best services often receive the poorest quality.

116. Although some regulation is provided (generally through a Children's Act), initial training, in-service training or quality improvement initiatives have no statutory right to funding in for profit systems. Frequently, the providers are not subject to any quality control, and are under no obligation to be trained, or provide a professional programme for the young children in their care. Parents too are confused by the multiplicity of providers and have little means of distinguishing quality except through rather external criteria such as hearsay, brochures or the appearance of premises. In addition, audits show that parents often are unable to access the childcare benefits offered by government, e.g. a recent analysis by the Daycare Trust (2003) shows that only 3% of English families

---

[26] For several reasons, market failure is inevitable where the care of children is involved, as explained by Cleveland and Krashinsky, OECD, 2003

receive the Childcare Tax Credit, which averages, according to the survey, only about a third of the cost demanded for an average nursery place. Recent figures from the US indicate also that faced with the uncertainties of childcare access and quality, a growing number of American parents (that is, women) are simply leaving the labour market to care for their children at home. [27]

117. Because of the present split auspices of the system in Ireland, we shall provide in Chapter 4 our recommendations concerning access, first for the Childcare sector and then for Education. This does not imply any preference for the split system, which in many respects is wasteful of resources and inhibits coherent policy. In fact, given the underdeveloped state of ECEC on the ground in Ireland and the magnitude of the challenge to create a national system (including sub-systems for disadvantaged and special needs systems), there is a strong case to be made for a single and accountable leadership for the field. An integrated system would cover all children from one to six years,[28] and include an out-of-school care system for children aged 3-12 years.

3. Access issues

118. Issues of access to early childhood services came up regularly during the course of the visit. As stated in the *Irish Background Report* 2002, access is a complex issue, linked to questions of affordability, geographical location, and the appropriateness of different kinds of services with regard to both cultural preference and the specific needs of individual children and families. It is also inextricably linked to quality issues. Many of the related concerns are outlined in the *Irish Background Report* 2002. In this section we shall focus on some of the most urgent issues from a review team perspective.

Weakness of access

119. In Chapter 2, we outlined the support of the three main ministries to access across the age range 0-6 years. Total access for children in government-financed half-day or full-day services came to approximately 56% of children from 3-6 years and from 10% - 15% of children (estimate) from 0-3 years. By EU standards, total coverage in Ireland is low, and falls far short of the targets set by the Presidency conclusions of the Barcelona European Council (16-17 March 2002). These conclusions state that Member States should remove disincentives for female labour force participation and strive to provide childcare by 2010 for at least 90% of children between 3 years and mandatory school age and at least 33% of children under 3 years of age. It is only in the year immediately preceding obligatory schooling that Ireland approaches the EU average for any one year. Table 9 in Appendix 1 shows in contrast the coverage rates of other small, northern European countries: Denmark, Flanders and Scotland.

Reasons for low access in Ireland

120. The low access rates for Ireland may be explained as follows:
- The very rapid transformation of the Irish economy and society in the last decade, resulting in policy and delivery gaps where young children were concerned;
- An initial policy option of relying on informal childminding to fill the gaps, which effectively places much of the childcare provision in Ireland outside official financing, accreditation and monitoring – and international recognition;
- A high barrier of affordability: most of the available childcare places are located within the private sector and rely heavily on parental fees. Because governmental subsidies do not exist, the costs of childcare have become prohibitive for low-income or even middle-income families;
- The failure to expand the early education system to include all children from 3-6 years. Compared

---

[27] Employment rates for women in the USA and the UK still remain significantly higher than above those in Ireland.

[28] If parental leave can be extended to one year, then the pressure to supply services to children under that age is much lessened.

with its European neighbours, the infant school in Ireland has hardly developed over the last decades;

- Irish parents prefer to keep their children at home until the age of 5 years. As the OECD team did not have access to parent surveys, it has no means of judging the plausibility of this reason or its underlying causes. Whatever the case - given that 60% of women are expected to be in the labour force by 2010 (implying that well over 70% of women 25-34 years will be employed) - it is an untenable option in the future.

Access challenges for the childcare sector

1. Children 0-3 years (from birth to 3rd birthday)

121. In terms of the European targets, a first access challenge for the childcare sector in Ireland is to multiply the number of subsidised places for children from birth to 3 years before the year 2010. We are obliged to be vague about the exact numbers of places to be subsidised, as the OECD team has not had access to national needs assessments or to reliable data giving the actual percentages of children from birth to three years of age who are at the moment in subsidised services. This type of information is now being drawn up, and no doubt in coming years, it will be possible to formulate concrete plans for young children with detailed benchmarks, targets, financing and deadlines.

122. From the *Irish Background Report* and information received during the review, we believe that most DJELR subsidised places so far have been created for three and four year old children (see, for example, Table 7 in Appendix 1). Part of the reason is that with the exception of the National Childminders' Association, the main provider networks, such as IPPA, Montessori, Naíonraí, etc., tend to cater for the older children, generally on a sessional basis. In sum, EOCP programming may be contributing more to provision for the 3-6 year olds than to provision for the 0-3 year olds. If this is true, it suggests that DJELR may need to focus more on the providers who can contribute to reaching targets set for the younger age group, viz. on *parents, childminders and community or county* services.

123. *Parents* - Maternity and parental leave is considered in almost all modern economies as a key step to ensuring that young infants have individualised attention and support during the early months of life. Paid, flexible and job-protected maternity and parental leave schemes of at least one year are seen as an essential component of any comprehensive strategy to support working parents with very young children. Leave benefits for mothers and fathers help reduce the need and demand for investment in infant provision (which because of the necessary high adult/child ratios is very costly), while acknowledging the primary role of the family in rearing young children. A generous measure in this sense from government would almost certainly be more attractive for the majority of Irish parents than large-scale investment in collective infant care. In addition, if well-administered and backed up by early childhood services, the measure would be helpful in retaining the attachment of young women to the labour market, and in encouraging male partners to invest more time with their children.[29]

124. However, from the perspective of an economy seeking high employment/population rates, parental leave schemes need to be time-limited and clearly linked with work. Evidence from other countries (Norway, Czech Republic...) shows that home carer allowances or a prolonged, low-paid parental leave stipend tend to take certain groups of women out of the labour market, more or less permanently. They result in a confirmation of traditional gender roles, in reinforced social welfare dependency, and a progressive isolation of some groups from employment and the life of the community. Home carer allowances also work against the rational expansion of labour markets, which for optimum functioning should rely on the best qualified people available, who increasingly are women.

---

[29] Because of traditional social expectations and present wage differentials, leaves are almost exclusively taken up by women, unless conditions are included that can attract fathers, such as "use it or loose it" clauses.

125. *Increasing access through accrediting and subsidising the quality childminders:* Because of the lack of early childhood centres in Ireland and population dispersion in rural communities, most families have to rely for childcare on non-registered, untrained childminders operating in the informal sector. This can be a real strength in that local access is available, but also raises challenges where affordability and quality are concerned. Since most of the available places are located within the private sector and rely heavily on parental fees, the costs of childcare can be prohibitive for low-income or even middle-income families. The review team was informed that fees are not usually income-related and that parents may have to pay in excess of €170 per week for the full-time care of very young children. This raises serious problems of equity of access. According to the *Report of the Expert Working Group on Childcare,* the cost of services in Ireland as a proportion of average earnings is among the highest in Europe.

126. Faced with a situation where there is little guarantee of quality and where it becomes increasingly difficult for low- and middle-income parents to find affordable childcare, some means of regulating childminding needs to be found, and local childminding arrangements transformed into recognised *family daycare networks.* In many instances in France, for example, local childminders are supported from a professionally-run, central *family crèche.* The director and professionals in this central crèche provide training once or twice a week to local childminders, allowing them to gain a diploma, an improved professional status and better earnings from their work.[30] The advantages for the local community and families are likewise significant: higher quality services for children, control of fees and subsidies to families most in need, better data on where children are, and the possibility of including in the official statistics for the county and country, children attending this family-type service.

127. Funding will be needed, however, to bring childminders into a properly accredited network. Without advantages, support and subsidies, it is difficult to see why private sector childminders would want to join a regulated network, which requires the use of a developmental programme, conducted by qualified staff with adequate remuneration and in-service training. A weighted operational grant attached to each child who uses an accredited service may be an effective means of financing such a transformation, and could radically expand provision in the coming years, through bringing the non-notified providers into the regulated system. If sufficient responsibility were given to them, City/County Childcare Committees could administer the scheme, and provide the necessary training and support to enable childminders to meet the standards set by the subsidising authorities.

128. *The communities and counties* – The third group that can contribute to the goal of increasing provision for children 0-3 years are the counties and communities. In all countries, access levels for younger children grow in accordance with the growing trust of parents in the quality and management of the services offered at local level. In Ireland, the City/County Childcare Committees have potentially a central role to play in this field if a means of funding and of enhancing their responsibility for the management of childcare can be found. In addition to collecting reliable data, co-ordinating and managing service provision (including accrediting and monitoring the childminder networks), the CCCs may be able to undertake two further measures to improve access for the younger children and their families, viz.

-   *To provide each county with a dedicated Child and Family Centre:* Plans have been announced by the Department of Family and Social Affairs to build family centres for family support purposes. Significant savings, a useful synergy and a much larger capacity could be achieved if the early education and care ministries were associated in the endeavour. Although equally a managerial and quality measure, the county centres could increase access significantly for

---

[30] In other countries, e.g. Belgium and Denmark, *family daycare providers* are part of the official municipal childcare networks, and receive training from municipal co-ordinators. These providers have been successful in providing education and care services for young children and families, particularly in rural areas.

disadvantaged infants and toddlers in the larger towns, and could act as the administrative centres for child and family policy within each county. They would also help to provide models of successful outreach programmes to families who are in need of support in carrying out parenting responsibilities. If associated with accredited training colleges, they could also provide management training and professional development, and model exemplary programmes. The financing of such centres is discussed in the section on funding below.

- *To create light county and community structures:* Light drop-in structures based around health care centres, social welfare offices, school, community centres, libraries, etc. are found useful in many countries, not only for women working part-time, but also for women who are at home looking after children. When the person facilitating a service is well-trained, and when appropriate programmes, information and educational materials are supplied, the links with society and world of work are kept intact for women who might otherwise leave the labour market permanently. In other countries, such facilities are used also in the afternoon and evening for after-school care and adult education. County and municipal services are best placed to decide on need and location, but it would seem helpful if the planning of these services and for facility building could be financially supported. Again, co-operation with the Family Support Agency could be a means of sharing the costs of such structures and of increasing their outreach.

2. Children 3-6 years (from 3rd birthday to 6th birthday)

Access to out-of-school services and an appropriate extension of the infant school day

129. Whether talking to parent representatives, union officials, experts and practitioners in both sectors, the lack of out-of-school provision for children came up repeatedly as one of the urgent issues needing policy attention during the coming years. Services for children before and after school hours and during the school holidays are virtually non-existent. For the few services that do exist, there is no kind of regulatory framework and there are no stated quality standards.

130. In all forms of provision offered by the DES for children under statutory school age, the period of time that children can attend is relatively short. As previously stated, the *Early Start* units and *Traveller Pre-Schools* are open for only $2^1/2$ to 3 hours. In the primary schools, infant classes finish at around 1:40 p.m. This limited time frame raises not only questions about the curriculum balance during those hours, but also about the quality of children's experiences after school hours if working parents are largely dependent on non-formal and unregistered childminding services. In the meantime, the solutions are half-time work for women or recourse to childcare either informal or regulated, where both quality and a continuing shortage of places are continuing issues.

131. What are other countries doing to meet the challenge? Some few countries, e.g. the Netherlands, promote part-time employment. The weakness of this solution is that it quickly becomes a gender issue, as the female partner generally takes on part-time work, often at low rates of remuneration. The Netherlands, too is experimenting with shared employment, that is, the "two-times three-quarters" model in which both partners work three quarters of their time, releasing one or other partner for the care of children on a half-day basis. This model seems to be unique to the Dutch.

132. In an effort to keep women in employment, other countries prefer to build up long-day care and after-school services based around the school. The reasons for the choice of the local school are partly practical (it is much easier for parents and young children if the service is based in the same location where the morning educational service takes place), partly cultural (by its association with the school, out-of school and long-day services become more acceptable to parents) and partly economic (to set up an infrastructure and system parallel to the school is extremely costly). Thus, most countries are increasingly experimenting with educare and recreational programmes for children on school premises in the afternoon. A free educational session is provided in the morning

for all 3-6 year olds at the local school, extended in the afternoon, on school or adjoining premises, by appropriate programmes – rest, arts and music education, sports and physical education, games, nature study, reading clubs etc. - provided by the community and voluntary sector. From the perspective of the child, it matters little who runs the service as long as it is of quality, provides continuity and does not involve bussing or disruption. Some cost recuperation through parental fees is practised for such programmes, and children are free to attend or not according to the contract made by the school with parents.

133. In Ireland, a beginning could be made by transforming the *Early Start* programme into a full-day service provided for children in all disadvantaged areas. For this close co-operation between DES, DJELR and the voluntary sector would be necessary. In extending the day, due care would need to be given to the best interests of children – their rhythms, emotional and physical needs, and the quality of the premises and programmes that they are offered. The role of DJELR and the County Childcare Committees would be vital here, to guarantee that children's interests are protected, that proper infra-structure is in place and that the community and voluntary organisations are adequately funded to carry out this type of work.

134. The measure would also provide an official and much expanded role for the voluntary and community agencies, especially if linked with subsidies, training opportunities and proper career profiles. Supported by appropriate funding (see section below on Funding) and training, these agencies could provide the afternoon programmes for children within the school precincts. A whole-day, integrated service would also remove pressure on teachers in the *Early Start* morning classes, improve quality and make place for a more appropriate pedagogy for these groups. At the same time, the extended day would provide an enriched learning environment for disadvantaged children throughout the day, and reinforce contact with parents who need support and job training.

135. The Department of Justice, Equality and Law Reform has already taken a proactive stance by setting up a Working Group in School Age Childcare, which is preparing proposals for the development of school age childcare services on an all year round basis. However, the response to an EOCP initiative in early 2002 inviting applications from community/not-for-profit childcare providers, parents' groups and school managing authorities for capital and staffing grant assistance for the establishment of School Age Childcare was quite disappointing. The DJELR is hoping that the publication of the Report of the Working Group will stimulate interest in the provision of much needed out-of-school care services for children aged 3-12 years.

Access challenges in early education

1. Improving general access for children

136. Taking account of the Barcelona targets, expectations are strong that by the year 2010, most European countries will have provided services for over 90% of children aged 3-6 years. Present coverage for the age group in Ireland stands at just 50%. Can it be argued – as the OECD team heard on several occasions - that the 3-year olds are not the responsibility of the Education sector and that Education should continue to concentrate on the 4-6 year olds? The practice of other countries runs contrary. Apart from the Nordic countries which have fully integrated services for *all* children under one ministry, and the Netherlands, which, like Ireland, begins the infant school at 4 years, the 3-6 year old age group is the responsibility of the ministries of education in the great majority of OECD countries. Moreover, in the Netherlands, the Ministry of Education is investing massively at the moment in morning education sessions all over the country for 2-4 year olds from disadvantaged backgrounds. These sessions are often attached to the local school.

137. Will Ireland opt for free public services for three-year old children? The OECD team was informed that when *Early Start* was launched in Ireland in 1994, the voluntary and community providers protested, seeing this better-funded programme run by trained teachers as unfair competition, particularly in

areas where voluntary and community bodies had been working for years previously. The lesson to be learned from the experience is not to pull back from expanded provision for 3-year olds, but through consultation and partnership, to find an equitable means of integrating the all too few local providers into a publicly subsidised system which would be ambitious for young children. At present, all energies are needed to create a quality, affordable, long-day ECEC system in Ireland. With government leadership, the community and voluntary bodies can be integrated fully into the official system, and receive recognition, subsidies and training support.

Educational access for children at 3 years

138. Net enrolment in pre-primary education (infant school) in Ireland for 3 year olds is around 4% (Figure 6, Appendix 1). This contrasts with the situation in most other OECD member states. In over half of these countries more than 50 % of 3 year olds attend some form of state-funded provision designed to foster learning. In others, e.g. Belgium, France, Italy, over 90 % are enrolled (Figure 6). Introducing free, universal access for all 3 to 6 year olds is a goal which many countries are working towards, as they see it both as a human capital investment and an important measure in reconciling work and the care of children. For the moment, the Irish government is committed only to providing educational services for a small proportion of 3-year olds coming from socially and economically disadvantaged backgrounds.

Access for children aged 4 years

139. While 4 year olds officially qualify for enrolment in junior infant classes, the coverage level for this age group in primary schools is only 56%, a surprisingly low enrolment rate by OECD standards, given that the provision is free of charge. Reasons advanced for the low enrolments were:

- Children are admitted to the infant school once a year only (in September), if they have reached the age of 4 years by September 1st. This particular form of intake policy excludes children born between September and Christmas, and since waiting lists for 5 year olds are considerable, schools tend to enrol by seniority of age, thus effectively limiting the intake of 4 year olds.

- Irish parents do not find the infant school attractive as a learning environment. Child-staff ratios are high, imposing a directive role on teachers, inhibiting child initiative and leaving little opportunity for free play and peer interaction. If this is the case, low attendance is a clear signal that quality needs to be improved.

Whatever the reason, these two areas – intake policy and quality – need to be addressed by the inspectorate and the local schools, if the European targets are to be reached. Teachers would be greatly helped in managing the increased intake if a Child Assistant were appointed to each infant school class. This would also have the advantage of reducing child-staff ratios to 15:1 or less for every infant class – an acceptable maximum level in the European context. In the section on financing, we shall discuss how this measure could be financed.

Recognition of selected pre-school providers

140. To increase access levels for the 3 and 4 year olds, the Department of Education and Science may also wish to consider recognition and support to accredited pre-school providers, as mentioned in the White Paper, 1999. Several of these groups have been working with young children in Ireland for generations. The different approaches that they bring enrich early childhood theory and pedagogy. In addition, they contribute to the national network for young children, providing places for some thousands of children. The question is often raised in countries where public services predominate: why should public funds flow toward private groups? It is a fundamental question, but solutions can be found, in particular where non-profit groups are willing to accept a quota of children from disadvantaged backgrounds, and keep fees at a level within a range defined by the public authorities. Again, the measure has the advantage for governments of regulating the sector more efficiently, and of including the children served in national statistics.

2. Access for children from disadvantaged backgrounds

141. The issue of child poverty in a country is always delicate, but it is an important one for early childhood administrators. No matter how good an early childhood service is, it cannot "inoculate children in one year against the ravages of a life of deprivation"(Kagan and Zigler, 1987). Commentators note, for example, that the fair start provided by Head Start programmes to disadvantaged young children in US cities is often set at naught by the living conditions of these children as they mature, and not least, because they remain in demoralised neighbourhoods and are obliged to enrol in under-performing primary schools.

142. In recent years, Irish society has become more sensitive to child poverty issues, and many initiatives are now being taken to support children from disadvantaged families and neighbourhoods, e.g. the creation of a National Anti-Poverty Strategy and the governmental obligation on building promoters to include a percentage of social housing in all large building developments.[31] In the education sector, similar initiatives have been made, such as the *Breaking the Cycle* initiative in primary schools and the *Early Start* programme in early education. In addition, significant parts of the Education Act of 1998 and particularly, the Education (Welfare) Act of 2000 are devoted to the issue of dropout and measures to encourage regular attendance at school. Likewise, the present social partnership agreement, *Sustaining Progress*, acknowledges that in tackling "educational disadvantage and procuring social inclusion, we must address disadvantaged conditions in childhood which are known to increase the likelihood of early school leaving and poor school performance."

143. Yet, inequality at the starting gates of education remains a critical challenge for Ireland. Figure 3 in Appendix 1, based on 1997 UNICEF figures (since confirmed by figures from 2000) shows the extent of child poverty in the country. To meet the challenge, the Department of Education and Science (DES) established during the 1990s, two targeted interventions to address the issues of educational disadvantage and social exclusion among young children, viz. *Early Start* and *Pre-schools for Traveller Children.* Surprisingly, there does not seem to be a strong policy commitment to expanding these programmes, and they are still described as "pilot interventions", i.e. they have not been established as an integral part of the early childhood system.

144. In addition, an initial evaluation of *Early Start,* based on assessment tests of children's cognitive, language and motor skills in the junior infant classes, failed to show progress greater than in children who had not experienced the programme.[32] Several reasons have been advanced for the unexpected result of the initial evaluation: the newness of the programme when the evaluation was launched; irregular attendance by children, inadequate curriculum support, insufficiency of specific training (at that moment in the programme) leading to inappropriate or unfocussed pedagogy (Kelleghan, 2002; McGough, 2002). In contrast, as evidenced from Box 6 above, parent and practicioner perceptions of the *Early Start* programme are much more positive, which suggests that evaluations might also include wider social impact measures.

145. In this context, it may be useful to recall the evaluation results of similar programmes for disadvantaged children from different countries (see, for example, Braithewaite, 1983, (Australia); McCain and Mustard, 1999 (Canada); Jarousse et al, 1992 (France); Kellaghan and Greaney,[33] 1993,

---

[31] Such a measure is particularly effective in combating the spatial segregation of the poor, which generally destines their children to low performance expectations and attendance at inferior schools.

[32] A more recent analysis by the Educational Research Centre indicates more positive developments in planning, curriculum and pedagogy.

[33] The Kelleghan-Greaney study researched the original Rutland Street Project, the first targeted intervention in Ireland toward children from disadvantaged backgrounds. Early evaluation studies failed to show any significant positive outcomes in the early years of schooling, whereas later follow-up studies showed that the Rutland Street cohort stayed longer at school, and were more likely to take a public examination than other children from the same area.

(Ireland); Kagitcibasi et al 1986 and 1991 (Turkey); Osborn and Milbank, 1987, (UK); Berrueta-Clement et al , 1984 (USA); McKey *et al* 1985 (USA); Schweinhart *et al,* 1993 (Perry Pre-school, USA) - cited in OECD 1999, 2001). In summary, the research carried out across these countries suggests that well-funded, integrated socio-educational programmes in disadvantaged areas do improve the cognitive functioning of disadvantaged children, and almost always yield positive outcomes with regard to socio-emotional development and ability to live with other children. If properly linked to the labour, health and social services, they can also be expected to deliver additional outcomes, such as enhanced maternal employment, parenting skills, greater family and community cohesion.[34]

146. Because of this research, and our experience of successful programmes across the OECD countries, the OECD team encourages the continuation of *Early Start,* especially in a reformed and expanded version. Certain steps would seem necessary, e.g.

- *To expand the present Early Start session to a full-day educare service for disadvantaged children, in partnership with the voluntary and community agencies:* Not only do cognitive and social outcomes improve (see Leseman above), but the choice of a full-day programme can help resolve the concern: what happens to these children, who are largely growing up under difficult circumstances, when they leave the present $2^1/_2$ hour service for the rest of the day? For instance, in the *Early Start* unit visited, the review team was informed that there was no other early childhood provision in the area. Families in which the parent(s) is employed outside the home are dependent on care arrangements through relatives, neighbours or (mostly unregistered) childminders in the informal sector. This means in reality that many children are experiencing poor quality and disjointed care arrangements in at least two or even more settings. In sum, for young children living in areas designated as disadvantaged, access to full-day quality service would seem to be one of the most urgent issues for policy development.

- *To improve the quality of Early Start programming:* In the section on quality that follows, the OECD team raises a number of concerns concerning structural and process conditions of quality in early childhood programmes, e.g. child-staff ratios, the undue dominance of teacher intervention, the relative poverty of classroom environments, the notion of play…

- *To strengthen parallel intervention supports: Early Start* was originally conceived as a socio-educational model of intervention, that is, as part of a wide range of intervention supports, including health, nutrition, social services, family support… and dovetailing with community development initiatives. However, these supports – according to teachers interviewed - have not always been present in Early Start areas in any comprehensive fashion. Teachers urgently need to receive sufficient support both to run an appropriate learning experience for the children and to establish the links with the social, family and community agencies, necessary in this type of work.

147. In this context, research from other countries suggests that interventions toward disadvantaged children are more effective when:

- *Early learning programmes take place within a general framework of anti-poverty and community development policies.* (Kagan and Zigler, 1987, Morris et al., 2001, Sweeney, 2002). To break the poverty cycle and thus protect the socio-emotional development of young children from disadvantaged homes, wider issues such as employment and jobs training, social support, income transfers, housing policies, substance abuse and community resources need to be addressed.

- *Programmes are multi-functional and engage families as well as children:* that is, programmes are strong on family engagement and support as well as providing high quality learning experiences to the children. A national evaluation of the Early Excellence Centres in England has

---

[34] See the outline of the British Sure Start project in Box 9 below.

shown that integrated socio-educational services bring multiple benefits to children, families, and practitioners (Bertram et al., 2002; Pascal et al., 2002).

- *Programming is intensive:* research indicates that the effectiveness of programmes for young children is enhanced by intensity (Leseman, 2002) and year-long duration (Consortium on Chicago School Research, 2003). There is evidence to show that a structured, half-day, early learning programme on a term basis can be effective, and should be incorporated into all full-day services.[35]

- *Programmes are pedagogically sound and conducted by appropriately trained professionals.* A high quality programme in early childhood implies child–initiative, play and involvement. If a programme is over-focussed on formal skills, it is more likely to provide opportunities for children to fail, and to develop a higher dependency on adults, promoting in them negative perceptions of their own competencies (Stipek et al. 1995).

- *Depending on the degree of disadvantage, enriched health and nutrition inputs may be necessary to ensure that young children can take full advantage of the early childhood service.*

3. Access for children with special needs

148. During the course of the review, the OECD team was particularly impressed by the well-organised environment, the individualised teaching strategies, careful documentation and record-keeping observed in a Special School for 56 children aged 6 to 18 in Galway. According to the teaching staff, the school was well supported by the local community and by voluntary contributions. However, we were informed on several other occasions that the general situation for children with special needs in Ireland is far from satisfactory. Despite the optimism generated by the National Forum on Early Childhood Education in 1998 (Report of the Forum, 1998), the raising of the issue in the White Paper on Early Education (1999), and the overwhelming case for early intervention with regard to these children (Guralnick, 1998), there is still, it seems, no national plan for early intervention for children under four years. The situation compares poorly with other countries, e.g. with the United States where from 1975, services for special needs children were expanded with the *Education for All Handicapped Children Act* (Public Law 94 142), further revised in 1997 under the title *Individual with Disabilities Education Act* (IDEA). According to this law, states receive funds from the federal government to assist in the education of those with special needs from age 3 to 21, and a further grant - *Grants for Infants and Toddlers* - may be used to implement state-wide early intervention services for children under age three and their families.

149. In addition, the right of American parents to be active participants in decision-making regarding educational services for their children is clearly recognised. Parents must be included in the development of a child's Individualized Education Plan (IEP), which lays out the goals and objectives for children from 3 through 5 years of age. Families of children from birth through two years of age are to have an Individualized Family Services Plan (IFSP), which is designed to build on each family's strengths, and provide the supports required to ensure that each young child with special education needs receives the appropriate supports and services. The legislation also establishes specific programs for educating parents about their legal rights by establishing a network of parent training and information centres across the US.

150. Routinely, young American children with disabilities are assessed by medical services, mental health professionals and by local school district child study teams, and if necessary are referred to the most appropriate services. The law requires placements in the "least restrictive environment", and insists

---

[35] The Dutch research conducted by Leseman indicates that five half-day, structured programmes per week produces more effective learning than shorter sessional programmes. Full-day programmes are even more effective especially in at-risk circumstances. The Chicago research underlines the efficacy of bridging programmes across holiday periods.

that, in so far as possible, children with disabilities should receive supports and services in natural environments with typical children, and not in segregated settings. Programme staff and family child care providers in most states are encouraged to enrol children with special needs, and most find it beneficial not only to the child but to all the children in the programme. Head Start programmes in particular offer health and mental health services to their children and families, and 13% of children enrolled have disabilities.

151. In Ireland, official policy states that children with special needs should be integrated into regular infant classes wherever possible. However, with the exception of children with visual or hearing impairment, DES does not take responsibility for the great majority of children with disabilities under 4 years of age. DES informed the OECD team that mainstream primary schools catered for some 9,092 children with special educational needs, out of a total of 423,344 children, that is, just over 2% of children with special needs are included. The team was not provided with figures concerning the numbers of special needs children in infant classes or the specific measures taken to ensure for them appropriate educational support. It seems that when enrolled in the mainstream school, special needs children can receive periodic tuition from a special needs teacher who may or may not have a specialisation to treat a particular disability. Moreover, these teachers report that they do not have sufficient supports to assist these children adequately. Certainly, the Department, the Irish National Teachers Organisation and school principals are aware of the issues, but despite policy initiatives and advocacy documents, a national plan does not exist to provide from birth structured public intervention in favour of children with disabilities, and to include them in a systematic and appropriate way in the mainstream school. In sum, the institutional support given to Irish children with special needs and to their families is, according to information received, irregular, under-funded and in the great majority of cases, not inclusive. Recommendations with regard to children with special needs are summarised in chapter 4.

4. Access for children from the Traveller community

152. From our interviews and the literature available, one group of children in Ireland seem to live in abject poverty, namely, children from the Travelling community. The team did not receive information on the annual per capita income of the group, but the figures for infant mortality, life expectancy, health and education status of children from the Traveller community are a matter of real concern (Pavee Point, 2000). All the predictors of poor health and future school failure were present in the small Traveller pre-school that the OECD team visited: low family income and low parental education, combined with one or more of other at-risk features, such as, large family size, unemployment, and at-risk living conditions. Our reading of the recent *National Evaluation Report* (2003) of Travellers pre-schools would suggest that conditions are better in other Traveller pre-schools, but it seemed to the review team that an energetic national approach to the well-being and education of young Traveller children is urgently needed, in close partnership with the Traveller community and its representatives.

153. The recently published national evaluation report, *Pre-School for Travellers* underlines that significant resources will be required to ensure the development and enhancement of the education provided in Traveller pre-schools. The report makes a number of far-reaching recommendations concerning: guidelines for the management of the pre-schools; provision for local involvement and a range of management models; the management and the local co-ordination of pre-school provision; improving the work of management committees; admission, registration and recording of attendance, the organisation of the pre-school; the development of a standard for pre-school buildings and their locations; improving funding arrangements; professional development of teachers and childcare assistants; sharing and developing good practice; planning, pedagogy and curriculum; assessment and record-keeping; linkages with primary schools.

154. The OECD review team welcomes this document, and the future work that it foresees. We would propose also that the successful inclusion of Traveller children into mainstream primary and secondary schools will depend not only on high quality early childhood programmes, but also on significant upstream measures. A systematic and co-ordinated approach needs to be adopted in favour of the Traveller community, which will deliver in coming years anti-bias treatment, appropriate housing, employment, and enhanced funding of special services for Traveller children. In these services, a delicate balance needs to be struck between inclusion and the right of Travellers to recognition as a special group. Recommendations with regard to Traveller children are summarised in the next chapter.

4. Quality issues

Quality discussions and initiatives in Ireland

155. The overall picture in Ireland is one of a focus on quality issues, with ongoing developments at various levels. The National Childcare Strategy - building on the recommendations of the National Forum - favours a view of quality assessment as a dynamic, ongoing process linked to indicators such as appropriateness of provision and learning environments; low child/adult ratios; trained, registered and adequately remunerated staff; partnerships with parents and local community; diversity; accessibility (Government of Ireland, 1999a). The *White Paper* (1999), while recognising that conceptualisations of quality cannot be fully standardised, recommends defining a set of core criteria which should include both structural (tangible) and process-oriented (non-tangible) elements of quality.

156. As a concrete measure for evaluating the quality of early childhood services outside the Education sector (primary), the *White Paper* (1999) recommended the introduction of a Quality in Education (QE) Mark. In its proposed form, the QE Mark is seen as an external evaluation measure against which provision will be assessed. It is to be awarded to "providers who reach minimum standards in a number of key education-related areas" (Government of Ireland, 1999b, p.54). These areas are defined as curriculum, methodologies, staff qualifications and training. It is planned that the standards will dovetail with the Department of Health and Children requirements as laid down in the 1996 and 1997 Child Care Regulations which focus on matters of health and safety, since under the present system, centres wishing to be assessed for a QE Mark would be inspected by two separate government agencies, each looking at different aspects of a centre's functioning. The *White Paper* proposes a combination of both sets of expertise and the varying perspectives into one set of inspection procedures. The QE Mark is to be developed by the Centre for Early Childhood Development and Education (CECDE).

157. Besides the above-mentioned approaches towards developing a quality framework for early childhood curriculum issues, the DES inspectorate is also currently working on "objectively defined evaluation and quality criteria" (*Irish Background Report* 2002, p.61) to help primary schools, including the infant classes, in conducting self-evaluations and to assist the inspectorate in external evaluations. Quality initiatives are also being funded under the EOCP, both at the level of the County Childcare Committees and in support of the work of the National Voluntary Childcare Organisations. A number of self-evaluation (e.g. by IPPA) and externally validated self-evaluation procedures have been developed (e.g. by the National Children's Nursery Association).

158. A number of issues are raised by these initiatives, e.g.

- Although the focus on quality is welcome and necessary in the present Irish context (see next section, and proposals concerning inspection in Chapter 4), a vision of quality as a matter of regulation, divorced from other system considerations, may be insufficient. There is the assumption that centres – in order to remain competitive – will wish to be awarded the QE

Mark. This raises several questions: How can centres be persuaded to take part in a voluntary quality improvement programme? How will quality of provision be guaranteed in the centres that opt out of a voluntary procedure? How will the costs of maintaining an extensive system of external evaluation be met?[36]

- Again, although national guidelines concerning programmatic and process requirements are important to elaborate, they would seem less urgent in the present context than a *National Goals and Quality Framework.* A national quality framework should be distinguished from a national curriculum dealing with learning areas, learning objectives and how to reach them. A quality framework focuses more on what Irish families and young children should be able to expect from accredited services whether public or private, that is: the passing of challenging accreditation procedures, adequate facility requirements, a sufficient number of highly qualified staff, favourable child-staff ratios, certified structured programmes, quality targets with regular monitoring and evaluation, certain modalities of parent participation and community outreach.

- From a review team perspective, the proposal by the White Paper to combine the expertise of DHC and DES in inspection procedures under a specialised inspectorate is interesting and cost effective. It is also far-reaching in its implications, implying that the early childhood sector is specific. If this is so, a case should also be made for the sector to have more autonomy with regard to facility needs and teacher training profiles.

- There is also the issue of possible overlap between different government agencies. Not only does the CECDE have a remit to develop a framework of learning goals for the age group 0 to 6, but also the National Council for Curriculum and Assessment (NCCA), a statutory body advising the Education minister, is working on a curriculum document for the same age-group entitled *Framework for Early Childhood Learning.* The document will cover various developmental domains (physical, cognitive, linguistic/communicative, social and emotional). Although not planned as a mandatory or prescriptive document, the NCCA sees the *Framework for Early Childhood Learning* as an integral part of the assessment procedure for gaining the QE Mark. Consideration is needed as to how these proposed frameworks interface with the quality standards laid down in the national Child Care Regulations (1996, 1997) under the Department of Health and Children, or with other curricula in use in Ireland, such as High/Scope, Montessori, Froebel…

The reality of quality on the ground – the education sector

159. The OECD team was able to experience a number and variety of early childhood settings during the course of the review visit. However, the overall impression of our brief visits in school settings for young children was one of whole class teaching, with children sitting quietly at tables. The approach appeared to be directive and formal compared to practices observed and theoretically underpinned in various other countries, where more explicit emphasis is placed on exploratory learning and self-initiated, hands-on (as opposed to table-top) activities. In addition, the teacher/pupil ratio (currently one teacher to a maximum of 29 pupils) and class size in the infant classes is one which compares unfavourably internationally. If the aim is to meet the learning needs of children in an individualised way, it constitutes a considerable barrier to quality. Although the DES is making every effort to improve this situation, Table 10 in Appendix 1 shows that over 54 % of Junior Infants and 57 % of Senior Infants are in classes of 25–34 children.

---

[36] This is a characteristic challenge for demand-side systems in which governments indirectly subsidise but do not engage in direct management of provision. In market conditions, for-profit providers are tempted to respect the minimal quality levels and cut back on hiring qualified ECEC staff. In such instances, non-profit providers may be a surer option as they may be less inclined to engage in opportunistic behaviour. However, if governments only give subsidies to non-profit providers, then for-profit providers have a significant incentive to masquerade as non-profits, and disperse profits under a variety of other names, e.g. management or rental fees. A solution often adopted is to invest in a heavy supervisory framework and inspectors, and to require that all ECEC providers are governed by a board of directors dominated by parents and public representatives. A more effective solution may be for governments to assume the funding and management of a public or mixed system of early education and care.

160. From the experience of the review team, DES-funded ECEC provision was characterised by an overt focus on literacy and numeracy related activities, possibly a consequence of teachers feeling pressured because of parental expectations and the short length of contact time. In discussions with practitioners and researchers, the team noted that the evaluation criteria chosen tend to be narrowly focussed on cognitive outcomes, and from early on, the introduction of written symbols is noticeable. The arrangement of classrooms into areas or corners which children can freely choose was not evident. In few schools did we find a role-play area, a nature or biology area, sand and water, an art area (broader than painting), a construction area or recycled material... 'Play' was often used as a means of delivering a curriculum goal or a pre-academic skill, and the place of 'free play' in the schedule of the day seemed rather limited. In general, the pedagogy was not focussed on the observed interests of children but sought to interest them in the concerns of the teacher. 'Open framework' programmes, which, internationally meet with wide acceptance, were not in evidence. Problems that related specifically to *Early Start* were the general high rate of pupil absenteeism, insufficient in-service training and teacher support measures, and inadequate allocation of time for staff to review their work.

Quality in the childcare sector

161. The team visited an excellent family daycarer in the Dublin suburbs, who showed much empathy and expertise in dealing with the young children in her care, and whose house was well-appointed to receive infants and toddlers. In general, however, the private centres we visited (charging fees of around €120 per week for full-day care) showed insufficient understanding of how to interact with and stimulate young children in group settings. Though often well-resourced in terms of rooms and equipment, again with an over-abundance of ready-to-buy plastic toys, there was again an observable emphasis on table-top games, puzzles and work cards rather than on inter-active, self-directed learning. In no instance did we see children engaged in the preparation of food, eating together or playing outdoors. In reality, outdoor facilities were generally token, and pedagogical activities that encouraged children to explore the outdoors and nature were not in evidence.

162. Again, the regulatory framework in place in Ireland seems weak in comparison to other countries. It is basically a licence to practice, but does not include sufficient incentives to train, employ qualified staff or continually improve expertise. Other countries regulate more stringently or, like Australia, introduce voluntary quality improvement and accreditation schemes. It may be noted, however, that the strength of a voluntary accreditation system depends on what the providers are offered in return. In several countries, accredited providers can receive, either directly or indirectly, normative grants or subsidies attached to young children and families who wish to avail of childcare or early education. This presupposes that a grant or subsidy scheme is in place, sufficient both to make care affordable for the low- and modest-income families, and to attract a maximum number of providers into the official system.

163. There is also the issue of childcare providers working in isolation, with much effort going into administration and the search for clients, and insufficient energy invested in training and quality improvement. To overcome this weakness, some countries such as the Nordics and Flanders, insist on family daycarers working in networks. The network structure is able to take on many of the administrative functions, organise training and enter into negotiation with the local authority on issues of salaries, training, holidays, insurance and the setting of parental fees.

164. The team visited also a community-based, not-for-profit playgroup/pre-school in an area of high unemployment, with a growing number of refugee families. A real lack of resources, trained staff and materials was apparent. Fourteen boys and girls aged 3 and 4, many of whom are classified as 'special needs' (including autistic) children, were grouped round one table with about 6 young trainees (college students on a youth employment scheme) cutting out Christmas trees according to a given pattern. The décor was old and unattractive, there was almost no heating (in mid-

November), with little equipment or play / creative materials to be seen. A "parents' room" we were shown was cold, dark, and uninviting. Despite a very committed stance, the director and her staff are faced with an almost impossible task. The centre had received a staffing grant from ADM, but the Health Board grant had consequently been cut, despite the fact that there is a long waiting list. A capital grant had not yet been applied for. With appropriate resourcing, this playgroup could be transformed into a vibrant intercultural learning environment in an area with great need of family and community support structures.

Staffing and training

165. A particularly pressing staffing problem in Ireland which is closely related to quality issues is the generally low level of training and remuneration in the Childcare sector combined with a low level of staff retention. In most of the services the review team visited, whether private for-profit or community-based not-for-profit, the difficulty of recruiting well-qualified - or even qualified - practitioners and high staff turnover was referred to as a significant problem. A related issue is that of representation for childcare workers. While the early years staff in primary schools (i.e. those working with 4 and 5 year old children) have strong union representation through the Irish National Teachers' Association (INTO), there is no such organisation advocating in the same way for practitioners in the Childcare sector.

166. The generally low level and the disparate forms of training in the Childcare sector is a policy concern that has been acknowledged by the DJELR. In our discussions with stakeholders, there was much support for the recent policy initiative to establish a training framework through the *Model Framework for Education, Training and Professional Development in the Early Childhood Care and Education Sector* (Government of Ireland, 2002). Improving training, professional development and career prospects in the Childcare sector must be seen as a key issue for the future. The Certifying Bodies Sub-Group of the National Childcare Co-ordinating Committee is working on this issue with the National Qualifications Authority. (See Abbott & Pugh, 1998, for a description of similar problems in the UK and proposals for meeting the challenge.)

167. A significant contribution has been made to the delivery of childcare, particularly in community groups, by workers participating in 'return to work' and other employment creation schemes. However, these workers are frequently untrained in childcare. Some have been encouraged to undergo childcare training to enhance their own prospects within the sector and to ensure that they understand the basic principles of quality childcare in delivering their daily work. An equally pertinent issue is that of consensus building on conceptualisations of the professional role profile considered necessary for work with young children up to statutory school age. At present the stances on professionalism and pedagogy range considerably, from a highly formalised, subject-oriented school teaching approach to a play-based, informal approach with little learning taking place.

168. In *Early Start* units, primary school teachers work alongside childcare workers in the same group. This collaboration was commented on as a "partnership challenge" because of the difference between professional perspectives and a very tangible divergence in terms of compensation. The team was informed, however, that recent analyses of *Early Start* show that collaboration between teachers and childcare workers functions well in most cases. In practice, the team perceived a need for stronger links between those working in *Early Start* units and teachers in the Infant classes. We became aware that the childcare workers, although part of the planning and review of ES activities, were not involved in the overall school planning. In terms of working conditions, the time structure of the ES programme allows practically no time for reviewing work and consultation with colleagues.

169. The current minimal focus on early childhood education and care in the Education sector training for teachers (46 hours total, all during the first year of study) is a further issue which the team sees as demanding policy attention. Training is strongly oriented towards the demands of compulsory

schooling and is organised around curriculum subject areas. The kind of inter-disciplinary approach needed for conceptualising and developing appropriate pedagogies for work with young children appears to have no clear place in this kind of training format.

170. The problem of insufficient time allocation for the early years has been noted in other countries where pre-school teachers are trained alongside primary school teachers (Oberhuemer & Ulich, 1997). Compulsory schooling proves to have higher status when designing the training curriculum, with inevitably negative consequences for the quality of student expertise in early childhood education and care. A recent reform in Sweden, where a unified framework of training has been adopted for pre-school teachers[37] and primary teachers (and leisure time pedagogues), will possibly develop new ways of addressing such imbalances. A policy goal set and explicitly pursued by the Swedish government - that of a co-ordinated education system which emphasises upward integration, with pre-schools influencing schools in terms of pedagogy and methodologies - will presumably have a positive impact on the status of the early years within the training curriculum.

5. Parental engagement and information services

171. Parental engagement in early childhood services differs widely from country to country. In some countries, parents may form an automatic majority on the board of centres, control the finances and co-operate with the professional staff in elaborating the broad lines of the annual programme of a centre. In all countries, even in those in which parental input is token, it is generally admitted that good relations between teaching staff and parents are more easily formed when children are very young. Communication with parents is often considered a necessary feature of early childhood work, a prelude to winning parental support for education. Opening and closing hours are often organised to begin a half-hour or so before and after the formal programme for children, so that parents can meet and discuss with staff. Parents are also made welcome during daily 'settling-in time' and in the critical first weeks of a child's arrival at a centre.

172. In Ireland, the Education Act provides for the establishment of a Parents' Association in each school, and according to DES, parental involvement is one of the underpinning principles of *Early Start*. In the Home-School-Community Liaison scheme, specific attention to parental involvement is part of in-service training for staff, who are expected to visit children's homes. However, from our observation of Irish schools and centres, we saw little evidence of parental presence in the hallways, classrooms or activities. This may indicate that though formal participation measures are in place, informal opportunities for contacts between staff and parents may be limited in Irish settings. If this is the case, greater focus on parental involvement will be necessary, particularly in schools and centres in disadvantaged areas, where parents need both support and greater access to education opportunities.

173. According to recent research (Bowman et al. 2001), the need to include parents in learning activities with children probably depends on the situation. In some circumstances, parents acting as teachers may be effective, e.g. parents can provide real learning support to children with certain types of special need. In general, however, the appropriate conduct of activities by trained professionals in an enriched learning environment seems to be the key variable in children's learning in a programme. What is required most of all from parents is that they provide a stable and caring home environment for the child. This may imply that other types of family support - unrelated to the issue of parents as teachers - may be more critical for achieving positive child outcomes, e.g. in areas where there are many disadvantaged parents, the implication is that alongside the high quality early childhood programme, integrated, multi-functional services should be offered in which the health,

---

[37] In Sweden, pre-school teachers work in centres with children aged one to six years.

social and family agencies are involved. In other areas, it may be sufficient for ECEC centres to model for parents how to interact with young children, and provide them with regular information about what is expected of parents or how to access useful courses and services.

Box 9. Outreach to parents with young children and sensitivity to community needs

New conceptions of early childhood intervention in Britain encourage strongly parent and community involvement. For example, *Sure Start* services seek first to establish partnerships of parents and professionals who will work together and will share skills and expertise. The aim is to build a community's participation and capacity around its young children. Activities organised by local groups are linked with available health, family, educational and social welfare programmes. Supportive and preventive services are made available to families with children under the age of four years, thereby identifying and addressing potential difficulties at the earliest possible age. Parents are supported in the process of accessing and utilising services.

Area programmes for children are often facilitated by an Early Excellence Centre (a pre-school/parent centre), from which networks of Carer and Toddler Groups are organised. Priority needs, identified by parents, are met through the provision of child care services, support groups, vocational and other training, within a context of contributing to the processes of social and economic regeneration, e.g. the well-known Pen Green centre in Corby has four major strands of activity: 1) High quality early years education and care; 2) Parent Education; 3) Community health and family support services; 4) Training and research. The Centre has a comprehensive parent partnership programme, and over 4,000 parents have been involved over a period of 15 years. Staff at the Centre have established a model of co-operative working that respects both the learning and support needs of parents, and children's right to high quality early years education with care. This model of working with parents is underpinned by the belief that parents are deeply committed to their children's learning and development.

---

174. Where formal engagement as a group is concerned, Irish parents are represented on most County Childcare Committees, but they do not appear to have a strong voice at the national level. The *National Parents Council Primary* is a member of the NCCC, but, being a school-oriented organisation and short-staffed (3 staff in the Dublin office, and 20 trainers around the country to reach 500 primary schools) it cannot effectively represent parents with children in childcare facilities. This must be seen as a weakness of the system as a whole, since partnership between early childhood services and parents is necessary for future school support, and can contribute to quality provision (see also White Paper, 1999, page 114 ff).

175. During our visit we were informed that effective information policies for parents on early education and childcare issues need to be developed, both at the local and the national level. Altogether, considerable resources and training are needed to ensure that parents can effectively participate in consultative measures and management positions. This includes organised parent representation within the Childcare sector and for training opportunities for parents within the Education sector to help them become more vocal in articulating their interests and needs on School Management Boards. (The present training budget of the *NPC-Primary* was recently cut from €340.000 to €150.000.). It would seem also that parental representation across the early childhood sector could be significantly stronger than its present inclusion within the wider remit of the National Parents Council Primary in the context of statutory schooling.

6. Research, evaluation, information systems

176. The *Irish Background Report* 2002 and subsequent discussions during the review visit made visible a number of insufficiencies in data collection at the national level. Educational statistics on primary education are generally not disaggregated in their published form. For example, there is no

breakdown of the 4 year olds in infant classes in terms of socio-economic background, ethnicity, family structure. In sum, it is not possible to say who among the 4 year old population is gaining (or not gaining) access to early education. Some data is collected by Health Boards, but this is done in non-standardised ways. It seems also that in order to gain information on registered facilities inspections and their outcomes at a national level, each of the 10 Health Boards has to be contacted separately. A special module of the Quarterly National Household Survey has just looked at childcare, but with a strong perspective on female participation in the labour force (see QNHS Module on Childcare Arrangements in the *Irish Background Report* 2002).

177. Further insufficiencies are reported at the county level. A National Childcare Census co-ordinated by ADM – another of the DJELR policy initiatives - is for the first time collating data in a standardised format across the 33 counties/cities, helping to provide a baseline for the effective planning of services. However, there are – so the review team was told – considerable discrepancies between counties as to the methods of data retrieval used and the quality of data assembled.

178. While a number of short-term evaluation studies on the effects of specific pre-school pilot interventions (e.g. *Early Start*) have been carried out, we were informed that there is no tradition of evidence-based policy making in the ECEC field in Ireland. It is to be hoped that the newly established CECDE will itself contract research and direct the attention of the university departments to the key issues on which evidence-based research is needed. As in many countries, little research has been carried out on important issues on a long-term basis. In this respect, the proposed longitudinal study of 18,000 children – put forward by both the National Children's Strategy and the Report of the Commission on the Family and accepted by the Minister for Social, Community and Family Affairs and the Minister for Children in April 2002 – is to be seen as a particularly forward-looking step towards collating systematic data on children growing up in Ireland.

179. In our discussions with researchers, several research priorities for the coming years were pinpointed:
   - To continue the analysis of labour force participation and patterns (half-time, temporary…), and to monitor family-friendly measures, parental leave and their use patterns;
   - To examine financial supports and incentives granted to working parents in other countries;
   - To identify the typical needs of parents vis-à-vis childcare and early education, broken down for different groups; parents of children with special needs; traveller families; low income groups (urban and rural); families with a second child… ;
   - To examine the effects of dual working parents on young children's development and school performance;
   - To examine the effects of lone parenting (in rural and urban milieus) on young children's development;
   - To develop a conceptual framework and refine the relevant indicators for comparative data collection on young children in Ireland, and the services available to them;
   - To map the density of ECEC services and schools across the country;
   - To overview the descriptive features of provision throughout the country, including the number of children having access, their attendance patterns in the different geographical areas, and the employment status and situation of parents using childcare services;
   - To elaborate a conceptual and comparative framework to undertake the evaluation of the quality of various ECEC settings in Ireland; structural features; process elements…;
   - To examine the types of curriculum in use, their validation and delivery implications, especially those used most widely in pre-school and the infant school;
   - To examine how parents may support young children's learning in the home;

- To examine the development of oral language and its links to school achievement;

- To identify how many trained personnel are working with children in Ireland, the extent of their training, etc. so as to set feasible standards for centres;

- To look more closely at how policy decisions concerning young children are implemented.

7. Funding

Public investment in young children and the funding of ECEC services

180. Figure 1 in Appendix 1 shows graphically the growth in the Irish economy from 1991 to 2001. During this ten year period, economic growth in Ireland surpassed that of all other OECD countries. As can be seen from Table 2 below, Ireland averaged a growth rate of 7.7% during the period, compared to the OECD average of 2.8%; to the USA rate of 3.4% or the UK at 2.7%. In 2001, 450,000 more people were at work in Ireland than in 1989 – a remarkable achievement in such a small economy. The new job situation has brought an enhanced standard of living to the majority of families and children, and has changed irreversibly patterns of work for Irish women.

181. However, growth rates are relative to a starting point, and as many of the comparative tables in this report demonstrate, young children in Ireland are starting from a position of relative disadvantage compared to their northern European counterparts. Public expenditure in general is relatively low in Ireland (see Figure 2 in Appendix 1), not least in the health, social and education fields (see Table 12, Table 2 and Figure 4 in Appendix 1). This is a feature that hinders Ireland's showing in the United Nations Human Development Index, where it is 18th in the world, but last among the northern European countries.[38] From 1985 onwards, social expenditure in Ireland increased considerably in volume, but decreased significantly as a percentage of GDP. Within this generally low expenditure, young children receive a small share in comparison with their counterparts in other EU countries.

182. Economic analyses from many other countries indicate that investment in early years services brings not only proven benefits to the children and families they serve, but also to governments and national economies (Leseman, 2002, Cleveland and Krashinsky, 2003). The following paragraphs list some of the more recent evidence:

Analyses showing educational returns from early childhood investment

- *Success For All: long-term effects and cost-effectiveness* (Borman, G. and Hewes G. in AERA Educational Evaluation and Policy Analysis, Washington, Vol. 24, No. 4, Winter 2002). Success For All is a comprehensive elementary school reform programme designed to promote early school success among at-risk children. It is widely replicated in the USA, and serves over 1 million children in 2000 schools. In addition to offering an intensive, pre-K and K programme, it provides mechanisms to promote stronger links between the home and the school, and to address social behavioural and health issues. Relative to control groups, and at similar cost, Success For All children complete elementary school at an earlier age, achieve better learning outcomes, have fewer retentions or special education placements. The authors underline that for success to continue, similar programmes need to be used throughout primary and lower secondary schooling.

- *The Title I Chicago Child-Parent Centers* (Reynolds et al. 2002) – Opened in 1967, the Centers are located in public schools and provide educational and family support to low-income children from ages 3 to 9 years. Using data from the Chicago Longitudinal Study, and

---

[38] Ireland performs strongly on the GDP indicator, but more weakly on social spending, health (life chances for girls and women are low by EU standards) and education (persisting functional illiteracy, and school drop-out among poor children).

comparison group children born in 1980, Reynolds and his team show that participation in the Centers was significantly associated with greater school achievement, higher rates of school completion, with significantly lower rates of remedial education, juvenile delinquency and child maltreatment. Cost-benefit analyses indicate that in 1998 dollar values, the programme provided to society a return of $7.14 per dollar invested by: increasing economic well-being and tax revenues; reduction of public expenditure on remedial education; criminal justice treatment and crime victims.

Analyses showing social, economic and labour market returns from investment

- The Müller Kucera-Bauer study: *Costs and benefits of childcare services in Switzerland – Empirical findings from Zurich,* (2001) shows that the city's public investment of 18 million SF annually is offset by at least 29 million SF of additional tax revenues and reduced public spending on social aid (Müller Kucera and Bauer, 2001). Where affordable childcare was available, the rate of hours in work almost doubled, especially for single-headed households with one or more children. In sum, publicly funded childcare resulted in 1) Higher productivity and earnings due to maintaining productive workers in work. 2) Higher contributions to social security and savings; 3) Less dependency on social assistance during both the productive and retirement ages (without affordable childcare, many families would fall below the poverty line).[39]

- *The ongoing Berrueti-Clement et al. study* (1984, 1995-6, 2001) evaluates the educational and economic returns of a high quality pre-school programme (Perry Pre-school) on a sample of Afro-American children. Key findings were that the children from the Perry Pre-school programme had better school records, improved labour market entry and higher incomes than the control group of similar children. In a cost-benefit analysis of the data, Barnett (1995) estimated that the cost-benefit ratio for the investment in the programme was almost 1:7.

- *The North Carolina Abecedarian Early Childhood Intervention* (Masse and Barnett, 2002), which began in 1972, has been subject to numerous studies. The various researches show positive cognitive and social results for the children (mostly disadvantaged) in the project, some of whom gained entry into four-year university programmes. The Masse and Barnett cost-benefit study of 2002 finds that every dollar invested in high quality, full-day, year-round preschool generated a four dollar return to the children, their families and all taxpayers. Among the study's findings:

  □ Participants are projected to earn about $143,000 more over their lifetimes than those who did not take part in the programme.

  □ Mothers of children who were enrolled can also expect greater earnings - about $133,000 more over their lifetimes.

  □ School districts can expect to save more than $11,000 per child because participants are less likely to require special or remedial education.

  □ The next generation (children of the children in the Abecedarian project) are projected to earn nearly $48,000 more throughout their lifetimes.

- *The 2001 report issued by the National Economic Development and Law Center* in the US assesses the impact of the childcare industry on the economy of California. Apart from enabling parents to work and earn higher incomes, the childcare industry contributed $65 billion to the total value of goods and services produced in California - just over four times as much as the motion picture industry. Licensed childcare directly employed 123,000 people, including teaching

---

[39] An interesting conclusion of this paper is that as most of the returns on ECEC investments go back to the Federal authority, cantons and municipalities in Switzerland are reluctant to invest in ECEC services.

and non-teaching staff, and maintained a further 86,000 jobs in transportation, publishing, manufacturing, construction, financial services, real estate and insurance (S. Moss, 2001).

- *The Canadian cost-benefit analysis* issued in 1998 by a team of economists at the University of Toronto estimates the costs and benefits of establishing a national quality childcare system for Canada (Cleveland and Krashinsky, 1998). Although the authors make conservative assumptions about the magnitude of positive externalities, they conclude that the substantial public investment envisaged would generate important net benefits for Canadian society.

- *Labour market/taxation studies:* The provision of education and care services has allowed most OECD countries in the last decades to maintain the labour market participation of women, with a corresponding widening of the tax base. In Norway, for example, the increase has been from about 50% female participation in 1972 to well over 80% in 1997 (Kornstad and Thorensen, Statistics Norway, 2002). In particular, women of 25 to 40 years have greatly increased their participation.

183. In sum, a strong economic rationale exists in favour of establishing national networks of early childhood services (ESO/Swedish Finance Ministry Report, 1999; Sen, 1999; Urrutia, 1999; Van der Gaag, 2002; Vandell and Wolfe, 2000; Verry, 2000). Significant employment can be generated immediately, tax revenues increased, and important savings made in later educational and social expenditure, if children – especially from at-risk backgrounds – are given appropriate developmental opportunities early enough in life. The consequences of not investing sufficiently in services can also be considered. If childcare is regarded as a private family responsibility, the result will be – in modern economies - insufficient supply of services for those who need them, a fragmentation of services, a lack of equity vis-à-vis poorer families and overall poor quality of provision.

184. The economic argument in favour of greater investment in young children is perhaps particularly strong in Ireland, from both labour market and human capital perspectives. Unless the state provides more supports and services, many working women in Ireland may continue to leave employment for family reasons. Both OECD and CSO figures (see Table 11 in Appendix 1) suggest that this is already happening on a large scale, and may eventually create a vicious circle: a decrease in taxation revenues leading to an inability to fund public services, and a reinforcement of the culture of low employment rates among women. In turn, lack of income leads to social dependency and poverty, especially in single-headed households, with extremely negative consequences for young children.

The funding situation in Ireland – childcare and education

Childcare

185. At the beginning of the decade, childcare in Ireland received the greatest funding boost ever in the state's history through the National Childcare Strategy and the Equal Opportunities Childcare Programme (EOCP). European Structural Funding, matched with significant governmental allocations, has been a major step forward in the development of childcare in Ireland. As mentioned in para. 28 above, the main body of funding is channelled through the two Regional Operational Programmes of the National Development Plan which together make €328 million available (including €170 million of EU funding), while the Exchequer has supplemented this funding with a further €109 million making a total of €436.7 million available to develop childcare over the life of the Programme, 2000 - 2006. Within this framework, one measure provides capital grant assistance to create new and quality-enhanced childcare places while two sub-measures support staffing grants where there is a focus on disadvantage and provide grants for quality enhancement initiatives through the national voluntary childcare organizations.

186. The recent NDP evaluation of EOCP performance has not been fully positive (NDP/CSF Evaluation Unit, 2003), and states that "in terms of its key objectives, the performance of the programme to

date has been disappointing". Expenditure and physical progress are running below target; deadweight has occurred in the process of providing capital grants to private providers; insufficient numbers of childcare places have been created; problems have arisen with programme indicators and reliable data; and there have been deficiencies in monitoring the quality improvement sub-measures.... From the perspective of the review team, these are teething troubles, which, of course, need to be addressed. To have been able to launch such an ambitious programme is already a real achievement in the Irish context, where few or no models were available. Moreover, as the evaluation acknowledges, the programme has been able to maintain a focus on equality of opportunity, staff support, affordability and social inclusion (92% of funding going toward the community sector).

187. From our understanding, the approach adopted has been to build up the community sector and the profession of childcare worker, while offering incentives to private providers to provide additional or enhanced childcare places. To our mind, this is a realistic and sound option in the present circumstances. Given the dearth of public services in the field, except for the early primary school service, the government has little choice other than to attract voluntary and private providers into the field, and through funding mechanisms, encourage them to become part of a regulated system. Because the initiative is government led, it has enabled the EOCP to focus to some extent on quality, which ultimately comes from the quality of the workers employed and from those inputs that government traditionally can supply: legislation, regulation, management, a national framework, equity for the poor, evaluation, training and research.

Education financing

188. Again, as in other sectors, public expenditure on education has expanded greatly in Ireland over the past decade but, parallel to health and social expenditure, it remains weak compared to other OECD countries – see Fig. 4 and Table 8 in Appendix 1. Within that expenditure, an investment imbalance of almost 3:1 has occurred in past decades in favour of the higher levels of education at the expense of primary and early childhood education (see Table 8). As a result, *per capita* investment, child/staff ratios and regular funding to renew training and pedagogy in the Irish infant school remain far behind northern European standards. Sometimes, this has been due to the assimilation of the infant classes into primary schooling, e.g. the "international best-practice guideline of 20:1" for child-staff ratios quoted in the *Agreed Programme for Government* (page 21), is not true of early education. Ratios for children aged 3-6 years, in most European school programmes, range from 10:1 to 22:1, and in the Nordic countries are much lower.

189. As noted in Chapter 2, recent figures from the Department of Education and Science (DES) show that 24% of infant pupils are still in classes of 30 pupils or above (*Irish Background Report* 2002, p.62). With such ratios, it is difficult to engage in individualised learning activities with young children, or to ensure the children's well-being and social interaction. However, as we shall indicate later, resolving the high child-teacher ratio is one measure among others that needs to be addressed in reforming quality standards in early education. We shall propose in our recommendations in Chapter 4, that where quality improvement is concerned, measures such as more independence and accountability for the infant school, the restructuring of pre-service teacher training, and ongoing investment in in-service training are other measures that need to be employed.

Funding for young children from the Health sector

190. According to our interlocutors, a more significant health budget is now being devoted to children, and access to primary health care has improved. Because of the shortness of the visit, the OECD team was unable to analyse how this works out in practice for young children. However, the evidence from overall health spending (see, for example, Table 12 on *Health expenditure as a % of GDP* in Appendix 1) shows that although Ireland's expenditure on health has risen rapidly with its growth in

GDP, its public spending on health in relation to GDP is significantly less (4.9% in 2001) than the OECD average of 6.07% in 2001. Again, general data available from OECD and European sources present an assessment of perinatal care and infant mortality that is not reassuring.[40] Given the relatively high rate of child poverty in Ireland, and the difficulty of certain groups, such as Travellers, to access primary health care, the question merits a real focus in future early childhood policy.

---

[40] A comment received from the Department of Health notes that: The infant mortality rate can vary because of variations in practices relating to the registration of deaths. Variations observed in the perinatal mortality rate are determined to a significant degree by practice in relation to termination of pregnancy. Many foetal abnormalities are detected in the antepartun period in countries that permit termination and resultant terminations are reflected in lower perinatal mortality rates

Chapter 4

CONCLUSIONS

This concluding chapter of the OECD Country Note on Early Childhood Education and Care in Ireland draws on the descriptions and analyses presented in Chapters 2 and 3. The points presented for consideration concern labour market, gender and equity concerns; co-ordination; expanding access; improving quality; and financing new measures. We are fully aware that our suggestions are based on an external knowledge of the ECEC system in Ireland. Despite this, we are hopeful that our independent perspective, which draws on knowledge and experience of systems of early childhood education and care in other countries, may contribute to the debate on policy development for young children and their families in Ireland.

1. Labour market, gender and equity concerns

191. The early childhood period is the foundation stage of health, well-being, socialisation and lifelong learning. Increasingly, the period is recognised as the foundation stage of a sound human resources policy (see Appendix 3), and as the critical moment for ensuring the development and rights of the child. As such, early childhood services are a public good and receive significant state investment in all OECD countries. Private providers, community and voluntary bodies are partners in the early childhood field, and can be particularly effective in the climate of public-private partnerships that prevails in Ireland. At the same time – in order to promote equity, protect young children and ensure that all services support young children to reach their full developmental potential - State funding, regulation, policy guidance and development of the national system are necessary. The experience of many countries shows that without significant investment from the State in this field, market failure inevitably occurs, especially with regard to affordability and equitable access to quality services.

192. Because of the economic externalities created - such as labour market expansion and flexibility, a larger taxation base, the development of further training and education, and the creation of new jobs at local levels - early childhood services are a productive investment for a country (see paragraph 182 and appendix 3). Services are provided primarily to develop the potential of young children, but they also serve to support women and families, and to ensure of equality of opportunity in education for disadvantaged young children when they begin school. There is also a strong research consensus that the keys to ending family poverty and to giving a fair start in life to children is to build a strong family structure around them, through jobs for parents, social supports, income transfers toward the needy; adequate community resources (including housing); *and affordable, quality socio-educational services to children from the youngest age,* including, in contexts of disadvantage, strong outreach to families and communities;

193. The Irish government has committed significant funding to the expansion of childcare services until 2006. Such funding will be needed throughout the decade to support the creation of long-term ECEC institutions capable of delivering quality services and interventions, especially in disadvantaged areas. Key issues for government in considering such an investment are: Will investment improve the labour market situation? Will investment ensure equitable educational outcomes for children from disadvantaged backgrounds? How can investment be shared across ministries? How can expenditure be kept within budgetary limits? Are there opportunities for a fairer distribution of costs between government and beneficiaries, or across the various income groups?

194. *Will investment in early years services improve the supply and flexibility of the labour market in Ireland?* Recent analyses of the Irish labour market (see, for example, Collins and Wickham, 2001) suggest that for the moment participation by women is determined more by level of education and the opportunity to earn, than by the existence of childcare services. It is still possible for Irish women with young children to join the labour force, despite the shortage of services, because of informal networks of family and neighbours, which are still available to look after young children, at least for some hours during the day. In the medium term, this reserve pool may remain stable, especially in rural areas, but will inevitably decrease as the present cohort of working young women moves upwards in the age structure, while continuing to pursue their careers. With this change in the work patterns of Irish women, demand for publicly regulated childcare services must be expected to increase.

195. Already signs of strain can be clearly seen. Table 11 in Appendix 1, taken from the OECD Employment Outlook (2002), provides comparative figures for the drop-out of women from the labour market across European countries. Ireland shows a particularly high female drop-out rate after the birth of a first and second child. Many of these women are well educated and a real loss to the economy.[41] In addition to the OECD chart above, CSO figures corroborate that remaining in work is often not an option for Irish women when a second child is born (CSO, 2002). Typically, a second earner in a couple family with two young children in care, with earnings at two-thirds of average salary, has no net return from work after childcare costs (OECD, 2003). In terms both of labour market policy and the best interests of young children, affordability of childcare remains a critical issue in Ireland. Many working parents in average jobs cannot afford two childcare places in the private market, where ability to pay determines accessibility. Because of affordability barriers, they must then rely on informal arrangements with family, friends, and neighbours, or leave the labour market.

196. *A gender perspective* – It would appear that the policy implications of equality of opportunity for women are still not clearly recognised either in the labour market or family spheres (see Chapter 3). High drop-out rates from the labour market, the increasing number of women in part-time work, the low participation of older female cohorts are signs, among others, that traditional patterns of gender inequality still survive. Supports for women with children are few: parental leave is meagre, affordable early childhood services are scarce, and fiscal support for young children in childcare does not yet exist. The situation is particularly critical for young women earning modest salaries.[42] Yet, women (and their families) gain greatly, both at a personal and a professional level, from being in employment. Remaining at work enables women to take their rightful place in society, contribute to the national economy, and to build up independent pension benefits for their later years. In many

---

[41] Is the drop-out a loss to the child and family? There is a growing consensus in European countries that parental care for the young child for at least a year after birth is desirable, although there is no evidence to show that care by other caregivers harms young children *unless it is of low quality*. Research also shows that toddlers from 1-3 years benefit from quality programmes, especially where socialisation, motor and socio-emotional development are concerned. From the point of view of family economics, the loss of a salary is more or less significant, depending on circumstances. The additional wage brought to households by a (second) working parent can make a great difference to family well-being, when the wage of the principal earner is modest.

[42] These are often women in public sector employment, notably at the user/provider interface. According to the National Economic and Social Forum (1995) and Harvey (2003), there is a marked absence of women in policy-making and management areas.

instances also, regular employment allows women to avoid long-term poverty damaging for themselves and for their children, an important consideration in situations of lone motherhood, separation and divorce, when children are normally left in the mother's custody.[43]

197. From a child well-being perspective, the situation of lone mothers in Ireland is also of concern. Their employment rate compares unfavourably with levels found in other countries, that is, a 45% employment rate compared to an 81% employment rate in Austria; 76% in France; 84% in Japan. Welfare supports, a disregard of small earnings for temporary jobs, plus a lack of quality childcare ensure that it is not advantageous for lone mothers to seek regular half- or full-day employment. In consequence, long periods of unemployment are experienced, which can result in children growing up in poor, workless and even socially excluded households. In sum, more active policies concerning the participation of women are needed so as to enhance the possibility and the rewards of work both for married and single mothers with young children. At the same time, work needs to be balanced – when young children are present – by family-friendly workplace policies. We encourage the authorities to avoid the excesses of the initial *Welfare to Work* practices in the USA, when in some cases lone mothers were obliged to work long hours for little remuneration, separated from their children for 10 hours or more per day.

198. *Parental leave* – A key policy mechanism in European countries to make work more rewarding and less stressful for women with young children is the provision of maternity and work leave for parents after the birth of a child. Paid, flexible and job-protected maternity and parental leave schemes of at least one year are seen as an essential component of any comprehensive strategy to support working parents with very young children, and a necessary element in labour market and family policy.

199. The jury is still out concerning *when* mothers should return to work and place their infants in care either in an individualised or collective setting outside the home. In the Nordic countries, there is a consensus that children should not be in services before one year (Denmark) or eighteen months (Norway and Sweden), unless there is necessity. Consistent with this conception of child development and the right of parents to rear their child especially in the critical first year after birth, these countries offer a great deal of support to parents so that they can take care of their child at home during the first year of life. There is also a financial calculation involved. Few countries can afford to finance high quality crèche services for infants under one year with adequate staff-child ratios. From many points of view, remunerated parental leave for a year, with job protection, would seem to fit better with parental preferences and the economic calculation. Actual practice in Ireland, however, lags behind the parental leave levels found in many other European countries. The comparative place of Ireland in terms of maternity and parental leave may be seen in Table 4 in Appendix 1.

200. *Will early childhood investment ensure equitable educational outcomes for children from disadvantaged backgrounds?* According to the policy brief presented recently to the US Congress (Brooks-Gunn, 2003), mainstream research across countries agrees that:

  - High quality centre-based programmes enhance vulnerable children's school-related achievement and behaviour;

  - These effects are strongest for poor children and for children whose parents have little education;

  - Positive benefits continue into late elementary school and high school years, although effects are smaller than they were at the beginning of elementary school;

  - Programmes that are continued into primary school and that offer intensive early intervention have the most sustained long-term effects.

---

[43] In over 90% of instances, women are given custody of children in case of separation or divorce. Such situations affect over 40% of couples in some urban milieus.

201. With the exception of the infant school for children from four to six years, a critical volume of centre-based services has yet to be developed in Ireland. Collective and community services are still predominantly used by low-income parents, and have not yet received the long-term funding, regulatory and infrastructural support that a high quality network requires. In parallel, a system of informal, individual childminding has grown up, covering the great majority of children who need care outside the home. Evaluative research in other countries indicates that informal childminding is far from satisfactory, and is generally judged to be of poor quality (NICHD, 1997). The situation can be even less promising for children born into situations of disadvantage, in which women with low educational levels tend to remain unemployed and live in poverty.

202. According to OECD and European Union figures, the regular health, social, and education budgets are relatively low in Ireland (see Table 2 and Figures 2 and 4 in Appendix 1). Within these budgets, young children are often an overlooked group, as currently, they are subsumed under larger concerns such as labour market childcare policy, gender equality, public health, family or primary education. Yet, infants and young children form the base of society and are passing through the most critical stage of life cycle development, which will influence profoundly their health, educational and social outcomes. To support them adequately, the major social ministries – and the National Anti-Poverty Strategy - may wish to consider a significant shift in expenditure toward young children so as to generate the level of funding that integrated family and early childhood services will need in Ireland in the coming years.

2. Co-ordination issues

203. Early childhood intervention is multiple in its aims. Several important societal goals are attained through the investment. In addition to ensuring the holistic development of young children at a moment in the life cycle when physical development, brain growth, motor skills, language, intelligence and personality structuring are in full progress, the goals of equality of opportunity for women, social inclusion, family support, and readiness for school can also be achieved. For this reason, central co-ordination of services is ensured in different countries by different ministries, e.g. in New Zealand, Spain, Sweden and the United Kingdom by education ministries, in Denmark and Finland by ministries of social affair; and in many countries by two different ministries or agencies. However, in almost all countries, employers, municipal authorities, education, labour, health, social and gender equality ministries co-operate to supply early childhood education, and to extend it to a full-day, year-long service. An example of this trend can be found in the *Call To Action From The Business Community* in the USA, which is reproduced in Appendix 3.

What model for Ireland?

204. Obviously, this is a question that Ireland must answer for itself. In view, however, of the urgent need to improve the present population/employment ratio in Ireland (especially with regard to women's participation) and to establish a coherent and affordable system for the early education and care of children outside the home – in a context where there is a dispersion of responsibilities across many ministries and agencies, and where general labour market conditions, preferences and cultural attitudes are not always supportive - the OECD team proposes for consideration:

- The integration of all early education and care policy and funding under one ministry or under a designated funding and policy agency. Ireland has much to gain – in terms of effective policy-making and economies of scale - by taking an integrated approach to early education and care for children from one to six years, conducted by one accountable agency, as is becoming the practice in many OECD countries.

- The urgent formulation of a *National Plan for Early Childhood Services Development,* rolled over on a three-year basis, with clearly spelt out goals, targets, time-lines, responsibilities and accountability measures from co-operating Departments. While universal in intent, the plan should include annual targets for the important subsystems, such as disadvantaged children, children from Traveller communities and children with special needs.

- Decentralisation of the planning and management of all early childhood education and care services at local level to an integrated agency or committee at the county/city level. Decentralisation to the local level needs to be backed by adequate regulatory powers and state funding.

Horizontal policy co-ordination across ministries

205. To achieve the Barcelona objectives, horizontal policy co-ordination across ministries will also be necessary. The recent NDP evaluation called for an overhaul of the existing National Childcare Committee, proposing to make it smaller and more focussed. The OECD team has noted the recommendation, and encourages DES to take a full role in the new Committee and in strategic planning at this level. The occasion may provide an opportunity to transform the present NCCC into a *National Policy Committee for Early Education and Care.* Benefits would include improved policy formulation, goal-setting and cost effectiveness. The Committee could also help to ensure, in formulating a *National Plan for Early Childhood Services Development,* that the different Departmental policies are consistent, interlocking and properly resourced. This would imply clearly spelt out objectives, targets, time-lines, responsibilities and accountability measures for the different Departments.

206. *County Childcare and Early Education Committees* - At the same time, the OECD team supports the subsidiarity in planning, budget and implementation that is now taking place. In parallel to the recommendation above, we propose a bringing together of childcare and education at local level through transforming the existing County Childcare Committees into *County Early Education and Childcare Committees.* If regulatory powers, stable funding and management expertise can also be transferred, the County Committees appear well capable of transforming national policy into concrete plans for each county, and of stimulating the necessary partnerships on the ground.

207. *Close co-operation between DJELR, DES, DHC and DSFA:* If an integrated ministerial structure is envisaged in Ireland bringing all ECEC under one ministry, the issue of co-ordination becomes much easier, especially if the lead ministry is open to a comprehensive approach, embracing the concerns of all the sectors involved and mobilising their respective strengths and competences. If administrative integration is not on the agenda, the OECD team would urge close co-operation between the major ministries engaged in early childhood services. In the context of the presidency of a new *National Policy Committee for Early Education and Care,* DJELR leadership may be envisaged for young children from birth to three, for parental leave measures, for afternoon services for children 3-6 years and for the development of out-of-school care. In like manner, DES would have responsibility for ensuring that a morning (3-hour) education session is made available for all children aged 3-6 years. This would mean moving away from an exclusive focus on the primary/infant school, and integrating the voluntary, community and private organisations capable of delivering high quality programmes and willing to follow the basic requirements of public child services. The contributions of both DHC and DSFA should also be sought, and leadership on certain issues given to them.

208. *Effective DES engagement in early childhood policy both at national and county levels:* The DES will continue to play a major role in the education and care of young children in Ireland. As the largest provider for children in the country, its collaboration will be essential if European Union targets are to be achieved, which presupposes that almost all 3-, 4-, and 5-year olds will be enrolled in regulated, half-day or full-day services by 2010. In addition, as the *White Paper* (1999) notes, DES has responsibility for training, for the development of a framework curriculum for 0-6 years, for

accreditation and for the development of quality standards. Its expertise will likewise be needed for children with special educational needs, for whom early intervention is a national responsibility and ethical priority. On several occasions, the wish was expressed to the OECD review team that the DES should play a fuller role in the co-ordinating committees both at central and local levels. The good offices of the DES vis-à-vis the School Boards will also be crucial in establishing a safe and cost-effective out-of-school care policy, and to extend the infant school day, using qualified providers from the community and voluntary sectors.[44]

209. This - and other measures proposed above to expand access - will require not only greater investment in young children from the Department than at present, but also an enhanced specialist presence. The need to create an *Early Years Development Unit* (EYDU) within the DES - as initially proposed by the National Forum for Early Education (1998) and recommended again in the *White Paper* (1999) – seems an urgent priority. A specialised Unit would seem critical to ensure from the Department a policy orientation in early education more specifically linked to the needs of young children and their families, and in tune with the efforts of other major stakeholders. A DES policy unit could also guarantee effective representation of educational perspectives on inter-Departmental, policy co-ordination bodies, and ensure through local delegation, regular representation on the County Committees. Until such expertise is present, it would seem urgent to devolve responsibility to the CECDE or other body to engage in official co-ordination with the other ministries, in particular with DJELR, DHC and DSFA.

210. *Pooling resources:* From the perspective of the review team, the pooling of resources across Departments will be necessary, if a high quality network of services is to be established, particularly in disadvantaged areas. In every county and city, a number of common tasks are undertaken for families with young children, e.g. developmental screening of young children; family healthcare; family outreach and support services; daycare and education of young children; pre-training and professional development of contact and support staff... Government departments such as DES, DHC, DJELR and DSFA may wish to consider co-operative funding toward the County Development Boards to build 50 or so multi-functional *Child and Family Centres* across the country, to administer and integrate services for young children and families.[45] Jointly funded administration/training /service provision centres - located in centres of disdvantage in the county towns and cities, and linked to regional and training colleges - would provide high quality service and play a major role both in training county level staff, and in modelling innovative programmes.

3. Expanding access

211. The Presidency conclusions of the Barcelona European Council (16-17 March 2002) present a major challenge for Ireland. They state that Member States should remove disincentives for female labour force participation by striving to provide childcare by 2010 for at least 90 % of children between 3 years and mandatory school age, and for at least 33 % of children under 3 years of age. The OECD team recommends that the ministries concerned should take on the challenge of meeting these targets, but with a due regard for quality. At present, coverage in half- or full-day, subsidised, regulated services stands at perhaps 10-15% for children under 3 years, and at about 56% for children aged 3 to 6 years in half-day services.

---

[44] In many countries, organised after-school care allows children who wish to play, study or engage in sports or recreational activities to do so in programmes within school precincts that are professionally facilitated and supervised.

[45] The Early Excellence Centres in England, piloted in 1997, have been developing such services with success, either as a 'one-stop-shop' for children and families or as multi-agency collaboration centres.

212. In order to reach the European goals quickly and without excessive cost, the OECD recommends for the consideration of the Irish authorities - in line with the *White Paper on Early Childhood Education* (1999) - the expanded use of the institutions in place. The general lines we present for consideration are: enhanced parental leave; the development of accredited family daycare and age-integrated centres for children 1-6 years; an operational subsidy for each child who uses an accredited childcare or pre-school service; the development, based on the local school, of a morning education session for all children from 3–6 years, with pre-school/educare added in the afternoon. Clearly, these suggestions are long-term, but if progressively implemented, they may offer a realistic response to the European Union challenge.

213. In the proposals that follow, we speak separately for the Childcare and Education sectors. We believe, however, that Ireland would have much to gain by taking a unitary approach to all services from one to six years, as is becoming the practice in several OECD countries. Centre-based services for young children from 1-6 years have much in common with each other, and the psychology and learning patterns of toddlers and children under six years differ significantly from those of older children. In addition, services for young children under six years – whether in care or school settings - have a triple function: viz. to ensure the well-being and global development of the child, including social and cognitive development according to age; to ensure care for children for some hours, especially if parents are employed ; and thirdly, to integrate children at-risk as early as possible into full-day tailored programmes based on family outreach and community building.

Access challenges for the childcare sector

214. From the perspective of the OECD team, two major challenges face the Childcare sector. To increase the number of full-time places for children aged 0-3 years; to co-operate with DES to lay the foundation of a full-day service and out-of-school care for children aged 3- 6 years and beyond.

1. Children 0-3 years (from birth to third birthday)

215. From the *Irish Background Report* and information received during the review, we believe that most DJELR subsidised places have been created for three and four year old children (see, for example, Table 7 in Appendix 1). This would suggest that DJELR may need to focus more on the providers who can provide for the younger age group, viz. parents; *childminders; and community and county services.* If this proposal meets with acceptance, significant funding will need to be oriented toward these groups.

216. *Parents – provision of a year-long maternity/parental leave linked with work.* The second principle of the National Children's Strategy states that measures toward young children should be family oriented, as the family generally affords the best environment for raising children. "External intervention should be to support and empower families within the community." Where the care of infants is concerned, maternity and parental leave are considered in almost all modern economies as a key step to ensuring that young infants have individualised attention and support during the early months of life. Paid, flexible and job-protected maternity and parental leave schemes of at least one year are seen as an essential component of any comprehensive strategy to support working parents with very young children. Leave benefits for mothers and fathers help reduce the need and demand for investment in infant provision (which because of the very low child/staff ratio is very costly), while acknowledging the primary role of the family in rearing young children. The issue is discussed more fully in paragraphs 103-106; 123-124 of Chapter 3.

217. *Childminders - increasing accredited access through integrating the childminders:* Because of the lack of early childhood centres in Ireland and population dispersion in rural communities, most families have to rely for childcare on non-registered, untrained childminders operating in the informal sector. The situation is positive in that local access is available, but becomes problematic where affordability and quality are concerned.

218. *Family daycare networks:* The need exists to transform childminding arrangements into recognised *family daycare networks* that can be accredited and will take in charge quality control and improvement. Networks also have the advantage of being able to take in charge initial administrative procedures and negotiations with the licensing authority concerning initial training, salaries, holidays, insurance, social security, parental fees and other issues. In many instances in France, for example, local childminders are supported from a professionally-run, central family crèche. The director and professionals in this central crèche provide training once or twice a week to local childminders, allowing them to gain a certificate, an improved professional status and better earnings for their work.[46] A further reward for childminders is that accreditation gains them access to subsidies paid to children using an accredited service. Because of these subsidies, the public authorities are able to cap fees charged to parents – a measure that we recommend strongly in the Irish context, where many women are forced to leave the labour market because childcare is unaffordable. Policies with regard to accreditation, subsidisation and fee capping exist in several OECD countries, for example, Canada.

219. *City/County Childcare Committees - building access levels through rigorous management:* In all countries, access levels grow in accordance with the growing trust of parents in the quality and management of the services offered at local level. In Ireland, the County Childcare Committees have potentially a central role to play in this field. Their mission is to examine all questions relevant to childcare policy, and to convene regularly the major actors in childcare, including the representatives of the ministerial agencies. So as to bring early education into the picture and work toward the integration of services, the OECD team recommends the further development of these committees to become *County Committees for Childcare and Early Education,* with enhanced powers to co-ordinate policies at county level for all children from 0-6 years, within the national frameworks established by the ministries. If given the necessary powers – including perhaps the authority to raise revenues for ECEC and set conditions for spending those funds – the County Committees can deliver:

  - *Needs assessments, reliable data and local training.* Guided by ADM, the Committees are well placed to gather information on the development of access in each county, its suitability to the needs of parents, its quality and equitability; and provide necessary information and orientation to parents. If financial flows can be matched to give these committees a strong management and steering role, within a clear accountability framework, the integration of services for children at local level can take place naturally.

  - *Light drop-in structures for mothers and young children* – As many Irish women remain at home to look after young children, consideration may be given to the creation of light drop-in structures based around health care centres, social welfare offices, school, community centres, libraries, etc. County and municipal bodies are best placed to decide on need and location, but will need the support of a ministry in planning these services.

  - *A purpose-built Child and Family Centre in each county:* In addition to the local childminder networks animated by a professional centre, we recommend also the creation of a network of purpose-built Child and Family Centres in the larger county towns and cities. Plans have been announced by the Department of Family and Social Affairs to build similar centres for family support purposes. Significant savings, a useful synergy and a much larger capacity could be achieved if other ministries were associated in the endeavour. Although having primarily a management and training purpose, the centres would increase access for disadvantaged children in the larger towns, and could act as the administrative centres for child and family

---

[46] In other countries, e.g. Belgium and Denmark, *family daycare providers* are part of the official municipal childcare networks, and receive training from municipal co-ordinators. These providers have been successful in providing education and care services for young children and families, particularly in rural areas.

policy within each county. They would also help to provide models of successful outreach programmes to families who are in need of support in carrying out parenting responsibilities. If associated with accredited training colleges, they could also provide management training and professional development, and model exemplary programmes. The financing of such centres is discussed in Section 5 on financing below.

2. Children 3-6 years (from 3rd birthday to 6th)

220. From the perspective of the OECD team, a second important task is for the Childcare and Education sectors to co-operate in gradually building up a full-day service for the 3-6 year olds, and in laying the foundation of a quality out-of-school service. Historically, "childcare" has often had little to do with "education", especially where the emphasis has been on social welfare or caring for a small minority of children while their parents worked. These features of the care sector are changing radically today, as increasing numbers of young children from all backgrounds need early childhood services and full-day care. Conscious of this change, the OECD review team suggests that a strong partnership between Childcare and Education can have a number of advantages, notably:

    - To ensure recognition of childcare as part of mainstream public provision;

    - To create shared goals for early childhood programmes;

    - To underline the common goals and educational methods of early childhood services; and

    - To organise in a coherent manner the recruitment, training and career structures of staff in both sectors.

221. Services for children before and after school hours and during the school holidays are virtually non-existent in Ireland. For the few services that do exist, there is no kind of regulatory framework and there are no stated quality standards. Yet, in all forms of provision offered by the DES for children under statutory school age, the attendance hours of children are few.[47] *Early Start units* and *Traveller Pre-Schools* are open for only 2^1/$_2$ to 3 hours daily. This limited time frame raises not only questions about the curriculum balance during those hours, but also about the quality of children's experiences after school hours if working parents are largely dependent on non-formal and unregistered childminding services. In the meantime, the only solution on offer seems to be half-time work for women or recourse to childcare either informal or regulated, where affordability, combined with a continuing shortage of places, remains a key issue.

222. To meet similar challenges, other countries are increasingly experimenting with educare and recreational programmes for children on school premises in the afternoon. Recent figures from the U.S. Census Bureau show that enrolments in full-day kindergarten has increased from 25% of age-eligible children in 1979 to 60% in 2000. In the last three years, a further 20 states introduced legislation related to increasing access to and funding for full-day kindergarten. A formula adopted in many countries is to provide at the local school a free educational session in the morning for all 3-6 year olds, extended in the afternoon, at school or on adjoining premises, by appropriate programmes – rest, leisure activities, motor development, music, dance, games, nature study, reading clubs etc. - provided by the community and voluntary sector. From the perspective of the child, it matters little who runs the service as long as it is of quality, provides continuity and does not involve bussing or disruption. Some cost recuperation through parental fees is practised for such programmes, and children are free to attend or not according to the contract made by the school with parents. In extending the day, due care needs to be given to the best interests of children – their rhythms, emotional and physical needs, and the quality of the premises and programmes that they are offered.

---

[47] Sessions for young children in the infant school are generally for 180 days annually, finishing about 1.10 p.m. daily. Working parents are obliged to rely on informal care or move their children to other services during school holidays and in the afternoons.

223.   The OECD team recommends a move toward full-day services and out-of-school care for 3-6 year olds. This would require not only policy leadership at central level but also close consultation at local level between the local authorities, voluntary sector and the local primary school. A start could be made in the already designated *Early Start* areas, inviting the school and the accredited voluntary and other agencies to plan together so as to provide a full-day, seamless service to children in these areas. If supported by appropriate funding, the measure could provide a more effective service for young children and families, and provide an official and much expanded role for the voluntary and community agencies.

Access challenges for the education sector

1. A morning educational session for all young children from the age of 3 years, extended in the afternoon by fee-paying pre-school and out-of-school services

224.   Keeping in mind, the targets set by the European Union and the large – and relatively permanent – drop-out rates of Irish women from the labour market, the main thrust of expansion in Ireland in the coming years should be the provision of a morning educational service for young children from the age of 3 years, extended in the afternoon by pre-school/educare services. Who provides the morning session should not be an issue, as long as it is provided by an accredited educational service. Learning from the first *Early Start* initiative, consultation and partnership at local level will do much to ensure that a comprehensive local service can be established to cover a high percentage of children in the age group, in the best possible conditions. With the co-operation of the local school, the challenge is not insuperable. From our interviews with teachers, parents and community leaders, we believe that the institution is capable of adapting itself to the new situation of parents in Ireland, to working with community agencies and to meeting eventually the targets set by the European Union.

225.   Part of this adaptation will be to prolong the day on school premises, as discussed in Chapter 3. A fair division of labour could be an educational session provided in the morning to 3-6 year olds at the local school by DES, or on their own premises by accredited providers of structured learning programmes, with appropriate afternoon programmes being provided by the community and voluntary sector on school or adjoining premises. Such a move could begin in the present *Early Start* areas, with partnerships between the school and the community and voluntary agencies to provide a full-day service for young children. The measure has a number of advantages:

   -   It would align Irish practice on the European model, where policy makers try to ensure that afternoon sessions for younger children take place in the same centre that hosts the morning period. In France, for example, different early childhood services work effectively side by side on the same premises. A sole location for services has obvious advantages both for young children and their parents. From the point of view of the child, the auspices of a service are of far less important than its continuity and quality.

   -   A full-day, integrated service would remove pressure on teachers in the *Early Start* morning classes, improve quality and make place for a more appropriate pedagogy for these groups. At the same time, the extended day would provide an enriched learning environment for disadvantaged children throughout the day, and reinforce contact with parents who need support and job training.

   -   A full-day would provide an official and much expanded role for the voluntary and community agencies, especially if linked with normative grants or a child education subsidy attached to each child participating in the afternoon session. With assistance from the county authorities, these agencies could provide the afternoon programmes for children within the school or pre-school precincts.

226.   *The enrolment of all 4-year olds* - The review team also recommends that all 4-year olds, irrespective of the month in which they were born, should have an entitlement to an education place in an infant

class or other accredited educational programme at agreed points during the year (at present, only 52% of 4 year-olds are enrolled in the infant classes). Teachers would be greatly helped in managing the increased intake if a Child Assistant were appointed to each infant school class. The presence of a Child Assistant would also reduce child-staff ratios for this age group to 15:1 – thus bringing Irish practice closer to European norms.

227. *DES accreditation and financial support for selected pre-school providers* - To increase access levels, the Department of Education and Science may wish to consider the recognition and support of accredited pre-school providers, as mentioned in the White Paper, 1999. Several of these groups have been working with young children in Ireland for generations, particularly with 3- and 4-year old children. Many teachers /educators in these groups have three- or four-year university qualifications. The different approaches that they bring enrich early childhood theory and pedagogy. In addition, they contribute to the national network for young children, providing places for some thousands of children. The new QE mark to be developed by the CECDE could have a section referring to the accreditation of the pre-school providers, outlining the facility, programmatic, recruitment and qualifications requirements needed to be a recognised early education institute. The measure has the advantage for governments of regulating the sector more efficiently, and of including the children served in Irish national statistics.

2. Strengthening Early Start and general provision for children from disadvantaged backgrounds with the community/voluntary providers

228. Ireland's attention to child poverty is noteworthy, and the situation of many young children born in poverty has improved in recent years. There is a strong NAPS strategy in place, a small *Early Start* programme in 40 schools in disadvantaged areas, and a further 270 areas of education disadvantage designated. Yet, according to our interlocutors, much more remains to be done (see also, Fig. 3 in Appendix 1). The OECD team recommends that *Early Start* should become a full day programme, and extended in agreement with the community/voluntary providers. Lessons should be drawn also from the research provided from other countries (see para. 147 above) concerning how to improve the effectiveness of this type of programme with regard both to parental/community outreach and to classroom practice.

229. In the effort to enrol all 4-year old children into the infant school, it will be helpful also to undertake research on the socio-economic background of children missing out on enrolment. The policy of designating priority education areas is a useful tool in that it allows intervention at the community level, but it is also a blunt instrument in that it fails to identify the many disadvantaged or at-risk children who live outside low-income areas. In sum, supplementary measures need to be taken to identify at-risk children who may not be enrolled or who may not be receiving the individualised attention they need in regular settings.

230. Disadvantage is a multi-dimensional phenomenon, "resulting from the interactions of deep-seated economic, social and educational factors." (Kelleghan, 2002). Effective responses are also multi-dimensional. In disadvantaged areas, early childhood services need to be intensive, multi-functional and co-ordinated with other services and agencies. To break the poverty cycle, attention to wider issues, such as anti-bias policies, employment opportunities, social support, income transfers, housing policies and community resources will be critical. For some groups, e.g. the Traveller community, well-resourced, early childhood and family services managed conjointly by Traveller parents may be necessary, so that young children from this special milieu can join mainstream education in the best possible conditions.

3. Children with special needs

231. As discussed in the previous chapter - and despite some excellent schools, supportive local bodies and an increasing number of specialist teachers in primary education – the OECD team was not

informed of any systematic plan, based on legal entitlement, for special education provision in Ireland for young children from birth. According to information received, the majority of children with disabilities below the age of four years do not have an entitlement to educational intervention and their parents lack the support of a professional service to reinforce the energy and optimism needed to conduct the intensive, individual learning programmes that children with special needs require. As the education and inclusion of children with special needs is a question of basic human rights, and as there is significant evidence of the positive effects of intensive intervention from birth and during the critical early years (Guralnick, 1997), the OECD team recommends urgent consideration and implementation of the recommendations made in the course of the National Forum of Early Childhood Education, 1998. The creation of a comprehensive national system of early years services for these children is urgently needed, with specific legislation to protect their human rights and provide entitlement to priority in enrolment in public services. In practice, these children should receive structured and regular educational support from birth, or at least from the time of identification of the disability. Crucial time is lost if educational intervention starts only at the beginning of infant or primary schooling. When children with disabilities are enrolled in mainstream schools, we encourage the DES, communities and school principals to ensure that these children receive, on a regular basis, individualised learning programmes and adequate support services.

4. Children from the Traveller community

232. Children from the Traveller community in Ireland urgently need enhanced access to all levels of education. Early education and care is no exception. Thanks to the voluntary bodies in charge of the special pre-schools for Traveller children, and to dedicated teachers and principals in primary schools, much progress has been made. However, the further development of early intervention programmes and of successful educational outcomes for children from the Traveller community in mainstream schools will be the acid test of national policies to combat poverty and achieve social inclusion.

233. The recently published national evaluation report, *Pre-School for Travellers*, is a key policy instrument. It underlines that significant resources will be required to ensure the development and enhancement of the education provided in Traveller pre-schools. The report makes a number of far-reaching recommendations concerning national policy on Traveller pre-schools; guidelines for the management of the pre-schools; providing for local involvement and a range of management models; the management and the local co-ordination of pre-school provision; improving the work of management committees; admission, registration and recording of attendance, the organisation of the pre-school; the development of a standard for pre-school buildings and their locations; improving funding arrangements; professional development of teachers and childcare assistants; sharing and developing good practice; planning, pedagogy and curriculum; assessment and record-keeping; linkages with primary schools.

234. The DES faces also the challenge of going beyond the collection of enrolment data, and to evaluate annually the actual outcomes for Traveller children. The drop from 5,500 child enrolments in primary school to only 1600 in secondary school needs urgent investigation. Measures need to be taken to set realistic annual targets and ensure the integration of all Traveller children into secondary education. A contributory element to the successful inclusion of children from the Traveller community at all levels of education will be anti-bias teacher training, and attention in schools to issues of diversity and identity (Derman-Sparks, 1989).

235. Throughout primary education and especially, through the delicate transition into secondary school, the DES may wish to put into place an accompaniment or mentoring service for Traveller children. With the permission of parents, a mentoring service could track and support each child, ensuring in particular that all Traveller children pass into secondary education. The low number of Traveller children in pre-school suggests that most Traveller children are entering primary school already at a

great disadvantage – a hypothesis which is strengthened by the huge drop-out of Traveller children on entry to secondary school.

236. As participation is a catalyst for change, the government may also wish to consider the appointment of a representative from the Traveller community to the relevant policy bodies concerned with the first three levels of education. The purpose would be to improve and expand programming for young children and their families; to ensure the meaningful inclusion of Traveller children into primary and secondary mainstream education and later, their successful transition from education to salaried employment. Within each Traveller pre-school, and in the primary schools that receive significant numbers of Traveller children, it would seem necessary – as is the custom in other countries - to ensure that a growing number of Traveller Child Assistants are trained and recruited. In line with the 1999 White Paper sections on *Qualifications and Training,* the DES may wish to begin consultations "on the most appropriate means of assisting... professionals to obtain qualifications which would enable them to hold mainstream posts in national schools". Having teachers from the Traveller community can be expected to give a real motivation to Traveller children, in particular to young girls.

237. The Inspectors' report also recommends better integration of Traveller parents on pre-school management boards. Traveller parents and their organisations should be given the opportunity to define the type of programmes that they need for their children. Further involvement of the Travelling community and the families of the children would also be helpful, in line with good practice in this field. Not least, the agencies involved in pre-school management may wish, in co-operation with Traveller parents, to reinforce adult learning opportunities and training in occupational skills for the parents and community of Travellers who use a particular pre-school on a regular basis.

4. Improving Quality

238. The National Childcare Strategy - building on the recommendations of the National Forum of Early Childhood Education (1998) - favours a view of quality as a dynamic process linked to indicators such as: trained, registered and adequately remunerated staff; appropriate learning environments guided by national frameworks; adequate adult/child ratios; partnerships with parents and local community; diversity and accessibility (Government of Ireland, 1999a). All these indicators are recognised in international research as necessary to building up quality in a system, and they are equally valid for the two existing systems in Ireland. However, as differences in the history and organisation of the systems exist, we shall propose separate quality recommendations for each, except for the first recommendations – a national goals and quality framework, which is applicable to both sectors.

A common national goals and quality framework for both sectors

239. The 1999 White Paper on *Early Childhood Education: Ready to Learn* recommended the granting of a Quality in Education (QE) mark to "providers who reach minimum standards in a number of key education-related areas." Although a useful idea to be retained, the proposal remains premature until national goals and a quality framework for ECEC services are elaborated, and adequate evaluation and inspection mechanisms put into place. A national goals and quality framework is a major guarantor of quality and system coherence. In conception, a quality framework is wider than the traditional notion of curriculum (learning areas and outcomes for children), and focuses more on agreed standards for all services, so that parents can have confidence in what is being offered. If the growing example of other countries is followed, a national goals and quality framework would include a description of what young Irish children can expect from *all* centres, whether public or private: that is, proper accreditation, adequate facility requirements, a sufficient number of highly qualified staff, favourable child-staff ratios, validated programmes, quality targets with regular monitoring and evaluation, appropriate modalities of parent participation and community

outreach… It would include also the core values that should inspire the life and practice of centres dealing with young children, as for example, the six operational principles of the National Children's Strategy:

Child-centred - *the best interests of the child shall be a primary consideration and children's wishes and feelings should be given due regard*

Family oriented - *the family generally affords the best environment for raising children and external intervention should be to support and empower families within the community*

Equitable - *all children should have equality of opportunity in relation to access, participation in and derive benefit from the services delivered and have the necessary levels of quality support to achieve this. A key priority in promoting a more equitable society for children is to target investment at those most at risk*

Inclusive - *the diversity of children's experiences, cultures and lifestyles must be recognised and given expression*

Action oriented - *service delivery needs to be clearly focused on achieving specified results in agreed standards in a targeted and cost-effective manner*

Integrated - *measures should be taken in partnership, within and between relevant stakeholders, be it the state, the voluntary / community sector and families; services for children should be delivered in a coordinated, coherent and effective manner through integrated needs analysis, policy planning and service delivery (Government of Ireland, 2000).*

Broad goals related to child socialisation, development and learning may also be outlined, with brief guidelines to management, staff and work teams concerning how to reach these goals *through a global approach.* The OECD team sees as necessary, widespread consultation among the major stakeholders, and close co-ordination between DJELR, DES, CECDE and NCCA on a national goals and quality framework.

Improving quality in the childcare sector

240. *A voluntary accreditation system linked to a childcare subsidy* – Another urgent need in terms of quality monitoring is to provide a basic accreditation system for the childcare sector, where both regulation and monitoring are weak. Regulation has come to mean the obligation on childminders or centres who care for three or more children, to notify their local health board. Health and safety checking is then undertaken, but in fact, there is little reason for providers to conform to national policy goals, pedagogical standards, or outcome goals.

241. The OECD team proposes the elaboration of a voluntary quality improvement and accreditation system for the childcare sector linked to funding, e.g. on the lines of the Australian QIAS[48] or other scheme that focuses on management, staffing, programme, developmental goals, ongoing pedagogical monitoring and support.

242. *The development of Child and Family Centres:* Opportunities for Irish professionals to experience integrated services of high quality are limited. For this reason, we suggest that the relevant government Departments may wish to come together with the City/County Boards to build or nominate 50 or so model centres around the country. These centres could be used for the administration of family and early childhood services in each county, and have both service provision and training units attached. They would provide high quality early childhood and family programmes, in which developmental screening, family outreach and innovative social inclusion programmes

---

[48] The QIAS system is a national, government supported accreditation system for centre-based care that is directly tied to the provision of funding.

could be piloted. They would also have training units for professionals in the early childhood field, including for the family daycare networks in rural areas. Depending on their location, e.g. located in areas of disadvantage and/or attached to regional colleges or other training institutions, the centres would generate different kinds of expertise for the system as a whole.

Staffing and training in the childcare sector

243. The present situation of staffing and training in the childcare sector is unsatisfactory. In the past, the sector relied heavily on committed individuals willing to work voluntarily. While strong efforts are being made to train and professionalize, the sector is still characterised by high staff turnover (with negative effects on young children), low pay, weak professional profiling, limited access to in-service training and limited career mobility. Making the profession more attractive is therefore a key concern. Some of the questions the review team raised were: How can the National Voluntary Organisations be supported effectively in this respect? What kinds of incentives should be put in place in order to encourage staff retention? Can the professional associations come together in one body to represent more effectively staff across the sector and advocate for appropriate wages, higher qualification requirements and better working conditions?

244. The review team acknowledges the progress made through the introduction of the *Model Framework for Education, Training and Professional Development in the Early Childhood Care and Education Sector* (2002). A co-ordinated structure of training for the childcare sector, easily available in all counties, would help to consolidate this initiative and bring together the work of the various training providers (IPPA, High/Scope, National Children's Nursery Association, regional colleges...). The nomination of an administrative/training/service-provision centre in each county (see section on Co-ordination below) for family support and early education and care could provide the infrastructure for this training. At some future stage, as is happening in other countries, an agreed accreditation scheme may be envisaged to enable practitioners - through a credit-based framework of qualifications - to move upwards and across sectors.[49]

Staffing, training and quality in the education sector

245. The structures for quality definition, good practice and monitoring have been in place in the education sector for decades: stable financing, school buildings and materials, management structures, trained professional teachers with good conditions of work, an active inspectorate, curriculum units, an educational research unit... However, of real concern to the OECD review team was the lack of specific quality guidelines for the reception of younger children, and our observation of a predominantly didactic approach towards early development and learning in the primary school infant classes.[50]

246. *Quality guidelines for the reception of younger children in the primary school.* With the exception of the White Paper on Early Childhood Education (1999), the specific needs and learning patterns of young children have not always received attention in primary school regulations and policy guidelines. In fact, there is no specific policy unit for the younger children in the Department of Education. The lack of specific policy guidelines sorely impacts on quality in the infant school. An example is the allocation of teachers to schools, calculated on staffing ratios for primary school children. 37% of junior infants in Ireland find themselves in classes of 25-29 children, cared for by one teacher. In contrast, the childcare regulations require for children aged 3-6 years, one care staff

---

[49] The OECD review (2002a) identified a cross-national trend towards at least a three-year tertiary degree for ECEC staff with group / centre responsibility. In many countries this is the case for work with children from 2 or 3 years upwards, and in some countries (Denmark, Finland, Sweden, Spain) for work with children from one to six years.

[50] Some direct instruction is helpful for young children, in particular, direct instruction to particular children on specific issues. It is the predominance of the model that is of concern. Didactic programmes have been found to be less effective than child-centred programmes in producing cognitive results, and compare poorly with regard to socialisation (see Bauman et al., 2001 for a fuller discussion).

for 8 children (full-time) or one to 10 children (sessional). Likewise, there are no specific regulations for the training of teachers of the younger children, or for classroom design and organisation – elements that ought to be differentiated when catering for young children. A recommendation to establish an expert policy unit in the DES with expertise in this and other ECEC fields is made in the section on *Co-ordination,* paragraph 209.

247. *An adequate pedagogy.* Of real concern to the OECD review team also was its observation of a predominantly didactic approach towards early learning in the primary school infant classes.[51] The model of the teacher as the source of learning, from whom young children receive knowledge, is still strongly felt within the system, while the notions of the well-being and involvement of children or the construction of knowledge through play, participation and choice, need to be developed. In sum, a more active and experientially-based pedagogy would improve learning and quality in the junior infant classes, and could even be extended – as in other countries - through the senior infants into the first years of compulsory schooling.

248. *An organisation of the infant school favouring autonomy and accountability.* In the past three decades, the infant school has developed little in Ireland compared to other countries, a result perhaps of the inclusion of early education within the primary school branch. Although a strong link with primary education is advantageous, the education authorities may wish now to improve quality and visibility by giving early education a clearer profile and more independence within the primary school. The OECD team would encourage the provision of a separate budget for the infant school at local level, and specific management responsibility given to its senior teacher. This teacher would be responsible: for managing facility requirements for the well-being of young children; for the layout, furnishings and materials of the infant school classrooms; for the provision of an exploratory outdoor environment; for the elaboration of the annual project and programme with her staff and parents; for regular team planning of activities; for organising professional development days for teachers and child assistants, and, in co-operation with the local school inspectorate, team-evaluations of quality and outcomes. She would also organise liaison with parents and community bodies, with the community/voluntary bodies responsible for afternoon activities, and with the relevant health, social and educational services. If the recommendation is acceptable, support for these teachers could be provided at national level by the proposed Early Childhood Education Agency.

249. *Teacher training:* The review team recommends a thorough reassessment of teacher training for the early childhood classroom. Teachers working with young children should have considerably more exposure to research-based ECEC pedagogy, and in so far as possible, prolonged practical training in model early childhood programmes. Several validated programmes are already practised in Ireland; High/Scope, Montessori, Froebel, Steiner... to which, no doubt, Reggio Emilia, Experiential Education and other programmes may be added. The OECD review suggests reviewing the three-year B.Ed. teaching degree, with a possible lengthening of it to four years, but above all, ensuring that a focus on ECEC-related theories and methodologies are included in all three (four) years of the training. The current two hours weekly during the first year, accounting for roughly 5% of total training duration, is totally inadequate to change the predominant teaching model or to allow students to learn the practical-aesthetic skills that characterise good practice in the early childhood field. The teacher training authorities may also wish to consider holding classroom practice in centres outside the present school system, which implement some of the validated programmes mentioned above. On a long-term basis, an education degree course, with the possibility of specialising in early childhood education and care (covering the age-group 0 to 8), may be more appropriate to the needs of the field.

---

[51] Some direct instruction is helpful for young children, in particular, direct instruction to particular children on specific issues. It is the predominance of the model that is of concern. Didactic programmes have been found to be less effective than child-centred programmes in producing cognitive results, and compare poorly with regard to socialisation (see Bauman et al., 2001 for a fuller discussion).

250. *Intensive professional development:* As a change of pre-service training takes ten years or so to be felt on the ground, professional development (in-service training) needs also to be established on a regular basis for early childhood staff. The third–level colleges and the professional associations, including the INTO, may be in a position to ensure such training if funding is provided.

251. Where *Early Start* is concerned, several teachers expressed the need to reinforce the newly developing collaborative teamwork between staff from differing professional backgrounds - between primary teachers and childcare workers in the *Early Start* units; and between primary teachers and special needs assistants in schools; and between early childhood teachers and educare staff. For *Early Start* teams, an essential measure would be targeted in-service training, e.g. on teamwork with disadvantaged families, on multi-professional collaboration, on self-evaluation techniques, on outreach strategies... A further supportive measure would be the establishment of a networking system for *Early Start* workers across the country. This would not only encourage professional exchange and clarity of focus, it would also enhance the status of inter-professional work teams and thus contribute to a wider perspective on the professional role of ECEC practitioners.

Inspection, monitoring and evaluation

252. *Supportive inspection* – Supportive inspection is critical to raising quality in schools. National reports, such as the recent inspectorate report on the Pre-schools for Traveller children, are very useful, helping to set future goals and policy. Local inspection visits will also be vital to improving quality in individual schools. Until the Early Childhood Education Agency is founded and can recruit its own inspectorate, as outlined in the 1999 *White Paper on Early Childhood Education: Ready to Learn,* the education authorities may wish to ensure that at least one inspector at regional level has the necessary background and training in early childhood programming, pedagogy and evaluation methods. Chapter 10 of the White Paper provides many useful suggestions concerning inspection and evaluation, which if implemented could do much to improve quality across the whole early childhood spectrum.

253. *Formative, self-evaluation procedures* – Related to the question of inspection and external evaluation is that of formative self-evaluation. In a mixed public-private system, the development of externally validated, self-evaluation procedures would seem to be not only a professionally sound policy step but also a pragmatic means of building up a culture of quality improvement in the system. Individual national voluntary organisations such as NCNA or IPPA are adopting this approach. When linked with advisory support services, the approach has been found in other countries to be both cost-effective and motivating for professionals (Bertram, 2001).

Child-staff ratios

254. *Child-staff ratios* – The issue was raised with the team on several occasions. Unfavourable ratios were often evoked as the cause of didacticism and of the formal teaching of pre-academic skills in the infant classes. Although the trend in the reduction of child-staff ratios is positive, the actual ratios for 4-year old children practised in Ireland are unacceptable in terms of active, open framework pedagogies. The OECD team wishes to underline the general principle of providing the lowest ratios for the youngest children, with a gradual child ratio increase as young people mature. In recent research (see DfES, London, 2001), a ratio of 15 children to one adult is cited as maximum ratio, if individualised and small group learning strategies are to be supported in the early childhood classroom.

255. It is unlikely, however, that a practical resolution of high numbers of children per class can be reached in Ireland in the immediate term through the recruitment of more teachers. A significant increase in the numbers of public servants is not on the agenda. In addition, there are trade-offs to be considered, such as the need to fund morning education sessions for all children from the age of

three onwards. We would recommend therefore for consideration the employment of a trained Child Assistant in each early childhood classroom, thus reducing present ratios to 15:1. We are conscious that significant expenditure will be needed to achieve this goal, and for this reason, we outline in Section 5 below, some funding mechanisms used in other countries to cover such expenses.

Other quality measures

256. In addition to the crucial issues of strengthening the autonomy of the infant school, appropriate training of staff, and a reduction in child-staff ratios, the review team wishes to draw attention to three further quality initiatives in the education sector, viz. appropriate programming for children from disadvantaged backgrounds; parental engagement and information service; and the reinforcement of research, evaluation and data collection systems:

257. *Appropriate programming for children and families in disadvantaged areas* – In Chapter 3, the features, identified by research and evaluations, of effective programmes for disadvantaged children and families were discussed, namely:

   - Effective early learning programmes take place within a general framework of anti-poverty and community development policies. (Kagan and Zigler, 1987, Morris et al., 2001, Sweeney, 2002).

   - Programmes are multi-functional and engage families as well as children: that is, programmes are strong on family engagement and support as well as providing high quality learning experiences to the children (see the entire Head Start literature). Linking early education programmes with child and family services, with primary health and nutrition programmes increases their effectiveness;

   - Programming is intensive: research indicates that the effectiveness of programmes for young children is enhanced by intensity (Leseman, 2002) and year-long duration (Consortium on Chicago School Research, 2003);

   - Programmes are pedagogically sound and conducted by appropriately trained professionals. A high quality programme in early childhood implies well-being, child–initiative, play and involvement. If a programme is over-focussed on formal skills, it is more likely to provide opportunities for children to fail, and to develop a higher dependency on adults, promoting in them negative perceptions of their own competencies (Stipek et al. 1995);

   - Depending on the degree of disadvantage, enriched health and nutrition inputs may be necessary to ensure that young children can take full advantage of the early childhood service.

258. *Family support, parental engagement and information services:* The review team experience in Ireland suggests that family support, parental engagement and information may be weak in the ECEC system as a whole. There was little evidence of parental presence in the hallways, classrooms or activities visited. We were informed, however, that the effective support provided by centres to parents at risk was improving steadily, but was still far too rare. Moreover, the *White Paper on Early Education* (1999) and Departmental regulations foresee strong parental participation. Quality early years centres that we have seen in other countries offer, as a matter of course, family support, referral, educational and recreational courses, and up-to-date information on all matters of concern to parents. In sum, supports, information and engagement policies for parents could be further developed in the Irish early childhood field both at local and national levels. The review team suggests that the Centre for Early Childhood Development and Education should be invited to make some practical recommendations for the early childhood field, based on the research already undertaken by Reardon (2001).

259. *Strengthening research, evaluation and data collection systems;* Ireland has no single child care information system. In Chapter 3, we noted considerable data gaps and a lack of disaggregated data

for many key indicators in the ECEC field. At the same time, two very significant research initiatives are being planned: the proposed longitudinal study of 18,000 children, put forward by both the National Children's Strategy and the Report of the Commission on the Family, and the proposed *State of the Nation's Children Report* to be produced on a bi-annual basis under the National Children's Strategy. By any standards, these initiatives must be seen as a particularly forward-looking step towards collecting systematic data on children growing up in Ireland. The OECD team recommends support for these ventures, with appropriate resources.

260. A stable research framework and a long-term research agenda are essential to providing the evaluations and in-depth studies necessary to inform policy making. The review team suggests that the National Children's Office examines the issue of insufficiencies in the national (and regional) data systems on children in general and on children in ECEC services in particular, recommending ways and means of standardising data collection across the Departments, so as to ensure both accuracy and conformity to international norms. We would also suggest that the Centre for Early Childhood Development and Education should become a clearing-house to collect and disseminate the best international research on topics of particular relevance to ECEC in Ireland.

261. The team also noted in previous chapters a number of issues for further research. Among the research topics recommended to us were:

- To develop a conceptual framework and refine the relevant indicators for comparative data collection on young children and families in Ireland, and the services available to them;

- To map the density and location of ECEC services and infant schools across the country;

- To collect reliable data on those services: the number of places by year of age available in each type of provision, the features of this provision; the characteristics of users (labour market attachment, socio-economic status; gender...);

- To overview the descriptive features of each kind of provision across the country, including the number of children having access, their attendance patterns in the different geographical areas, and the employment status and situation of parents using childcare services;

- To identify the typical needs of parents vis-à-vis childcare and early education, disaggregated for different groups; parents of children with special needs; traveller families; low income groups (urban and rural); families with a second child...

- To map the key target groups considered disadvantaged in Ireland;

- To research the values basis of ECEC policy-making in Ireland, with special reference to the participation rights of young children;

- To elaborate a conceptual and comparative framework to undertake the evaluation of the quality of various ECEC settings in Ireland; structural features; process elements...

- To disseminate research on cross-national systems policy

In addition, and perhaps more urgently, action research will be needed to elaborate some of the quality proposals made above, in particular:

- To elaborate a national quality framework;

- To organise a national accreditation scheme for childminders and other providers;

- To reform pre-service training for early childhood teachers, and provide validated in-service training programmes for teachers in infant schools;

- To produce an effective approach at the early childhood level toward children and families from disadvantaged backgrounds....

5. Financing new measures

262. The advantages of investing in the childcare field are outlined clearly in the Müller Kucera-Bauer study from Zurich (see Chapter 3). These authors emphasise the economic and social benefits that come from the maximum number of people being in work, and the employment opportunities offered to women at local level. The disadvantages are equally clear: a worsening of women's situation in the labour market; growing child poverty, especially in single parent families; prolonged social welfare dependency and its attendant ills. In Ireland, there is also the urgency of building up services, and the impossibility of reaching European targets unless a start is now made. The following is a short list of the financial challenges in the childcare field:

The childcare sector

263. - *Lengthening the period of parental leave to one year,* with a guarantee both of salary replacement and job protection;

   - *Providing a normative grant to accredited providers or a weighted subsidy to every child who uses an accredited childcare, educare or out-of-school place.* If the grants or subsidies are adequate, the measure could have the effect of raising the salaries and retention rate of staff in the sector, bring childminders into the official network, strengthen greatly the capacity of the voluntary and community sector to work, and enable the public and county authorities to require higher quality levels.

   - *Supply side financing,* for example, increased building grants and operational subsidies for communities providing childcare services in disadvantaged areas; financing to build or refurbish community and voluntary childcare facilities; tax breaks for family day carers/childminders (who account for over 85% of total provision for the under 4-s)…

   - *Building and staffing of a network of light drop-in structures for parents with young children,* based around health care centres, social welfare offices, school, community centres, libraries, etc.;

   - *Supporting communities and voluntary organisations to organise and take on afternoon sessions in schools and out-of-school care;*

   - In co-operation with DSFA, *enhancing access for disadvantaged children and families, through building a network of Child and Family Centres around the country.* These centres could also act as administrative centres at county level for family and ECEC policy, and become early excellence and training centres.

The education sector

264. The financial implications of increasing access and improving quality are significant also for the education sector. In sum, we propose for consideration the expansion of access to all 3-6 year old children (as in other European countries) on the basis of a free morning education session, followed by a subsidised, fee-paying pre-school session in the afternoon at the local school or adjoining premises, conducted by the community or voluntary sector. Private providers can also participate, and if accreditation has been given, receive likewise the normative grant or childcare/pre-school subsidy. In this way, full-day care for Irish children, on a sound educational basis, can be gradually built up. The benefits of so doing are clearly announced in the major research (see discussion in Chapter 3). The disadvantages of ignoring the challenge will be a further widening of the gap in comparison to other European countries; the reproduction of a cycle of educational failure among at-risk children in Ireland, leading to future low employment rates, social security dependence, and at times, wasted lives and delinquency (see, for example, the *Call to Action by the Business Community* in Appendix 3). The recommendations made include the following:

   - An entitlement for all 4-year olds to a free education place in school or pre-school settings, with expansion of access for the 3-year olds;

- Parallel improvement of child-staff ratios through the employment of a trained Child Assistant for every infant classroom;

- Gradual extension of the present half day *Early Start* and infant school to whole-day education and care based on the school, the afternoon session being in charge of accredited community and voluntary providers and funded by parental fees, communities, and normative grants or child subsidies;

- An increase in budget for each infant school, including the creation of a post of responsibility for the senior infant school teacher, as outlined in para. 248 above;

- Until a new pre-service training regime for early childhood teachers can be created and introduced, the organisation and funding of in-service training for all teachers in the infant classes, in particular for the senior teachers with managerial responsibility;

- The urgent implementation of the *White Paper on Early Childhood Education* (1999);

Each of these recommendations has significant funding implications, and we are conscious that all cannot be accomplished in a short period. However, if reaching the European targets is a real goal for Ireland, the present funding commitment must increase.

265. *A pooling of resources and sharing of costs across ministries and users:* As provision for young children is a concern shared across several government departments, a pooling of funding sources may also be suggested. The ministries involved – DES, DJELR, DHC, DSFA, DETE, DELG, DCRGA and the National Anti-Poverty Strategy – all have a stake in contributing funding toward high quality early childhood services for young children. Cost recuperation through light user fees – supplemented by county and municipal funding – can also be used to meet the costs of afternoon ECEC activities below the obligatory school age, with a waiving of fees for families most in need. Cost recuperation on a sliding scale from parents is practised in many countries, until the year when it is considered essential to have all young children enrolled in an early education programme. In publicly subsidised services, costs are generally much less onerous for parents than fee levels charged in the private sector;

266. *A transfer of some costs toward local communities:* Though infant classes have been free to parents for many decades, it was only in the school year 2001/2002, that primary schools became 100% funded by the state. Prior to this, the school management boards were required to raise a local contribution (at least 25% of the state grant) toward running costs. The Irish authorities may wish to consider the use of constitutional or statutory powers to provide legal authority for communities to raise revenues for non-obligatory education, and to set conditions for spending those funds;

267. *A shifting of educational financing toward early childhood:* As can be seen from Table 8, a real imbalance between early childhood and tertiary investments exists in Ireland and other countries. In response, an increasing number of education economists[52] are urging governments to channel more educational investment to the young children at the base. The argument is essentially one of equity and returns on investment. The personal economic returns from university education are such that it is in the interest of students and their families to invest. Subventions from the State at this level can be seen as "middle-class welfare" or, in economic terms, as dead weight, as student enrolments continue to grow even when subsidies are abolished. Australia is a case in point (Gallagher, 2003). In particular, analysts of the question point out that blanket subventions, such as free fees, are inefficient, as they take away the state's power to subvent needy students or to orient students

---

[52] For example, James Heckman, a labour market economist at the National Bureau of Economic Research in Cambridge, MA, joint winner of the Nobel Prize in economics in 1999, and a leading human capital policy expert.

toward certain disciplines to meet the changing needs of the economy. In contrast, early education is grossly under-funded. Yet it serves all children, and is especially effective where children from disadvantaged or dysfunctional backgrounds are concerned. In addition, early childhood services deliver other externalities important for an economy and society.

268. *The co-ordination of childcare and early education for the 3-6 year olds,* in particular, the co-ordination of services for the 3-6 year olds based on the local school. This would be a far more rational development for parents, and would help to reduce costs considerably. Rather than large investments in rented and other premises, it would seem more rational *in most instances* to invest significantly in school infrastructure and bring the early education, full-day and out-of-school care together in one location. It is to be hoped that as a public resource, the school building can be further developed for early childhood services professionally run by any qualified and accredited provider. An important lesson from the first *Early Start* initiative was the need to consult with the voluntary/community sector in the early education of the 3-6 year olds. Any centring of services for this age group around the school would have to ensure the involvement of the sector, and guarantee it an equal and subsidised role in building up the local network of care and education.

269. *A sharing of tasks with the voluntary early education bodies:* Official enrolment rates for 3- and 4-year olds would immediately increase in Ireland if recognition were given to a selected number of non-profit educational bodies who are now providing pre-school education to a significant number of children. Attracting private providers into the regulated network will require subvention, but this seems reasonable when the voluntary or private bodies provide expertise and share costs. Subsidies are particularly efficient when voluntary early education bodies are willing to accept a quota of children from disadvantaged or special needs backgrounds, and keep fees at a level within a range defined by the public authorities.

270. *Support from the corporate and business sector:* In many countries, as for example in the US, employers are one of the main supporters of early childhood services. Their reasons for so doing are outlined by the *American Business Round Table* in Appendix 3. In summary, business leaders are conscious that high-quality early childhood education is important for the development of young children and their future success in school. In addition, "employers increasingly find that the availability of good early childhood programs is critical to the recruitment and retention of parent employees." For these reasons, businesses in a wide range of countries supply workplace crèches and early education at the place of work, or purchase places in centres accredited by the public authorities. In the USA, grants from the large corporations toward early childhood services are also common, in particular, when tax concessions are granted by the public authorities for such donations. In yet other countries, e.g. Korea and Mexico, firms employing women are required by law to establish an on-site day care centre or subsidise child care expenses for their employers.

271. *Special funding initiatives:* By special funding initiatives are meant, the raising of funds for early education through special taxes, national lotteries and the like. In Belgium and Italy, a significant part (about 1%) of social security and/or corporate tax is channelled toward childcare. In Finland, the alcohol tax has been used for many years to subvention early childhood services, in particular, out-of-school care. In the state of Georgia in the US, the state lottery proceeds are used to fund early childhood services. In some of the Nordic countries, local authorities have powers to raise taxes, much of which is devoted to supplementing the State allocation for health, social welfare and early education services.

272. *Funding a Child Assistant in each infant class* - The salaries for trained Child Assistants in all infant classes will be a challenge but, as in other countries, a means of sharing that expenditure can be found, without breaching the present funding and hiring limits set by government. Grant aid for staff

costs for community-based/not-for-profit services is already a feature of the EOCP programme. Adequate salary levels for staff could be achieved through sharing costs with other relevant government programmes, the county, and the local community. Some responsibility for salaries may be placed also on parents who wish to have better child-staff ratios in the local community school, leaving DES and the NAPS to assume the responsibility of subsidising Child Assistants in the disadvantaged areas.

273. *Funding a whole-day service:* If adopted as a policy, a solution to reducing the cost to public finances of an extended full-day service for children aged 3-6 years needs to be found. The OECD has argued above that the use of the local school would greatly reduce expenditure on other premises and programmes. In addition, it would impose collaboration between the Education and the Care sectors, a goal that is important to achieve. To attempt to set up two parallel systems will lead to duplication and waste, with the probability – if we can judge from other countries - of childcare remaining a low quality service. Combined funding from the two ministries could build up a strong local school infrastructure, and bring together the education and care of young children from 3-6 years. Consideration may also be given as to whether designated lines of government expenditure, regional and local authority grants could be used for the refurbishing of local schools and support to the salaries of personnel. Again, as in the past, some local responsibility for school facilities may need to be envisaged.

This Country Note for Ireland represents the views of the OECD team after an intense five-day visit, aided by a comprehensive *Background Report* contracted by the Irish Department of Education and Science. Our reflective comment is offered in a spirit of professional dialogue, basing our judgements on our discussions and observations. During the visit, the OECD team was impressed by the approachability of the people we met at all levels within the system and their willingness to engage in a critical debate. We especially commend the manner in which the visit was organised by our host, the Department of Education and Science, the open access we enjoyed to all levels of the system and the richness and variety of the programme. Despite the shortness of our visit, we spoke to a wide range of providers and sectors at national, regional and local levels.

The National Co-ordinator, the author of the Background Report, the Steering Committee and all who contributed to the project are to be congratulated on their approach and professionalism. It should be noted, however, that the facts and opinions expressed in the Country Note are the sole responsibility of the review team. While we have received every help from the Department of Education and Science, and from many researchers and practitioners in Ireland, they have no part in any shortcomings, which this document may present.

REFERENCES

Abbott, L. & Pugh, G. (1998) *Training to work in the early years. Developing the climbing frame.* Buckingham, Philadelphia: Open University Press.

Barnett, W.S. (2003). PowerPoint presentation. J.P. Morgan Chase, New York, NY.

Barnett, W. S. (1996). Lives in the balance: Age-27 benefit-cost analysis of the High/Scope Perry Preschool Program. *Monographs of the High/Scope Educational Research Foundation, 11,* Ypsilanti. MI: High/Scope Press.

Bennett, J. "Starting Strong: The Persistent Division between Care and Education" in *Journal of Early Childhood Research,* Vol.1, No. 1 2003.

Bergmann, B. R.(1999) *Subsidizing child care by mothers at home,* New York, Foundation for Child Development, Paper Series, 1999

Bertram A., Pascal C., Bokhari S., Gasper M., & Holterman S. (2002) Research Report 361: Early Excellence Centre Pilot Programme Second Evaluation Report 2000 – 2001. London: Department for Education and Skills.

Bond, J.T, Galinsky, E., and Swanberg, J.E. (1998). *The 1997 National Study of the Changing Workforce.* New York, NY: Families and Work Institute.

Borman, G. and Hewes G. in AERA Educational Evaluation and Policy Analysis, Washington, Vol. 24, No. 4, Winter 2002

Bryant, D., Maxwell, K., Taylor, K., Poe, M., Peisner-Feinberg, E., and Bernier, K. (2003). *Smart Start and Preschool Child Care Quality in North Carolina: Change Over Time and Relation to Children's Readiness.* Chapel Hill, NC: Frank Porter Graham Child Development Institute.

Campbell, F. A., Ramey, C.T., Pungello, E., Sparling, J., and Miller-Johnson, S. (2002). Early childhood education: Young adult outcomes from the Abecedarian Project, *Applied Developmental Science,* 6(1): 42–57.

Carneiro, P. and Heckman, J. (2003) *Human Capital Policy* National Bureau of Economic Research, Cambridge MA. Working Paper 9495

Committee For Economic Development. (2002). *Preschool for All: Investing in a Productive and Just Society.* New York, NY: CED.

Chicago School Consortium (2003) *Ending Social Promotion: Results from Summer Bridge*

Daly, M. & Clavero, S. (2002) *Contemporary Family Policy. A comparative review of Ireland, France, Germany, Sweden and the UK.* Dublin: The Department of Social and Family Affairs, Institute of Public Administration.

Department of Justice, Equality and Law Reform (2002). Progress Report on Childcare. Unpublished paper. Dublin.

European Commission Network on Childcare and other measures (1996), *Quality Targets in Services for Young Children,* European Commission, Brussels

Fahey, T. & Russell, H. (2001) *Family Formation in Ireland. Trends, Data Needs and Implications.* Policy Reseach Series Number 43. Dublin: The Economic and Social Research Institute.

Friendly, M. (2000) in *Early Childhood Care and Education in Canada,* ed.s Prochner, L. and Howe, N. Victoria, University of British Columbia Press.

Fuller, B. et al. (2002) "Does maternal employment influence poor children's social development?", Pages 470-497, *Early Childhood Research Quarterly,* Volume 17, Issue 4, Pages 415-607 (2002)

Galinsky, E., and Bond, J.T. (1998). *The 1998 Business Work-Life Study: A Sourcebook.* New York, NY: Families and Work Institute.

Galinsky, E. and Johnson, A. (1998). *Reframing the Business Case for Work-Life Initiatives.* New York, NY: Families and Work Institute.

Gallagher, M. (2003) *Higher Education Financing in Australia,* OECD, Directorate for Education, 2003

Gardner, H. (1993) *Frames of Mind: The Theory of Multiple Intelligences* New York, Basic Books

Government of Ireland (1999a) *National Childcare Strategy: Report of the Partnership 2000 Expert Working Group on Childcare.* Dublin: The Stationery Office.

Government of Ireland (1999b) *Ready to Learn: White Paper on Early Childhood Education.* Dublin: The Stationery Office.

Government of Ireland (2002) *Model Framework for Education, Training and Professional Development in the Early Childhood Care and Education Sector.* Dublin: The Stationery Office.

Government of Ireland (2002c) *Ireland and the European Union: Identifying priorities and pursuing goals*

Guralnick, M.J. ed. (1998) The effectiveness of early intervention Baltimore: P.H. Brooks

Harkness, Susan and Waldfogel, Jane, (2002) *The Family Gap in Pay: Evidence from Seven Industrialized Countries.* Casepaper 30, Centre for Analysis of Social Exclusion, London School of Economics.

Hart, B., and Risley, T. R. (1995). *Meaningful Differences in the Everyday Experience of Young American Children.* Baltimore, MD: Paul H Brookes.

Hayes, N. (2000) "Early Childhood Education in Ireland. Policy, Provision and Practice" Paper presented at the Early Childhood Education Symposium, University of Malta, November 27 – December 1 2000.

Healy, T.(2001) *Is the future my responsibility?,* Ceifín Conference, 2001

Healy,T. (2003) *The policy implications of social capital in Ireland,* Forum Report No. 26, Dublin, National Economic and Social Forum

Heckman, James J. (1999) *Policies to foster human capital,* Washington, NBER Working Papers Series, No. 7288

Ireland Background Report (2002) *OECD Thematic Review of Early Childhood Education and Care.* Prepared by Carmel Corrigan for The Department of Education and Science. Dublin, October 2002.

Kahn, A.J. & Kamerman, S.B. (1987). *Child care: Facing the hard choices.* Massachusetts, IL: Auburn House Publishing Company.

Kellaghan, T. (2002) *Approaches to problems of educational disadvantage in Primary Education: ending disadvantage. Proceedings and Action Plan,* Dublin, St. Patrick's College.

Lee, V.E. and Burkam, D.T. (2002). *Inequality at the Starting Gate.* Washington, D.C.: The Economic Policy Institute.

Masse, L.N. and Barnett, W.S. (2002). *A Benefit-Cost Analysis of the Abecedarian Early Childhood Intervention.* New Brunswick, NJ: National Institute for Early Education Research.

McGough, A. (2002) "Addressing disadvantage: the role of teaching" in *Primary Education: ending disadvantage. Proceedings and Action Plan,* Dublin, St. Patrick's College.

McAleese, D. Ireland's *Economic Boom: the true causes,* OECD Observer, Jan. 2000

Müller Kucera, K. and Bauer, T *Costs and Benefits of Care Services in Switzerland – Empirical results from Zurich,* Department of Social Services, Zurich

Murray, C. (2002). "The Traveller Child. A Holistic Perspective", in: The National Children's Resource Centre (Eds.) *Diversity in Early Childhood. A Collection of Essays.* Dublin: Barnardos.

Morris, P. et al (2001) *How Welfare and Work Policies Affect Children: A Synthesis of Research.* New York: Manpower Demonstration Research Corp.

National Research Council and Institute of Medicine. (2000). *From Neurons to Neighborhoods: The Science of Early Childhood Development.* J.P. Shonkoff and D.A. Phillips, (Eds.). Board of Children, Youth and Families, Commission on Behavioral and Social Sciences and Education. Washington, D.C.: National Academy Press.

National Research Council. (2001). *Eager to Learn: Educating Our Preschoolers.* Barbara T. Bowman, M. Suzanne Donovan, and M. Susan Burns, (Eds.). Committee on Early Childhood Pedagogy, Commission on Behavioral and Social Sciences and Education. Washington, D.C.: National Academy Press.

NICHD (National Institute of Child Health and Human Development) (1997), *Mother-child interaction and cognitive outcomes associated with early child care: Results of the NICHD study.* Society for Research in Child Development meeting symposium, Washington, D.C., Author.

Oberhuemer, P. (2000) Conceptualizing the Professional Role in Early Childhood Centres: Emerging Profiles in Four European Countries. *Early Childhood Research and Practice (ECRP),* 2 (2), 10 pages, http://ecrp.uiuc.edu/v2n2/oberhuemer.html.

Oberhuemer, P. & Ulich, M. (1997) *Working with Young Children in Europe.* London: Paul Chapman.

OECD (1997) *Ireland: Managing across levels of government,* Paris

OECD (1999) *Ireland: Modernising the Public Service,* Paris

OECD (2001a) *Starting Strong: Early Childhood Education and Care.* Paris: OECD.

OECD (2001b) *Employment Outlook.* Paris: OECD

OECD (2002a) *Education Policy Analysis, Chapter 1:* "Strengthening Early Childhood Programmes: A Policy Framework" (pp. 9-34). Paris: OECD.

OECD (2002b) *Enhancing the effectiveness of public spending in Switzerland,* ECO/WKP/(2002)18, Paris

OECD (2003) *Economic Survey of Ireland, 2003,* Paris

OECD (2003a) Review of Family-Friendly Policies in Austria, Ireland and Japan, DELSA/ELSA, (2003)5/ANN2

Cleveland, G. and Krashinsky, M. (1998) *The Canadian cost-benefit analysis: early childhood care and education in Canada: provinces and territories 1998,* Toronto, CRRU, University of Toronto

Cleveland, G. and Krashinsky, M. (2003) *Starting Strong: Financing ECEC Services in OECD Countries* Paris, OECD

Pascal, C., Bertram, T., Holterman, S., Gasper, M. & Bokhari, S. (2002) Evidence from the Evaluation of the EEC Pilot Programme. University College Worcester: Centre for Research in Early Childhood.

Ramey, C.T. and Ramey, S.L. (February 23, 2003). Preparing America's Children for Success in School. Invited Keynote Address. National Governors Association, Washington.

Reynolds, A.J., Temple, J.A., Robertson, D.L., and Mann, E.A.. (2002). *Age 21 Cost-Benefit Analysis of the Title I Chicago-Child Parent Centers.* Madison, WI: Institute for Research on Poverty.

Reynolds, A.J., Temple, J.A., Robertson, D.L., and Mann, E.A. (2001). Long-term effects of an early childhood intervention on educational achievement and juvenile arrest- a 15-year follow-up of low-income children in public schools. *Journal of American Medical Association,* 285(18): 2339-2346.

Reynolds, A.J., Temple, J.A., Robertson, D.L., and Mann, E.A. (2002) *Age 21: Cost-benefit analysis of the Title I Chicago Child-parent Centers* in AERA Educational Evaluation and Policy Analysis, Washington, Vol. 24, No. 4, Winter 2002

Rolnick, A. and Grunewald, R. (2003). *Early Childhood Development: Economic Development with a High Public Return.* Minneapolis, MN: Federal Reserve Bank of Minneapolis.

Ryan, Anne, B. (2001) *How was it for you?: learning from couple's experience of their first year of marriage,* Dublin, ACCORD

Sabel, C.F. (1996) *Local Development in Ireland,* New York, Colombia Law School

Schweinhart, L. J., Barnes, H. V., and Weikart, D. P. (1993). Significant benefits: The High/Scope Perry Preschool study through age 27. *Monographs of the High/Scope Educational Research Foundation,* 10. Ypsilanti, MI: High/Scope Press.

Siraj-Blatchford, I. & Wong, Y. (1999) Defining and Evaluating 'Quality' Early Childhood Education in an International Context: **Dilemmas and Possibilities. Early Years, 20 (1), 7-18.**

St. Patrick's College (undated) *Review of Teacher Education. Submission to the Expert Advisory Group established to conduct a review of Teacher Education at Primary Level.* Drumcondra, Dublin.

Stipek et al. 1995 "Effects of different instructional approaches on young chidlren's achievement and motivation"in *Child Development 66*

Waldfogel, J. (2001) *International policies toward parental leave and child care* in The Future of Children, Vol.11:1, CA, 2001

West, J., Denton, K., and Reaney, L. (2001). *The Kindergarten Year.* NCES 2001-023. Washington, DC: National Center for Education Statistics.

Appendix 1

FIGURES AND TABLES

Figure 1
Comparative growth rates across OECD countries, 1991 - 2001

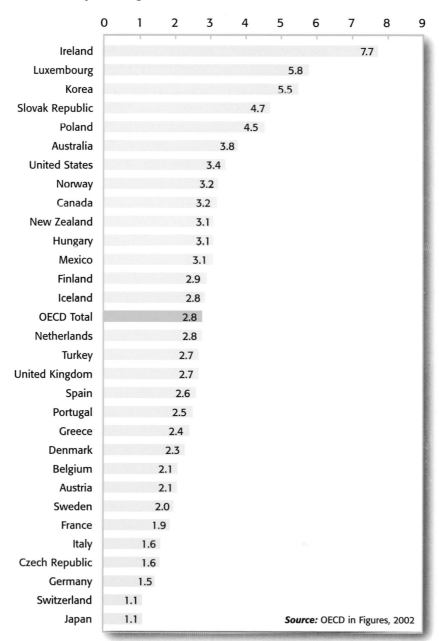

Source: OECD in Figures, 2002

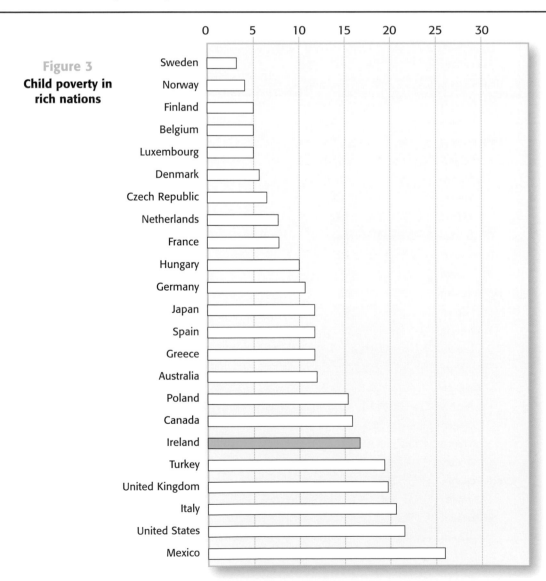

Figure 2

Public expenditure in OECD countries as a percentage of GDP, 2000

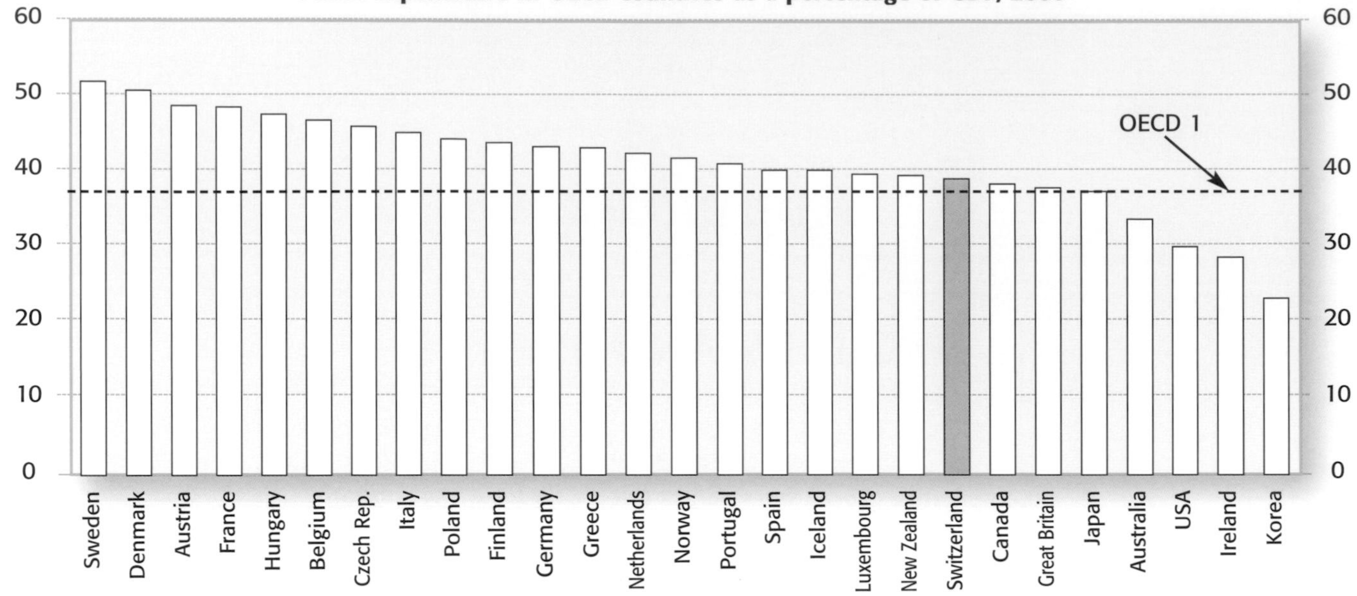

OECD 1

1. Weighted average.　　**Source:** Administration fédérale des finances and OECD *National Accounts.*
Note: Ministry officials have suggested to the OECD team that calculations in terms of Gross National Product
give a fairer picture of Ireland's investment effort in the social and educational domains

Figure 3

Child poverty in rich nations

Figure 4

Figure 4

Expenditure per student on public and private pre- and primary schools, based on full-time equivalents, and US dollars converted using PPPs.

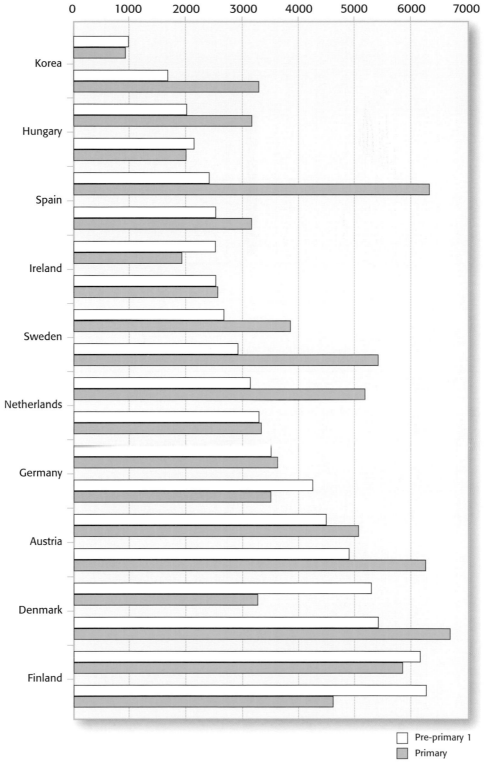

Source: OECD education data base, 2001

Note: The expenditures given for Denmark Finland and Sweden concern only the pre-school class for 6-7 year olds. In these countries, the average government/local government expenditure for children 3-6 years is significantly greater than for children in the pre-school class or in primary school, owing to the much lower child// staff ratios for the former.

Figure 5
Enrolments of 4-year old children in early education in selected OECD countries

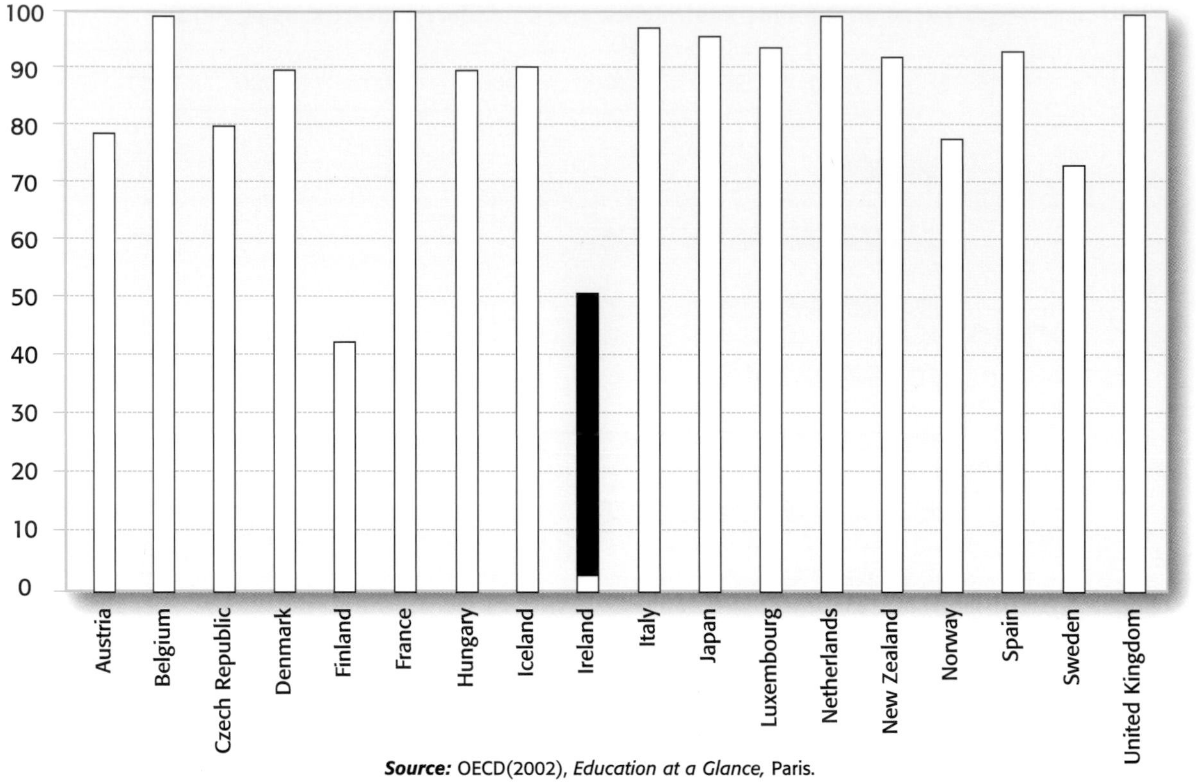

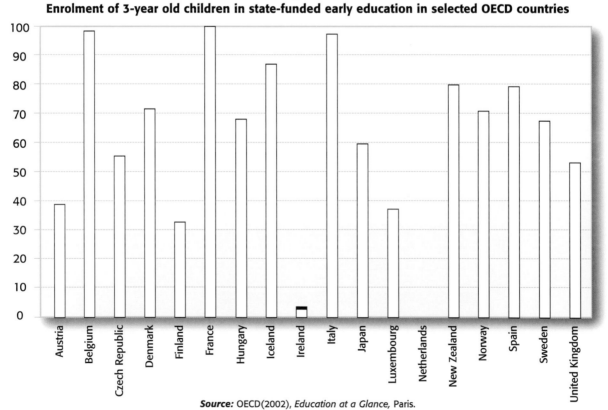

Source: OECD(2002), *Education at a Glance,* Paris.

Figure 6
Enrolment of 3-year old children in state-funded early education in selected OECD countries

Source: OECD(2002), *Education at a Glance,* Paris.

Note: Many 3-year olds attend some form of sessional education in Ireland. However, as these sessions are organised on a private basis and are unsupported by state funding, ministry statisticians do not include them in figures supplied to the OECD and other international organisations.

Table 2
Social expenditure in OECD countries as % of GDP

	1980	1985	1990	1995	1996	1997	1998
Australia	11.3	13.5	14.4	17.8	17.9	17.6	17.8
Austria	23.3	25.1	25.0	27.9	27.9	27.0	26.8
Belgium	24.2	27.0	24.6	25.1	25.5	24.2	24.5
Canada	13.3	17.0	18.2	19.2	18.4	17.8	18.0
Czech Republic	-.-	-.-	16.8	18.6	18.6	19.4	19.4
Denmark	29.1	27.9	29.3	32.4	31.7	30.7	29.8
Finland	18.5	22.9	24.8	31.2	31.0	28.7	26.5
France	21.1	26.6	26.5	29.0	29.3	29.3	28.8
Germany	20.3	21.0	20.3	26.7	26.0	26.4	26.0
Greece	11.5	17.9	21.6	21.2	21.8	21.9	22.7
Iceland	-.-	-.-	-.-	18.6	18.3	18.1	18.4
Ireland	16.9	22.0	19.0	19.6	18.5	17.2	15.8
Italy	18.4	21.3	23.9	23.7	24.4	24.9	25.1
Japan	10.1	11.0	10.8	13.5	13.9	14.3	14.7
Korea	-.-	-.-	3.2	3.7	3.9	4.3	5.9
Luxembourg	23.3	22.8	21.7	23.3	23.5	22.3	22.1
Mexico	-.-	1.8	3.2	7.4	7.5	8.0	8.2
Netherlands	27.3	27.4	27.9	25.9	25.9	25.5	24.5
New Zealand	19.1	19.4	22.5	19.3	19.7	20.8	21.0
Norway	18.5	19.7	26.0	27.6	26.5	26.2	27.0
Poland	-.-	-.-	16.2	24.7	24.9	24.2	22.8
Portugal	11.6	12.3	13.8	17.5	18.2	17.8	18.2
Slovak Republic	-.-	-.-	-.-	13.5	13.4	13.1	13.6
Spain	15.8	18.0	19.3	20.9	20.9	20.2	19.7
Sweden	29.0	30.2	31.0	33.0	33.0	32.3	31.0
Switzerland	15.2	16.2	19.7	26.0	27.3	28.3.	28.1
Turkey	4.3	4.2	6.4	7.5	10.4	11.7	11.6
United Kingdom	18.2	21.3	19.4	22.7	22.2	21.1	20.8
United States	13.1	12.9	13.4	15.4	15.3	14.9	14.6
OECD Countries	**18.0**	**19.1**	**19.2**	**21.1**	**21.3**	**21.0**	**20.8**
EU Countries	**20.6**	**22.9**	**23.2**	**25.3**	**25.4**	**24.6**	**24.2**

-.- Data not available.

Source: OECD(2001), CD-Rom on social expenditure database, 2001.

Table 3

Monthly Child Benefits in Ireland, UK, Sweden, France and Germany (Euros, July 2001 – France, 2003)

	Ireland	UK[a]	Sweden	France	Germany
1 child	85.7	108.2	105.4	160	138.0
2 children	171.4	180.5	220.0	288.8	277.1
3 children	280.6	252.8	355.74[b]	390[b]	430.5

a) Since child benefit is paid weekly in the UK, amounts have been calculated based on a 30-day month.
b) Supplements for large families are included in this figure.

Source: Daly & Clavero, 2002

Table 4

Childbirth-related leave policies in selected OECD countries

Country	Type of leave	Duration in months	Payment rate
Austria	16 weeks maternity leave plus 2 years parental leave	27.70	100 % of prior earnings 18 months unemployment benefit, 6 months unpaid
Canada	17 weeks maternity leave plus 35 weeks parental leave	12.00	55 % (ceiling) for maternity leave; unemployment rate + part-time earnings for parental leave
Denmark	28 weeks maternity leave plus 1 year parental leave	18.50	60 % of prior earnings 90 % of unemployment benefit
France	16 weeks maternity leave plus Parental leave to child's 3rd bd	36.00	100 % of prior earnings €334 (plus child allowance of €189), or €493 monthly.
Ireland	26 weeks maternity leave plus 14 weeks parental leave	9.30	70 % (ceiling) of wages for 18 weeks. All else unpaid
Norway	52 weeks parental leave plus 2 years child-rearing leave	36.00	80 % of prior earnings Flat rate
Sweden	Each parent entitled to 18 months parental leave	36.00	80 % for 12 months; 3 months flat rate; rest unpaid

Source: Waldfogel (2001) and Irish Background Report 2002

Table 5

**Subsidised access to ECEC services for children 0-6 years
provided by government departments**

	Typical service	Number of children covered	% of cohort 0-6 covered
DHC	Social Services nurseries from birth to 4 years	c. 7000	2 %
DJELR	Support to actual EOCP places from birth to 6 years	c. 23,466	7.3 %
DES	Provision (in primary schools) for pre-school children aged 3-6 years	104,437*	32 %

* Strictly speaking, there are 104,437 children in early education services, but another 21,656 children are already enrolled in 1st or 2nd class in primary school by January of the current year, when figures are collected. For the report, the smaller figure is chosen, and access data, financing data, child-staff ratios etc. are based on this figure.

Source: Irish Background Report 2002

Table 6

Percentage of children enrolled in early childhood services in EU countries

	% coverage for 3-6 years	% coverage for 0-3 years	Year of data validity
France	99	29	1998
Netherlands	90	(0)	1990
Belgium	97	30	2000
Italy	95	6	1998
Denmark	91	64	1998
Spain	84	5	1998
Sweden	80	48	1999
Norway	80	40	2000
United Kingdom	(79)	(34)	1997
Germany	78	10	1998
Portugal	75	2	2000
Austria	68	4	1998
Finland	66	22	2000
Ireland	56	(38)	2000
Greece	46	3	1999

Source: OECD Employment Outlook 2001. Brackets indicate data inaccuracies. Figures were provided by national sources

Table 7

ECEC services in the Childcare sector in Ireland

Type of service	Sessional	Full-day	Total number of services
Playgroup / Pre-school	1 276	252	1 528
Montessori school	402	229	631
Nursery / day care centre	–	414	414
'Other service'	113	118	231
Drop-in crèche	124	68	192
Naíonrai	159	3	162
Parent & toddler group	136	–	136
After school group	97	–	97
Workplace crèche	22	40	62
Homework club	43	–	43
Total			**3 496**
Total number of childminders (estimated)			**37 900**

Source: Forthcoming report of the ADM: *National Summary of the County Childcare Census* 1999/2000, cited in the *Irish Background Report* 2002, adapted. The figure for childminders is taken from Government of Ireland, 1999a.

Table 8

Expenditure on educational institutions per student, relative to GDP per capita, by level of education, based on full-time equivalents

OECD countries	Pre-school 3-6 years	Primary	Secondary	Tertiary level
Austria*	20	26	33	47
Belgium*	12	16	26	39
Denmark*	15	24	28	39
Finland*	16	18	25	35
France*	17	18	31	34
Germany*	20	16	27	42
Hungary 1*	21	19	21	51
Ireland	13	12	17	37
Italy 1	21	22	27	32
Netherlands 2	15	16	21	46
Norway 1	40	20	26	43
Portugal*	13	20	30	28
Spain	15	19	26	30
Sweden	14	24	25	61
United Kingdom*	27	16	24	41
United States 4*	20	20	24	57
Country mean	**18**	**19**	**25**	**44**

Source: OECD, *Education at a Glance, 2002.* The investment in early education of the Nordic countries is much greater than the table shows, as with the exception of Norway, the expenditure figures here were provided only for the "pre-school class", that is a special induction class for 6-7 year olds, which takes place in primary school in Denmark, Finland and Sweden. Sweden spends, in fact, over 2% of its GDP on integrated services for young children.

Table 9

Percentage access to publicly subsidised early childhood provision in small northern EU economies (2002)

Country	Children from 0-3 years	Children from 3-6 years
Denmark	48%	93%
Flanders	58%	97%
Ireland	15%	56%
Scotland	n.a.	96%

Table 10

Proportion of pupils in junior and senior infant classes by class size 2000/2001

	0 - 19	20 - 24	25 – 29	30 - 34	35 – 39	40+	Total
Group sizes in the Irish infant school							
Junior Infants	17.0 %	28.0 %	37.0 %	17.1 %	1.9 %	0.0 %	100 %
Senior Infants	14.5 %	26.4 %	34.2 %	22.8 %	2.0 %	0.1 %	100 %
Total	**15.7 %**	**27.3 %**	**34.8 %**	**20.1 %**	**2.0 %**	**0.1 %**	**100 %**
Total number of children according to group	16,349	28,319	36,120	20,932	2,072	40	103,832

Source: Department of Education and Science, forthcoming (cited in the Irish Background Report 2002, p.63)

Table 11

Women's employment rates by presence of children in 2000, as a percentage of cohort 25-54

	No children	One child	Two or more children
Austria	76.0	75.6	65.7
Belgium	65.6	71.8	69.3
Canada	76.5	74.9	68.2
Czech Republic	80.8	72.3	59.4
Denmark (1998)	78.5	88.1	77.2
Finland (1997)	79.2	78.5	73.5
France	73.5	74.1	58.8
Germany	77.3	70.4	56.3
Greece	53.1	53.9	50.3
Iceland	89.1	89.3	80.8
Ireland	**65.8**	**51.0**	**40.8**
Italy	52.8	52.1	42.4
Netherlands	75.3	69.9	63.3
Norway	82.9	83.3	78.0
Portugal	72.6	78.5	70.3
Spain	54.6	47.6	43.3
Sweden	81.9	80.6	81.8
Switzerland (2001)	84.3	75.5	65.5
United Kingdom	79.9	72.9	62.3
United States (1999)	78.6	75.6	64.7
OECD 23	**73.7**	**70.6**	**61.9**

Source: EULFS and OECD (2002), Employment Outlook, Chapter 2, *Women at work*

Table 12
Public expenditure on health, as % of GDP

	1960	1970	1980	1990	1991	1992	1993	1994	1995	1996	1997	1998	1999	2000
Australia	2.1	4.4		5.2	5.4	5.4	5.4	5.4	5.5	5.5	5.7	5.8	6	6.1
Austria		3.3	5.2	5.2	5.2	5.5	5.9	5.9	6.1	6.1	5.6	5.7	5.6	5.6
Belgium				6	6.2	6	6	6	6.4	6	6.2	6.2	6.2	6.2
Canada	2.3	4.9	5.4	6.7	7.2	7.4	7.2	6.9	6.5	6.3	6.2	6.5	6.4	6.5
Czech Republic				4.9	5.1	5.2	5.9	6.1	6	5.5	5.5	5.5	5.5	5.5
Denmark			8	7	7	7	7	7	6.8	6.8	6.8	6.9	7	6.9
Finland		4.1	5	6.3	7.2	7.2	6.3	5.8	5.7	5.8	5.5	5.3	5.2	5
France				6.6	6.7	6.9	7.2	7.1	7.3	7.2	7.1	7.1	7.1	7.1
Germany		4.5	6.8	6.5	6.7	7.7	7.6	7.8	8.1	8.4	8.1	7.9	8	7.9
Greece		2.6	3.7	4	3.9	4.3	4.8	4.8	5	5.1	5	4.9	5.1	5.3
Hungary				6.4	6.4	6.8	6.7	7.2	6.3	5.9	5.6	5.5	5.3	5.1
Iceland	2.5	4.1	5.5	6.9	7.1	7.1	7	6.9	7.1	7	6.8	7.1	7.6	7.7
Ireland	**2.8**	**4.2**	**6.8**	**4.4**	**4.8**	**5**	**5.1**	**5**	**4.9**	**4.7**	**4.8**	**4.7**	**4.6**	**4.7**
Italy				6.4	6.6	6.5	6.2	5.9	5.3	5.4	5.6	5.6	5.6	6
Japan	1.8	3.1	4.6	4.6	4.6	4.8	5.1	5.3	5.3	5.4	5.3	5.5	5.8	6
Korea				1.7	1.5	1.6	1.6	1.6	1.7	1.9	2.1	2.4	2.4	2.6
Luxembourg		3.2	5.5	5.7	5.5	5.7	5.8	5.6	5.9	5.9	5.5	5.4	5.4	4.9
Mexico				2	2.3	2.4	2.5	2.6	2.4	2.1	2.4	2.5	2.7	2.7
Netherlands			5.2	5.4	5.7	6.1	6.3	6.1	6	5.5	5.5	5.5	5.5	5.5
New Zealand		4.1	5.2	5.7	6.1	5.9	5.5	5.6	5.6	5.5	5.8	6.1	6.1	6.2
Norway		4	5.9	6.4	6.8	6.9	6.8	6.7	6.7	6.6	6.6	7.2	7.3	6.5
Poland				4.8	5	5.1	4.7	4.3	4.4	4.7	4.4	4.2	4.4	4.2
Portugal		1.6	3.6	4.1	4.3	4.2	4.6	4.6	5.1	5.5	5.6	5.6	5.9	6.2
Spain	0.9	2.3	4.3	5.3	5.3	5.6	5.8	5.6	5.5	5.5	5.4	5.4	5.4	5.3
Sweden		5.8	8.2	7.4	7.2	7.3	7.5	7.1	7.1	7.3	7.1	7.1	7.2	7.1
Switzerland				4.5	4.8	5.1	5.2	5.3	5.4	5.7	5.7	5.8	5.9	5.9
Turkey			0.9	0.9	2.2	2.4	2.5	2.5	2.5	2.4	2.7	3	3.5	3
United Kingdom	0.9	3.9	5	5	5.4	5.8	5.9	5.9	5.8	5.8	5.5	5.5	5.8	5.9
United States	1.2	2.5	3.6	4.7	5.2	5.5	5.7	5.9	6	6	5.9	5.8	5.7	5.8

OECD Health Data, 2003

Table 13

Comparative extent of child poverty across countries in relation to family type

Poverty Rates for Children by Family Type

Note:
* Poverty line is defined as 50% of median adjusted disposable income for all persons
* Equivalence scale is the square root of family size
* The definition of two parent and single mother households allows other adults to be present.

Country	Year	% Children in poverty	In Two-Parent Families	In Single-Mother Families	% of Children Living in Single-Mother Families
Australia	1994	15.8	11.9	46.3	10.6
Austria	1997	10.2	8.4	23.5	12.7
Belgium	1997	7.7	7.2	10.1	8.9
Canada	1998	16.3	10.5	49.6	14.3
Czech R.	1996	6.6	3.2	36.2	10.0
Denmark	1997	8.7	4.9	30.2	14.1
Finland	2000	2.8	2.1	8.1	12.8
France	1994	7.9	6.1	25.3	9.3
Hungary	1999	8.8	8.2	11.8	6.7
Ireland	1996	14.4	11.1	43.4	10.3
Italy	1995	20.2	19.6	30.6	5.2
Luxembourg	1994	4.5	2.9	19.3	9.6
Netherlands	1994	8.1	6.6	26.4	7.6
Norway	1995	3.9	2.0	13.5	15.2
Slovenia	1999	6.9	5.8	19.6	6.6
Spain	1990	12.2	11.5	25.4	4.9
Sweden	2000	4.2	2.3	12.9	17.8
United Kingdom	1999	15.4	10.0	34.0	21.7
United States	2000	21.9	14.8	49.3	19.5

Appendix 2

THE OECD REVIEW TEAM

Ms. Pamela Oberhuemer, Rapporteur
State Institute of Early Childhood Education and Research (IFP)
Munich
Germany

Ms. Anke Vedder, Senior policy adviser
Youth Policy Directorate of the
Netherlands Ministry of Health, Welfare and Sport

Ms Colette Kelleher, Head of Unit
Early Childhood Partnership Unit
Department for Education & Skills
London

Mr. John Bennett, Project Manager
OECD Directorate for Education
2 rue André Pascal
75775 Paris Cedex 16
FRANCE

Appendix 3

A CALL TO ACTION FROM THE BUSINESS COMMUNITY

WHY AMERICA NEEDS HIGH-QUALITY EARLY CHILDHOOD EDUCATION

Over the past two decades, business leaders have invested time, expertise, and resources in efforts to improve K-12 education in the United States. What we have learned leads us to conclude that America's continuing efforts to improve education and develop a world-class workforce will be hampered without a federal and state commitment to early childhood education for 3- and 4-year-old children.

As states implement the *No Child Left Behind* Act, designed to ensure that all students are proficient in reading and math by 2013-14, we also need to ensure that children enter school ready and able to succeed. Research shows, however, that far too many children enter school ill-prepared.

Studies document a wide gap between lower- and higher- income children before they enter kindergarten. When children begin school behind, they tend to continue to fall further and further behind. High-quality early childhood education can help close this gap. Long-term positive outcomes and cost-savings include improved school performance, reduced special education placement, lower school dropout rates, and increased lifelong earning potential (see the Appendix for a summary of this research).

Not only does high-quality early childhood education make a difference for children, it matters to their employed parents. Employers increasingly find that the availability of good early childhood programs is critical to the recruitment and retention of parent employees.

In today's world, where education and skill levels determine future earnings, the economic and social costs to individuals, communities, and the nation of not taking action on early childhood education are far too great to ignore, especially when the benefits far outweigh the costs. Estimates of the return on investment of high-quality programs for low-income children range from $4 to $7 for every $1 spent. However the research is clear: the return on investment is linked to quality; simply increasing participation without ensuring program quality will not produce positive results.

As business leaders, we see the discussion around early childhood programs for 3- and 4-year-olds as largely an education issue. Since states have primary responsibility for education, we believe that states need to take the lead in developing and funding a coherent early childhood education system from the patchwork of programs and services that exist today. The federal government also must play a leadership role. It must make high-quality early childhood education a national priority, and continue its historic role in focusing on the children most in need. Federal and state investments in early education must be coordinated in order to improve program quality and to serve more children.

Statement of Principles

The Business Roundtable (BRT) and Corporate Voices for Working Families (CVWF) believe federal and state efforts to develop early childhood education systems for 3- and 4-year-olds must be based on a set of guiding Principles that define the components of a successful system and high-quality programs. These Principles draw on current early childhood research, lessons from K-12 education reform efforts, and applicable lessons from the nation's experience in building a voluntary system of higher education. Although our focus is on 3- and 4-year-old children, we fully recognize the importance of quality improvement efforts for early childhood programs serving children under 3.

The six principles below are interconnected; they are not listed in priority order. BRT, CVWF, and others will use these Principles to assess existing early education programs, consider philanthropic priorities, evaluate policy proposals on Pre-K, Head Start, and other programs, and formulate policy positions.

1. Learning:

A successful early childhood education system views children's learning as the central mission. It should:

- ☐ Provide positive learning experiences that foster the interconnections among children's social, emotional, and cognitive development and nurture children's innate joy in learning;

- ☐ Engage children in developmentally appropriate experiences with English language literacy and numeracy, and encourage family literacy programs to reinforce these experiences;

- ☐ Hold the same high expectations for success for all children while also respecting and supporting the diversity of children's families, cultures, races, socio-economic backgrounds, as well as the different ways that young children learn and the rates at which they progress; and

- ☐ Include healthy nutrition, safe environments, facilities conducive to learning, and diagnostic screening with effective follow-up services to treat disabilities or health problems that might affect children's ability to learn.

2. Standards:

A successful early childhood education system articulates standards for children's learning and program quality that align with state K-12 academic standards. It should:

- ☐ Align the objectives of the early childhood education system and the state's standards in the early grades of school;

- ☐ Adopt research-based curriculum options and program standards that enable early childhood education to achieve and sustain results for children;

- ☐ Endorse research-based indicators for what children need to know and be able to do when they enter school that respect the diverse ways that children grow and learn; and

- ☐ Use the results of regular and appropriate diagnostic assessments of children's performance to improve instructional practice.

3. Teachers:

A successful early childhood education system ensures that teaching staff possess the skills, knowledge, and attitudes to help young children enter school prepared to succeed. It should:

- ☐ Employ skilled teaching staff who have a college degree and/or demonstrated knowledge and skill commensurate with the requirements of the position and meet performance criteria such as English verbal skills and the ability to connect with and teach young children;

- ☐ Require effective preparation as well as ongoing professional development that helps staff improve the quality of their teaching, become ongoing learners, and move through an articulated, degree-granting system, where appropriate; and

☐ Institute differentiated salaries based on the experience and competencies of teachers that, given the importance of consistent relationships to children's learning, are adequate to attract and retain a qualified teaching staff.

4. Parents:

A successful early childhood education system supports parents as their children's first teachers and provides high-quality program options to parents who choose to enrol their children. It should:

☐ Provide access to high-quality early childhood programs for families seeking out-of-home early childhood education for their 3- and 4-year-old children, regardless of their socio-economic status;

☐ Offer seamless ways to meet the need of some families for care during the time they are working as well as the need for early learning experiences for their children; and

☐ Promote practical and effective strategies for parents to be involved in and support their children's learning at home and in early education programs.

5. Accountability:

A successful early childhood education system embraces accountability for measurable results. It should:

☐ Collect the data and conduct the research needed to identify best practices, assess system performance, and report these results to stakeholders;

☐ Evaluate the progress of children who have participated in early childhood education programs on the state's annual assessments required by the No Child Left Behind Act;

☐ Implement continuous improvement processes that put the lessons learned from research and evaluation into program standards and practice; and

☐ Establish incentives for meeting or exceeding objectives as well as consequences for persistent failure to achieve intended outcomes for children.

6. Partnerships:

A successful early childhood education system builds crosscutting partnerships to govern, finance, sustain, and improve the system. It should:

☐ Create effective and efficient governance mechanisms that support community planning, program development and oversight;

☐ Involve key stakeholders at the federal, state, and local levels, and encourage public/private partnerships to improve effectiveness, efficiency, and accessibility;

☐ Include participation among all sectors of the early childhood field within the state, including public and private programs as well as those that take place in schools, centers, and homes; and

☐ Insist on adequate, efficient, and shared financing mechanisms that minimize duplication of effort and identify priorities for public investments in times of budgetary constraints as well as a blueprint for future expansion.

From Principles to Policy

In 1990, the nation's governors and the Administration set as their first National Education Goal, "By the year 2000, all children will start school ready to learn." Thirteen years later, there has been progress—45 states are now providing some early childhood education services and programs, using both federal and state funding sources. The reality of today's families—including those with working parents and those with a parent at home—is that 69 percent of 3-year-old children and 82 percent of 4-year-old children are in some form of early childhood program on a regular basis. Yet most of these programs are not high quality, despite the research that shows that only high-quality programs produce a strong return on investment. Thus, the goal of school readiness remains largely unmet.

Three groundbreaking initiatives pave the way toward realizing this goal. Two reports by the National Research Council of the National Academy of Sciences summarize current research on early development and early learning: *From Neurons to Neighborhood: Applying the Science of Early Childhood Development* in 2000 and *Eager to Learn: Educating Our Preschoolers* in 2001. In addition, the Committee for Economic Development developed a vision for applying this knowledge in its publication, *Preschool for All: Investing in a Productive and Just Society* in 2002.

The Principles outlined in this statement take us the next step in formulating federal and state policies. As noted earlier, education is largely a state responsibility, but the federal government has always played a very significant financial role in early childhood programs and must continue to do so. Although the federal role in early childhood is different from its role in K-12 and higher education, policymakers should examine relevant lessons from federal initiatives that have strengthened both higher education and K-12 education.

In higher education, the federal government's first priority is to help low-income students gain access to postsecondary studies. The federal government also helped states build a voluntary higher education system that is the envy of the rest of the world. The federal government could take a similar role in the early childhood arena, supporting low-income children's participation in high-quality programs while also helping states to build the infrastructure for high-quality programs—including building staff capacity.

In elementary and secondary (K-12) education, the federal government only provides 7 percent of the overall resources, but influences the entire system because these resources link their assistance for low-income students in low-performing schools with requirements for rigorous state accountability systems that include all students. Although early childhood education is very different from the public K-12 system because it is has a higher percent of federal funding and a mix of public and private providers, we believe that the federal government could use a similar model of linking resources with accountability by pairing federal investments with requirements for strong state accountability systems that measure results, ensure high program standards, and expand the numbers of children served.

We are well aware that economic conditions, budgets, and political considerations can hinder or hasten domestic policy initiatives. But even in uncertain times, we can begin to plan for the future. We urge decision makers in the public and private sectors—the U.S. Congress, the Administration, local and state governments, school boards, the business community, and other leaders —to make early childhood education a high priority by supporting and endorsing these Principles and launching a multi-sector planning process to identify incremental and additional revenue streams required for implementation. BRT and CVWF are committed to working with all stakeholders to build a quality early learning system for today's and tomorrow's young children.

> *The Business Roundtable (BRT) is an association of 150 chief executive officers of leading corporations committed to advocating public policies that foster vigorous economic growth and a dynamic global economy. In 1990, the BRT adopted a nine-point policy agenda, "Essential Components of a Successful Education System," which outlined the framework for standards-based education reform. One of the nine essential components includes high-quality pre-kindergarten education for disadvantaged children. BRT member companies created or joined state business coalitions to promote higher standards, and business leadership has been a critical factor in many of the states that have significantly improved student achievement. The BRT also strongly supported the passage of the No Child Left Behind Act of 2001, which creates a national imperative to raise student achievement and*

close the achievement gap, and the Roundtable's Task Force on Education and the Workforce is actively involved in the law's implementation.

Corporate Voices for Working Families (CVWF) *is a coalition of 36 leading corporations that have been engaged in listening to and addressing the challenges of their employee families for over two decades. The CVWF coalition was created in 2001 to bring this private sector voice and experience into the public dialogue on issues affecting their working families. CVWF is focused on communicating the business case for early learning to policymakers, corporations, and other stakeholders interested in strengthening working families. CVWF's partner companies believe that the care and education of young children is critical to the attraction, recruitment and engagement of today's parent employees as well as a key to economic growth. CVWF recently released an issue brief outlining why early education is an important business issue.*

Supporting Research

By the time children enter kindergarten, there already is a wide gap in their readiness for school.

☐ At age 3, high socio-economic status (SES)[1] children have average vocabularies of 1100 words, middle SES children have average vocabularies of 750 words, and low SES children have average vocabularies of 480 words (Hart and Risley, 1995).

☐ Lower SES children enter school with much poorer skills in the major areas of development and learning. Average achievement scores for kindergarten children in the highest SES group are 60 percent higher than those in the lowest SES group (Lee and Burkam, 2002).

☐ Only 47 percent of low SES kindergarteners are likely to have attended a center-based program (including Head Start) prior to kindergarten entry, compared to 66 percent of higher SES children. Moreover, higher SES children have access to higher-quality programs, further benefiting them (Lee and Burkam, 2002).

When children begin kindergarten behind, they continue to fall further and further behind.

☐ During the kindergarten year, children who are deemed at risk for later school failure because of their family backgrounds make gains in basic skills such as letter recognition, counting, and comparing object size. Yet these children remain farther behind children with fewer at-risk factors because the more advantaged children make even greater gains in reading and math skills in school than their less advantaged counterparts (West, Denton, and Reaney, 2001).

High-quality early childhood programs can make a difference in school readiness despite poverty and other risk factors in children's backgrounds.

☐ Children, including those of low and high SES, who attend high-quality centers, score significantly higher on measures of skills and abilities that are important for school success compared to children from lower quality centers. While children's abilities are typically related to their families' income level, the quality of the early childhood experiences can make a difference over and above the effects of family characteristics (Bryant, Maxwell, Taylor, Poe, Peisner-Feinberg, and Bernier, 2003).

---

[1] Throughout this report we refer to the effects of socio-economic status (SES) and family income, which are different. In addition to income, SES takes into account such characteristics as parental education and social status.

High-quality early childhood education programs have a high return on investment for low-income children[2]

☐ In the short term, longitudinal studies of high-quality early childhood programs, including the Perry Preschool Program, the Abecedarian Early Childhood Intervention Project, and the Chicago Child Parent Center Program find increased achievement test scores, decreased rates of being held back in school, and decreased placement in special education among low-income children. In the longer term, studies also find increased high school graduation and decreased crime and delinquency rates (Schweinhart, Barnes, and Weikart, 1993; Campbell, Ramey, Pungello, Sparling, and Miller-Johnson 2002; Reynolds, Temple, Robertson, and Mann, 2001).

☐ Cost-benefit analyses of Perry Preschool and the Chicago Child Parent Center Programs find a cost savings of $7 for every dollar invested (Barnett, 1996; Reynolds, Temple, Robertson, and Mann, 2002). Cost-benefit analysis of the Abecedarian Early Childhood Intervention Project finds a cost savings of $4 for every dollar invested (Masse and Barnett, 2002).

☐ When using an internal rate of return, which compares public and private return on investments, high-quality early childhood programs fare well. The internal rate of return for the Perry Preschool Program has been calculated at 16 percent, supporting the notion that early education can be a good investment (Rolnick and Grunewald, 2003).

There is evidence that high-quality programs will benefit middle-class children as well.

☐ At the beginning of kindergarten, the gap between middle and higher SES children is larger than the gap between lower and middle SES children in achievement scores assessing literacy and mathematics (Lee and Burkam, 2002).

☐ An indication that middle-class[2] children might substantially benefit from preschool education is that they have relatively high rates of being held back in school and school dropout rates— problems that early childhood education has been found to reduce. Middle-income children have a 12 percent rate of being held back in school compared to 17 percent for low-income children and 8 percent for high-income children. Likewise, middle-income children have an 11 percent school dropout rate, compared to 23 percent for low-income children and 3 percent for high-income children (Barnett, 2003).

High-quality early childhood education is important to business.

☐ Numerous studies reveal that there is a cost to business in not responding to its employees' need for reliable and good-quality early childhood programs. Employees are likely to miss work when they spend long hours trying to find early childhood programs or when they deal with the often-tenuous arrangements they have, especially when these arrangements fall apart. When employees with these problems are at work, they have difficulty concentrating because they are worried about their children (Galinsky and Johnson, 1998).

☐ Companies have also found that there are business benefits in providing their own employees assistance with early childhood programs, including improved recruitment and retention (Galinsky and Johnson, 1998; Galinsky and Bond, 1998). Employees with access to family-supportive programs and policies are more likely to be satisfied with their jobs, to be loyal, to go the extra mile to help their companies succeed, and to stay at their jobs (Bond, Galinsky and Swanberg, 1998).

---

[2] In this calculation, low-income children are in the bottom 20 percent of family income levels, middle-class children are in the 20-80 percent range, and high-income children are in the top 20 percent.

OECD Thematic Review of
Early Childhood Education and Care Policy

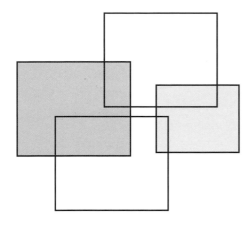

Background Report

IRELAND

October 2002

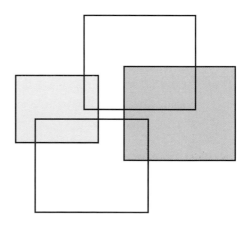

Prepared by Carmel Corrigan for
The Department of Education & Science

ACKNOWLEDGEMENTS

Many people contributed to this report by sharing their knowledge, experience and views. In the first instance, my thanks go to the members of the Editorial Group – John Fanning of the Department of Education and Science, Peter Archer of St. Patrick's College, Drumcondra, Noirín Hayes of Dublin Institute of Technology and Heino Schonfeld of the Centre for Early Childhood Development and Education. The inputs of Liam MacMathuna and Richard Byrne are also appreciated. I would like to thank the representatives of Area Development Management, the Childcare Division of the Department of Justice, Equality and Law Reform, the National Co-ordinating Childcare Committee, the Inspectorate Unit and the Social Inclusion Unit of the Department of Education and Science, the Department of Health and Children, the National Children's Office, the National Council for Curriculum and Assessment, the National Childcare Voluntary Organisations and the Centre for Early Childhood Development and Education that attended meetings and provided essential information and insights in to the issues addressed. The contributions of those organisations that made submissions – the Combat Poverty Agency, An Comhchoiste Reamhscolaíochta, the Irish National Teachers Organisation, the Catholic Primary School Managers Association and the Department of Community, Rural and Gaeltacht Affairs – are also gratefully acknowledged. Thanks are also owed to the many organisations and sections within Government Departments who provided invariably prompt replies to an array of requests for information.

I would particularly like to thank my colleagues in the Centre for Social and Educational Research, Dr. Lorna Ryan and Ms. Liz Kerrins, for their help and support in this work. Finally, my heartfelt thanks go to Antoinette Ryan of the Strategic Policy Unit of the Department of Education and Science who contributed in no small part to this report. Not only did she prove to be an administrator of some talent, but also proved extremely capable in the drafting and editing of text as well as a welcomed source of professional and personal support.

The views expressed in the document are those of the authors and do not necessarily reflect the opinions of the Irish authorities, the OECD or the OECD Directorate for Education.

GLOSSARY OF TERMS

After-school and Out-of-School Care: this refers to care provided for school-going children outside of school hours, including after-school hours and during school holidays.

Early Start Programme: this is a programme aimed at pre-school children in disadvantaged areas aged three to 4 years.

Childminders: these are private individuals who provide care for children predominantly in their own [minder's] home, providing full-day, part-time and after-school care to children of a wide variety of ages.

Infant Classes in Primary Schools: these are the first two years of primary school education and are usually comprised of 4, 5 and 6 year olds. This category also includes the small number of special infant classes that cater for children with special learning needs that are attached to some ordinary primary schools.

Naionrai: these provide pre-school education through the medium of Irish and cater for children aged 3 to 6 years.

Nurseries and Crèches: these typically provide full day services and many cater for children from 2 to 3 months up to school-going age. In addition, many of these provide after-school care for children of school going age.

Parent and Toddler Groups: typically these cater for children from birth to 3 years, are attached to other childcare services such as pre-schools or crèches and offer opportunities for play for children and social interaction and informal support to parents.

Play Groups and Pre-schools: these usually provide sessional services (that is, less than three hours per child per day) for children aged from 3 to 4 or 5 years.

Pre-School for Travellers: these cater for pre-school children from the Traveller Community.

Special Schools: this refers to schools that cater exclusively for children with learning and/or physical disabilities.

ABBREVIATIONS

ADM	Area Development Management Ltd
B.Ed	Bachelor of Education
CECDE	Centre for Early Childhood Development and Education
CLAR	Ceantair Laga Ard-Riachtanais
CSER	Centre for Social and Educational Research
CDB	County Development Board
CEB	County Enterprise Board
DCRGA	Department of Community, Rural and Gaeltacht Affairs
DES	Department of Education and Science
DELG	Department of the Environment and Local Government
DETE	Department of Enterprise, Trade and Employment
DHC	Department of Health and Children
DIT	Dublin Institute of Technology
DJELR	Department of Justice, Equality and Law Reform
DSFA	Department of Social and Family Affairs
EOCP	Equal Opportunities Childcare Programme
ERC	Educational Research Centre
ESF	European Social Fund
FETAC	Further Education and Training Awards Council
HETAC	Higher Education and Training Awards Council
HSCL	Home School Community Liaison
ICTU	Irish Congress of Trade Unions
INTO	Irish National Teacher's Organisation
ISPCC	Irish Society for the Prevention of Cruelty to Children
NAPS	National Anti-Poverty Strategy
NCCA	National Council for Curriculum and Assessment
NCCC	National Co-ordinating Childcare Committee
NCNA	National Children's Nurseries Association
NCO	National Children's Office
NEPS	National Educational Psychological Service
NVCO	National Voluntary Childcare Organisations
RAPID	Revitalising Areas by Planning, Investment and Development
SNO	Special Needs Organiser
VEC	Vocational Education Committee

TABLE OF CONTENTS

Chapter 1

CONTEXT AND CURRENT PROVISION

1.1 BACKGROUND TO IRELAND

1.1.1 Geography

Ireland is one of the smallest countries in Europe and occupies the most westerly, peripheral position. Geographically, the entire island is comprised of 32 counties, 26 of which make up the Republic of Ireland, (commonly referred to as the South), and 6 of which go to make up Northern Ireland (usually called the North), which forms part of the United Kingdom. This report is concerned with the Republic of Ireland only, which will be referred to as Ireland in the remainder of this report for ease of reading.

Ireland covers an area of some 70,282 square kilometres (27,136 square miles). It is comprised of 4 provinces: Leinster to the east, Connaught to the west, Munster to the south and Ulster, the majority of which (6 of nine counties) lie in Northern Ireland. Regional differences that broadly correspond to provincial divisions are commonly acknowledged. Leinster is the most developed part of the country in commercial and industrial terms, has the highest level of developed infrastructure and is the most urbanised and densely populated province. Connaught and the counties of Ulster are among the less developed regions of the country with less industry, less urban development (with the notable exception of Galway City) and an older and more sparsely distributed population. Munster, like Leinster, is mixed with some areas such as Cork and Waterford seeing high levels of economic and urban growth, but with large stretches of rural areas.

One particular feature of Ireland is its small size. At its longest the entire island, North and South, stretches 486 kilometres (302 miles) and is at most 275 kilometres (171 miles) wide. This is an important comparative issue in service location and provision as the distances or time spent travelling that are thought of as considerable in Ireland may seem insignificant in other countries. It is important to remember in this context that distance is not an absolute measure but is relative to what is considered normal or acceptable within any given culture as well as the travel opportunities, facilities and infrastructure available.

1.1.2 Population and Age Structure

The most recent national Census of Population took place in 2002[1] and only preliminary results are available at this time. The population of Ireland now stands at just over 3.9 million, an 8% increase on the previous Census figure of 3.6 million in 1996. (CSO, 2002a) Age breakdowns from the 2002

---

[1] This was originally scheduled to take place in 2001 but was postponed due to the foot and mouth crisis.

Census are not available at this stage. The number of children aged 6 years and under can be gleaned, however, from vital statistics records that provide the number of registered births. These figures are shown in Table 1 below. Using these figures the total number of children aged 6 years or under is 323,026, divided reasonably equally across the single year age groups. Although this figure does not account for inward or outward migration of children or infantile deaths, this is one of the most accurate estimates of the relevant age specific population currently available.

Table 1
Single Year Age Cohorts

	Births in 2001	Births in 2000	Births in 1999	Births in 1998	Births in 1997	Births in 1996
Age 1 Year	57,882	-	-	-	-	-
Age 2 Years	-	54,239	-	-	-	-
Age 3 Years	-	-	53,924	-	-	-
Age 4 Years	-	-	-	53,551	-	-
Age 5 Years	-	-	-	-	52,775	-
Age 6 Years	-	-	-	-	-	50,655

Source: *Vital Statistics available at* www.cso.ie/principalstats/pristat7.html#figure1

1.1.3 Economic Growth and Changing Employment Patterns

It is important to contextualise the current debate on early childhood education and care in the rapid and significant economic change that has occurred in Ireland over the latter half of the 1990s and the changes that this has both demanded and facilitated in family life. On the whole, the 1980s and early 1990s represented a period of economic recession in Ireland that was characterised by high unemployment. However, in the mid-1990s the emergence of what was to be called the 'Celtic Tiger economy' was becoming noticeable. The period from 1996 onwards saw substantial economic growth, with average annual growth rates in GNP[2] of 4.7% between 1990 and 1995 and 6.7% between 1995 and 2000 (Duffy, FitzGerald, Kearney and Smyth, 1999). Unemployment decreased from 13.2% in 1990 to 11.8% in 1998 and 3.7% in 2001, with corresponding increases in the employment rate from 87% of the labour force to 88.1% and 96.3% respectively. The significance of these increases is further highlighted when placed in the context of a labour force that grew by just under 450,000 people or 34% over this eleven-year period (Central Statistics Office, 2002b). However, the Irish economy has slowed in 2001 and the outlook for 2002 is for a further moderation in the rate of growth, which it is estimated will be in region of 3%. This will have an impact on the national budget. (Department of Finance, 2002)

This economic boom has also come at a time of demographic dividend for Ireland, which has one of the youngest populations in Europe. Ireland is now reaping the benefits of a small baby boom that occurred in the late 1970s and early 1980s. Once employment became plentiful in the mid- to late 1990s, Ireland began to witness substantial inward and return migration. This too has improved Ireland's demographic profile. However, these factors, as well as others such as the availability and usage of land, influenced the availability and cost of residential property. Nationally, the cost of new homes rose by just 4% between 1993 and 1994. Between 1997 and 1998 the

---

[2] Although GDP is the more widely used measure internationally, GNP is commonly used in Ireland due to the relatively large number of multi-national companies located here and the consequent significant repatriation of profits.

annual rate of increase had climbed to 23% and to 19% between 1998 and 1999 (Drudy and Punch, 2000). Although price increases have stabilised somewhat in the past two years, prices still rose by 8.1% between 2000 and 2001 (Department of the Environment and Local Government, 2002). These increases have resulted in many first-time buyers who traditionally bought houses in their mid-20s being squeezed out of the housing market until their late 20s or early 30s. In addition, many couples now require both parties to work in order to meet mortgage repayments, which, in turn, has had an impact on women's labour force participation (see 1.1.4 below). Rising house prices have also placed pressure on the private rented accommodation market, which has also seen a sharp increase in prices. These price increases have undoubtedly resulted in many young people delaying the formation of independent family units.

As the cost of accommodation is particularly expensive in the greater Dublin area, many young people seeking to establish their own homes have moved to the areas surrounding Dublin. This has resulted in an ever-widening commuter belt, which now stretches fifty kilometres and more around the Dublin area. This has had repercussions for childcare and education services in this commuter zone.

1.1.4 The Changing Role of Women

In Ireland, the traditional role of women was in the family home. This view was perpetuated by its inclusion in the country's Constitution (Article 41, Government of Ireland, 1999a) and also through the strong links between the Catholic Church and the Irish state. Following Ireland's entry to the EU (then the EEC) in 1973 and the implementation of legislation and policies necessary to meet EU directives that women's right to employment after marriage was established. Under the Civil Service (Employment of Married Women) Act 1973 and the Employment Equality Act, 1977 women were given a statutory right to remain in paid employment after marriage. Since then, as a result of the increased secularisation of Irish society, the industrialising economy and gender equality reforms, women in Ireland have experienced significant social and political changes. Some examples of the progress made are the fact that in 2000/2001, 54% of those in third level institutions in Ireland were women (Department of Education and Science, forthcoming 2002), and the current President of Ireland and her predecessor are female. However, it remains that fewer women than men participate in senior management, technical positions and high-ranking political positions. For example, less than 14% of the members of the current Irish Parliament are female.

Of particular concern here is the dramatic increase in female participation in the labour market. This is one of the key influences on the demand for early childhood care and education services. In the early 1990s Ireland had a low rate of female labour force participation relative to other EU member states. However, with economic growth came employment growth and an increasing demand for labour. Employment growth was not sector neutral and the services sector, which is traditionally labour intensive and dominated by women, grew in particular. Therefore, the labour market opportunities for women became plentiful. This 'pull' from the labour market, as well as the 'push' from a housing market that necessitated dual income households, had a substantial effect on women's labour market participation and employment.

Between 1990 and 1996 the number of women aged 15 years and over in the labour force grew from 456,500 to 573,700 and to 761,000 in 2002. This gives increases in the female labour force participation rate from 35.8% in 1990 to 41.4% in 1996 and 48.8% in 2002. (Table 2, CSO, 1990-1997, 2002b) The increasing participation of married women and, more specifically, mothers in the labour force should also be noted. In 1990, the labour force participation rate of married women was 31%. By 1996 this had increased to 40.8% and to 48.1% in 2002.

Table 2
Proportion of employed men and women in full and part-time employment and full and Part-Time Labour Force Participation Rates (ILO) for Persons Aged 15 Years and Over, 1990, 1996 and 2002.

	1990	1996	2002
Men	%	%	%
% Share Full-Time Employment	96.7	95.0	93.5
Full-Time Participation Rate	58.6	57.0	62.8
% Share Part-Time Employment	3.3	5.0	6.5
Part-Time Participation Rate	2.0	3.0	4.4
Unemployment Rate	12.5	11.9	4.6
Total Participation Rate	**69.3**	**68.1**	**70.4**
Women			
% Share Full-Time Employment	83.2	78.2	69.5
Full-Time Participation Rate	25.6	28.5	32.6
% Share Part-Time Employment	16.8	21.8	30.5
Part-Time Participation Rate	5.2	7.9	14.3
Unemployment Rate	13.8	11.9	3.7
Total Participation Rate	**35.8**	**41.4**	**48.8**
Married Women			
% Share Full-Time Employment	72.4	70.5	60.6
Full-Time Participation Rate	19.0	25.9	28.4
% Share Part-Time Employment	27.6	29.5	39.4
Part-Time Participation Rate	7.3	10.8	18.5
Unemployment Rate	15.0	10.0	2.4
Total Participation Rate	**31.0**	**40.8**	**48.1**

Source: *Central Statistics Office Labour Force Surveys 1990 and 1996, Quarterly National Household Survey, Quarter 2 Mar-May 2002.*

Historical data on the labour force participation of women with children, and in particular very young children, is somewhat sparser and less regularly available. More recent data is available is available in the Quarterly National Household Survey. Data from the 1996 Labour Force Survey shows that 27.3% of women in family units (that is, either living with a partner and/or with at least one child) and in work had at least one child aged less than 5 years. In the period March to May 2002, this rate had increased to 29.3%. In 1996, lone mothers with a child/children aged under 5 years accounted for 5.5% of women with a child/children in this age group and had an employment rate of 22.2%. By 2002, lone mothers accounted for 16.3% of women with at least one child aged under 5 years and had an employment rate of 41.7% (Central Statistics Office, 2002b).[3]

---

[3] It should be noted here that the data from the 1997 Labour Force Survey is based on Principal Economic Status (PES) while the more recent data is based on the more widely used ILO Economic Status. See National Economic and Social Council, 1999, pp. 411-412 for a fuller description of these measures.

As a consequence of these changes, the traditional view of the role of women in Irish society has changed to a 'dual' one. In a family where both parents want and/or need to work, the responsibility for childcare still falls predominantly on the woman. (Fine-Davis et al, 2002) Consequently, more and more women are striving to reconcile childcare and home responsibilities with formal employment. As a result, participation in part-time or atypical forms of work represents a continuing trend amongst Irish women. For example, in 2002 almost one third (30.5%) of women in employment worked part-time, in comparison to just over 6% of men (CSO, 2002b). Part-time work among married women was substantially higher, with the share of part-time employment standing at 39.4%.

In recent years, a number of Government initiatives have been designed to address the issue of equal employment opportunities and an increasing number of large employers have become aware of the benefits of supporting family friendly policies. However, small and medium employers, who employ up to 70% of those working in the private sector, cannot afford to offer the same policies as larger organisations. As a result, although some progress is being made, much work remains to be done to ensure that parents, and in particular mothers, can successfully and positively balance family and work commitments.

1.1.5 Changing Family Size and Structure

Ireland has one of the youngest populations in Europe and, correspondingly, one of the lowest and most favourable age dependency ratios. Recent fertility patterns would suggest that this favourable picture will remain for a while longer and that the dependency ratio worries currently facing many European countries will not affect Ireland for some time yet. This favourable position was supported by relatively unusual (by western European standards) family formation and fertility patterns found in Ireland up to the late 1960s, as well as the small baby boom of the late 1970s and early 1980s referred to above. Fertility and marriage patterns up to the late 1960s was characterised by a relatively low incidence of marriage, but high fertility and large families. This pattern has now changed to one similar to most western nations of higher incidence of marriage and smaller families.

Traditionally, Ireland has one of the highest fertility rates in Europe. In 1960, Ireland's total fertility rate (TFR)[4] stood at just below 4. However, the total fertility rate (TFR) declined substantially during the 1970s, '80s and '90s, but bottomed out in 1999 at 1.89. This still leaves Ireland with the highest TFR in Europe. Using information on birth orders from birth registrations, it is clear that family size also decreased significantly, if slowly, over this period.[5] In 1960, approximately one third of births were registered as the mother's fifth child or more. By 1999 this had fallen to 10.2%. In addition, fertility among women in their 30s, and particularly in the 30-35 years age group, has increased substantially in the 1990s, displaying a tendency towards delayed childbearing. (Fahey and Russell, 2001)

Also of interest here are recent trends in marriage, family formation and the incidence of lone parenthood. The 1980s and 1990s saw particular changes in family formation. In the 1980s a high incidence of marriage resulted in the formation of many new families. However, by the mid-1990s marriage had become less common and more women of childbearing age were reported as never married. (Fahey and Russell, 2001) This decline in the number of marriages coincided with the increase in births to unmarried, and in particular never married, parents. In 1986, just over 20% of lone parents had never been married, with just under half (47.5%) being widowed. Just 10 years later, 35% of lone parents had never been married and only one eighth (12.4%) were widowed.

---

[4] Total fertility rate refers to the number of children women of childbearing age can be expected to have if the fertility rates for any one year are applied.

[5] See Fahey and Russell (2001), p.11 for a discussion of the use of birth order data for determining family size.

The remaining lone parents had been married but were separated: in 1986 these accounted for one third (32.3%) of lone parent families but by 1996, this had increased to just over half (52.7%). (Fahey and Russell, 2001)

These changes in fertility, family formation and family structure are, in part at least, reflective of changing moral attitudes towards sexual activity, family and marriage. In addition, the legalisation providing for the ready availability of contraception in the 1980s and the introduction of divorce in 1995 played their part in these changing fertility and family formation trends. With respect to the latter, it is interesting to note that the number of marriages has increased substantially in the late 1990s. Much of this increase can be attributed to the incidence of second marriages.

While all of the above factors – economic growth, rising employment, increased female labour market participation and changes in family formation and fertility patterns – are of themselves of interest, it is their interaction that is central to issues of early childhood education and care. If fertility rates had declined in a period of recession, where the increased labour market participation of women would not have been so marked, the issues facing the early childhood education and care sector in Ireland would be substantially different to those faced today.

1.2 OVERVIEW OF EARLY CHILDHOOD CARE AND EDUCATION

1.2.1 Children, Family and Education in the Constitution

Ireland is a sovereign, independent, parliamentary democracy with a written Constitution (Bunreacht na hEireann, Government of Ireland, 1999a). The functions and powers of government derive from the Constitution and all laws passed by government must conform to the Constitution. The Constitution, originally enacted in 1937, is open to amendment or change only through national referenda. Article 41 of the Constitution says *The State recognises the Family as the natural primary and fundamental unit group of Society, and as a moral institution possessing inalienable and imprescriptible rights, antecedent and superior to all positive law. The State, therefore, guarantees to protect the Family in its constitution and authority, as the necessary basis of social order and as indispensable to the welfare of the Nation and the State* (Government of Ireland, 1999a, Articles 41.1. and 41.1.2). The critical importance of this Article is that it affords the family a degree of privacy and protection that has been interpreted as superceding the rights of its individual members, including children.

The roles of the family and of the State in the education of children are addressed in Article 42 of the Constitution. Under Article 42 the State recognises that the *primary and natural educator of the child is the Family and guarantees to respect the inalienable right and duty of parents to provide, according to their means, for the religious and moral, intellectual, physical and social education of their children* (Article 42.1). By allowing for the education of children in their home, the Constitution does not make it compulsory for children to attend schools. While children may be educated by their parents at home, Article 42.3.2 states that the State shall act as guardian of the common good and therefore *require in view of actual conditions that the children receive a certain minimum education, moral, intellectual and social* (Article 42.3.2). However, Article 42.4 obliges the State to provide for free primary education for every child whose parents wish them to avail of it.

The importance of these articles lies not only in their legal protection of the family and the promotion of education, but also in the national culture they reflect. This involves the overriding importance of the family in Ireland and the rights of families to privacy and independence in the conduct of their family responsibilities.

The Constitution also sets out the right of the various churches to provide educational services for their congregations. Article 44, paragraph 2.5 states that *Every religious denomination shall have the right to manage its own affairs, own, acquire and administer property, movable and immovable, and maintain institutions for religious or charitable purposes.* The Churches, and in Ireland the Catholic Church in particular, have played and continue to play a significant role in the development and delivery of education. The majority of primary schools in Ireland are denominational and, reflecting the religious denomination of the majority of the population, are Catholic. The principal model of primary education is one of State sponsorship where the school premises are owned by the Church and managed by a board of management that is, in a great number of cases, chaired by a local priest. All primary schools have patrons and this is primarily the bishop of the relevant diocese in the case of Catholic and Church of Ireland schools.

1.2.2   Changing Perceptions of Children: The Emergence of a Rights-Based Approach

One of the principal features in relation to children and their place in society, as defined in the Constitution and Irish law, is the passive role attributed to them and the assumption that their parents or other adults will provide for and protect them. It is only in *exceptional cases* of failure in meeting parental duties that the State intervenes in the protection of children in their family environment (Article 42.5). In addition, the Constitution contains no Article on the rights of the child as a separate individual or their active participation in society (Government of Ireland, 1998). It could be argued that the traditionally large Irish family did not allow for considerable introspection on children's development by parents who, in the majority of cases, were primarily concerned with the physical well being of their children. However, increasing wealth and prosperity, decreasing family size, as well as greater exposure to education, both formal and through mass media and Information and Communication Technologies, have undoubtedly led to an increase in more informed parenting in which the overall development of the child is considered. This issue was clearly reflected in the Report of the Commission on the Family, *Strengthening Families for Life,* which recognised the changing nature of parenting, the increased demand for parenting courses and the need for these to always hold the well being of the child as their central concern (Government of Ireland, 1998).

It is only in recent years that issues such as children's rights and participation have become important in Irish discourse and policy. The traditional dominant view of children as adults-in-waiting 'who should be seen and not heard' has been challenged through the emergence of a rights approach to children and childhood (Government of Ireland, 1998). This is based on the UN Convention on the Rights of the Child, which came into force in 1990. This Convention is based on a view of children as active participants in their own lives and who have rights that are distinct from adults. The 54 Articles of the Convention cover the civil, social, economic and cultural rights and the rights to protection of children. The Convention places a significant onus on parents, families, communities and the State to ensure that these rights are promoted and protected.

The Convention on the Rights of the Child was ratified by Ireland in 1992. On foot of its *First National Report* (Department of Foreign Affairs, 1996), in 1998 the UN Committee on Children's Rights commented on the lack of real commitment to an integrated approach to children and the absence of effective measures to eradicate child poverty. The Committee recommended that Ireland remove all constitutional barriers to the implementation of the Convention and to put in place a range of measures to promote children's rights and implement the Convention. Following this, the Government undertook a number of measures recommended by the UN in its Concluding Observations on the State of Children's Rights in Ireland, including the development of a National Children's Strategy (see 1.2.6 below). Following this, the government established the National Children's Office (NCO) and the Office of the Ombudsman for Children. These are crucial in the development among children as well as adults of the reality of the children's rights approach. What

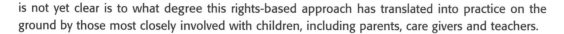

is not yet clear is to what degree this rights-based approach has translated into practice on the ground by those most closely involved with children, including parents, care givers and teachers.

1.2.3 Child Poverty in Ireland

The revised National Anti-Poverty Strategy (NAPS, see 1.2.6 below) identifies children and young people as one of the most vulnerable groups in Ireland today. Child poverty has long been a concern in Ireland and in the mid-1990s Ireland had the highest rate of child poverty in the EU. In 1994, the proportion of children under the age of 14 years living in consistently poor[6] households stood at 24%. Children living in households headed by a person who was unemployed, ill or disabled and / or in households in which there were three or more children were at a particularly high risk of poverty. (Nolan, B., 2000) Significant progress has been made on reducing child poverty since then and the most up-to-date data shows that this rate had fallen to 8% in 2000 (Combat Poverty Agency, 2002). The revised NAPS has a specific target of reducing the number of children who are consistently poor to less than 2% in the period to 2007 and, if possible, eliminating consistent poverty among children. This Strategy recognises that meeting these targets will require interventions across a range of areas, including education, housing and health. (Government of Ireland, 2002b)

As with most groups, children who experience poverty and social exclusion are not homogenous. The importance of this diversity is highlighted in the National Children's Strategy which states that particular children, including children with disabilities, Traveller children, the children of refugees and other immigrants, have special needs which have to be considered. (Government of Ireland, 2002). There is, however, relatively little known about the experience of such groups of children.

There are approximately 12,000 Traveller children aged less than 10 years in Ireland. These children experience poverty and discrimination, are vulnerable to ill health and poor physical development and are subject to disadvantages in emotional and cognitive development. (Pavee Point, 2002a). In terms of education, in 1999 approximately 6,000 Traveller children attended primary schools. (Pavee Point, 2002b) The number of Traveller children transferring to second level has increased in recent years, with more than 1,000 Traveller children in second level schools. (DES, 2002a) However, while the transfer rate to second level is high at 90%, more than half of Traveller children leave school before the end of the Junior Cycle.

Although there are no precise figures available, a substantial proportion of asylum-seekers in Ireland are children and there is evidence that many face very high levels of poverty and exclusion. In a study of 43 households in receipt of direct provision[7] most were found to be living on incomes that would place them below the 20% poverty line, with children experiencing extreme material deprivation. (Fanning, B, Veale, A. and O'Connor, D. 2001) This same study reported that many parents saw education, including pre-school education, as central in supporting their children's participation in Irish society, but identified a number of obstacles to accessing such services, including language and religion. Additional factors such a disrupted education, trauma and stressful living conditions impeded children's educational progress.

---

[6] Consistent poverty is defined as the proportion of households living on less than 60% of average disposable incomes and experiencing an enforced lack of at least one item on the following list of eight necessities: one substantial meal each day; chicken, meat or fish every second day; a 'roast' or equivalent once a week; two pairs of strong shoes; a warm coat; new rather than second hand clothes; and, being able to pay everyday household expenses without falling into arrears.

---

[7] Direct provision, introduced 2001, means that newly arrived asylum seekers ceased to be entitled to full rates of supplementary assistance, as was previously the case. Instead, adults dispersed into hotels, hostels and other reception centres around the country receive a weekly benefit of €19.50 per week, with €9.75 per week being paid in respect of each child plus child benefit. Some additional payments may be made for children aged under 3 years in exceptional cases at the discretion of community welfare officers. These typically live in hostels which make no provision for the needs of babies.

The Framework Document that supports the Revised NAPS clearly states that children experiencing poverty and exclusion do less well educationally and have reduced life chances that may lead to a cycle of deprivation and social exclusion that may also have intergenerational consequences. (Department of Social, Community and Family Affairs, 2001). Many of the interventions identified in this report are targeted at reducing educational disadvantage, thereby increasing life chances.

1.2.4 How Early Childhood Education and Care is Understood in Ireland

From birth to 6 years is the widely accepted age bracket for use when discussing early childhood education and care. This is a relatively straightforward issue and is further assisted in Ireland by the fact that the compulsory age at which children must starting primary education is 6 years. However, in determining what is meant by 'care' and 'education' is considerably less straightforward. Although perhaps not capturing all perceptions of early childhood care and education, official definitions exist. Based on extensive consultation, the Report of the Expert Working Group on Childcare defines childcare as

> "...daycare facilities and services for pre-school children and school-going children out-of-school hours. It includes services offering care, education and socialisation opportunities for children to the benefit of children, parents, employers and the wider community. Thus, services such as pre-schools, naionrai [Irish language pre-schools], daycare services, crèches, play groups, childminding and after-school groups are included, but schools (primary, secondary and special) and residential centres for children are excluded." (Government of Ireland, 1999b)

Early education is not as rigorously defined. The reason for this can be identified from the definition of childcare above. This is the view that early childhood education cannot be separated from early childhood care as the two are inextricably linked. This perception of a continuum of care and education for young children is to be found in all of the major policy documents dealing with provision and policy for young children. The Report of the Expert Working Group on Childcare clearly articulates this view by stating: "Care and education are inextricably linked elements in a child's holistic development...". (Government of Ireland, 1999b, p.45)

The White Paper on Early Childhood Education upholds this view and goes on to state that "Early childhood services will usually encompass both care and education, with the distinction between the two increasingly blurred as the age of the child decreases." (Government of Ireland, 1999c, p.3) However, the corollary of this statement also holds true and the White Paper expounds the view that education rather than care becomes increasingly important as the child matures and states that "Care is the dominant requirement of children aged less than 3 years and, because education is a more significant need of older children, the principal, though not exclusive, policy focus of this White Paper is on children aged between 3 and 6 years". (Government of Ireland, 1999c, p.4) In terms of provision, this understanding of early childhood education brings formal[8] primary school education in infant classes and specific pre-school education provisions of the DES for disadvantaged groups into the early childhood education and care arena.

1.2.5 The Irish Education System

Until recently much Irish education provision and policy was determined on an administrative rather than legislative basis within the Constitutional framework outlined above. In the past few years, important new legislation has been introduced, in particular, the Education Act, 1998. This Act establishes a statutory basis for the operation and continuing development of Irish education

---

[8] The term 'formal' is used here in relation to early education in primary schools, that is, infant classes, including classes catering for children with special needs. This distinguishes it from childcare as defined by the National Childcare Strategy, which takes place in other venues.

at primary and post-primary level. Its very existence reflects the increasingly interventionist role of the State in education. It also reflects of a decade of consultations and policy documents including the *Education for a Changing World - Green Paper on Education* (DES, 1992), the *Report of the National Education Convention* (National Education Convention Secretariat, 1994) and *Charting Our Education Future - White Paper on Education* (DES, 1995). The Act sets out a number of key objectives that the education partners are required to take into account in implementing the various provisions of the legislation. These objectives include:

☐ giving practical effect to the constitutional rights of children, as they relate to education, including children with disabilities and children with other special educational needs;

☐ promoting equality of access to and participation in education and developing the means whereby students may benefit from education;

☐ promoting the right of parents to send their children to a school of the parents' choice having regard to the effective and efficient use of resources;

☐ promoting best practice in teaching methods with regard to the diverse needs of students and the development of the skills and competences of teachers;

☐ promoting effective communication between schools and the wider community;

☐ contributing to the realisation of national education policies; and

☐ enhancing the transparency and accountability of the education system at local and national level.

Under the Act the Minister for Education has a statutory responsibility to determine national education policy and to ensure that, subject to available resources, there is provided to each person in the State, including a person with special needs, support services and a level and quality of education appropriate to meeting the needs and abilities of that person. The Minister is required to carry out these functions in line with the objectives outlined above.

The Department of Education and Science provides for education in primary and second-level schools and in third-level institutions. Although education provision has traditionally focused on these three levels, recent years have seen an expansion in the focus of provision to include pre-school education for children experiencing disadvantage or with special needs and further / adult education. The diagram at Annex 1 provides a brief overview of the education system in Ireland

Primary Education

Attendance at full-time education is compulsory for children between the ages of 6 and 16 years. Although children in Ireland are not obliged to attend school until the age of 6, a high proportion of children start school prior to this. Consequently, half (49.2%) of 4 year olds and virtually all (99.9%) 5 year olds are enrolled in infant classes in primary schools (Department of Education, forthcoming 2002). As a result, much of what is considered pre-school education in other countries (from age 4 to 6) is provided for all children in Ireland. (Government of Ireland, 1990)

State-funded primary schools include schools run by religious orders, multi-denominational schools and Gaelscoileanna (schools that teach the curriculum through the Irish language). All of these are managed by Boards of Management which are typically comprised of two nominees of the Patron, two parents of children enrolled in the school (one father and one mother), the principal teacher of the school, one teacher and two other members nominated by the Board to represent the local community (DES, 2000). The primary school cycle is 8 years long (2 years of infant classes, followed by 1st class to 6th class). There is no formal examination at the end of primary schooling and virtually all students proceed to post-primary level. In the school year 2000/2001, there were a total of 444,782 students in 3,286 primary schools in Ireland. (DES, forthcoming 2002)

Post-Primary Education

The second-level education sector comprises secondary, vocational, community and comprehensive schools, all of which are substantially funded by the DES. The majority of Irish students go to secondary schools, which are privately owned and managed and often run by religious orders. Vocational schools are administered by local Vocational Education Committees (VECs) while community and comprehensive schools are managed by Boards of Management of differing compositions. Second-level education consists of a three-year junior cycle followed by a two or three-year senior cycle. The Junior Certificate is taken at the end of the junior cycle. The Leaving Certificate is the terminal examination of post-primary education and takes place at the end of the senior cycle. In the school year 2000/2001, there were 349,274 students enrolled in 780 post-primary schools in Ireland. (DES, forthcoming 2002).

Third Level Education

The third level sector in Ireland comprises the university sector, the technological sector and the colleges of education that are substantially funded by the State and are autonomous and self-governing. In addition, a number of independent private colleges have developed in recent times. In 2000/2001 a total of 126,300 students were receiving full-time education at third level in Ireland. (DES, forthcoming 2002).

Further Education

The Further / Adult Education sector embraces education and training which occurs after second-level schooling but which is not part of the third level system. It includes programmes such as Post-Leaving Certificate courses, second chance education for the unemployed (the Vocational Training Opportunity Scheme - VTOS), and for early school leavers (in Youthreach and Senior Traveller Training Centres), adult literacy and basic education, and self-funded night-time adult programmes in second-level schools.

The Irish Language in the Education System

Under the Constitution, the Irish language is Ireland's first official language. While those using Irish as their first language are very much a minority in Ireland today, the language plays an important role in the cultural and educational life of the nation. The Irish language is taught in all primary and second-level schools. While the numbers of students receiving their education entirely through Irish are relatively small, there is evidence of growing interest among parents in having their children educated through Irish. Ireland currently has 114 recognised Gaelscoileanna (primary schools delivering education through the medium of Irish). In the school year 2000/2001 22,923 children were attending these primary schools. This represents 5.4% of all primary pupils. Unfortunately, it is not possible to break these numbers down further to determine the numbers in infant classes without contacting each of the schools. There are 3,359 3 to 6 year olds attending 292 Naíonraí (play groups providing services through the medium of Irish).

1.2.6 The Development of Early Childhood Care and Education Policy in Ireland

The development of national policy on early childhood education and care has been much discussed in Ireland since the beginning of the 1980s. However, these issues moved to the fore in Irish policy discussions and developments from the mid-1990s. Increasingly, the value of early childhood care and education for children, and specifically for those experiencing or at risk of educational disadvantage and the participation of women in the labour force were emerging as key factors in this debate. In this context, and spurred by the beginnings of the economic growth and labour force changes outlined above, a number of fora concerned with childcare and early education came into being. It is through these fora that national policy was developed in the form of various reports, strategies and one White Paper. In addition, these policies identified necessary institutional supports and have resulted in significant changes in the institutional landscape. These policy documents and reports are drawn on substantially throughout this report and are outlined below in chronological order. In addition, key pieces of legislation in early childhood education and care are also highlighted.

In looking at the policies derived from and contained in these documents, consideration of the context in which these were formulated is important. This involves the demographic, economic and labour market circumstances outlined above, as well as the place and role of the family enshrined in the Constitution, but also the level and type of childcare and early education provision that existed at the time. In this regard, it is particularly important to note that early childhood education and care was, and many would claim still is, under-developed in Ireland, with no history of comprehensive or universal State provision other than through infant classes in the primary schooling system. Until the late 1990s, support to childcare came mainly from the Department of Health through Health Boards. The majority of this support was provided through small grants to Community-based services catering for children at risk and in need of protection that were referred by the health services. Judged against this background, the progress made in terms of policy and provision in recent years has been significant.

Much of the gap in pre-school education and childcare provision was met by extended family members and local childminders. The gap in provision was also increasingly being addressed by private and community-based, not-for-profit providers. This sector has continued to grow in response to increase female labour force participation and the reduction in informal childcare. (IPPA, the Quality Childcare Organisation, 2001) Some of these services are based on well established early educational approaches, including Montessori, Steiner, Froebel and Highscope, but all include an educational component.[9] The contribution of these providers and their umbrella organisations – such as IPPA, the Early Childhood Organisation and the Montessori schools – to developing quality services should not be overlooked. At a time when there was little State support, such providers and organisations worked to develop and increase the capacity of the sector to deliver quality services. These organisations developed and delivered training, provided advice, information and support and worked for policy change in the various fora. Without the work of such organisations, there would have been little childcare provision for policies, programmes and funding to engage with in recent years.

The importance of appropriate early childhood care and education is clearly acknowledged in the various policy documents identified below. Within these documents, the role of such provision in combating educational disadvantage and promoting social inclusion is emphasised. Many of the commitments given in, or made in respect of the recommendations included in these documents, are reinforced in the current Programme for Government (2002a) and implemented through the various institutional structures and programmes identified in this report. The focus within these policies and programmes is clearly on the needs of the most vulnerable children, especially those with special education needs due to disabilities or those coming from disadvantaged socio-economic backgrounds.

The National Agreements: *Partnership 2000 and Programme for Prosperity and Fairness*

Since the mid-1980s Ireland has operated a number of three-year national partnership agreements that provide an agreed framework for economic and social policy. These are based on agreement between the social partners – the Government, the Trade Unions, Employer's Organisations, Farming Organisations and Social and Community Organisations. The nature of social partnership in Ireland has a number of unique features, not least of which is the recognition and inclusion of

---

[9] It is worth noting here that childcare services in Ireland are zero VAT rated on the basis that they services they provide are educational.

the community and voluntary sector as a full partner since the mid-1990s. Since their inclusion, the national partnership agreements have contained more detailed social chapters. These have set down the policy parameters and committed the government to a range of measures. These have included education, including early education, and childcare. Indeed, the Expert Working Group on Childcare and the National Childcare Strategy arose from the national agreement *Partnership 2000* (Government of Ireland, 1997), which ran from 1997 to the end of 1999.

The current national agreement, *Programme for Prosperity and Fairness* (PPF) (Government of Ireland, 1999d) sees lifelong learning as the key to a future of sustained economic growth and social development at a time of ongoing change. In this regard, one of the main objectives is to provide a continuum of education provision from early childhood to adult targeted at tackling educational disadvantage and promoting equality of opportunity and participation. In relation to Early Childhood Education, the Programme proposes extensive actions ranging from the implementation of the recommendations in the White Paper 'Ready to Learn' to early literacy strategies and a wide range of strategies to prevent early school leaving. To date, significant progress has been made in relation to many of the actions proposed. These include the establishment of the Centre for Early Childhood Development and Education (CECDE), the enhancement of the Home/School/Community Liaison Scheme, the expansion of the National Educational Psychological Service (NEPS), the establishment of a National Educational Welfare Service and a statutory Education Disadvantage Committee, and the implementation of an integrated plan to tackle educational disadvantage. These are returned to below.

The National Childcare Strategy

The national agreement of 1997, *Partnership 2000* (Government of Ireland, 1997) included provision for the establishment of an Expert Working Group on Childcare, convened by the Department of Justice, Equality and Law Reform. This Expert Working Group comprised over 100 individuals and received over 100 submissions in response to advertisements in the national press. The Expert Working Group worked in two Framework Resource Groups, one of which addressed the needs and rights of children, with the other deliberating on equality of access and participation. Six Framework Development Groups were also established, one of which addressed each of the following issues:

☐ maximising the job potential and financial implications of childcare;

☐ registration, training and qualifications;

☐ regulations and standards;

☐ early education;

☐ resourcing and sustaining childcare in disadvantaged urban areas; and

☐ resourcing and sustaining childcare in rural areas.

The outcome of the deliberations of these groups was the National Childcare Strategy, which was launched in 1999 (Government of Ireland, 1999b). This comprises discussions of the salient issues and 27 recommendations relating to notification and registration, staffing and employment procedures, training and pay, supporting and stimulating both the supply of and demand for childcare, and the structures and procedures necessary to implement and support the overall strategy. These structures will be returned to later (see 1.2.9 below).

The fact that this Expert Working Group had such a wide membership serves as an indication of the importance that the question of childcare had come to assume in Ireland. The National Childcare Strategy is important not least in that it represents the first concerted attempt to develop a coherent and comprehensive government policy that specifically addressed childcare. Nonetheless, one particular caveat should be noted here. The terms of reference of the Expert Working Group was to consider the needs of children whose parent/s were either at work or attempting to access work through training and/or education. Provision under the National Childcare Strategy is inextricably linked to labour market participation. Therefore, while the National Childcare Strategy states that the needs and rights of children should be a primary consideration, this has to be interpreted as the needs and rights of children whose parent/s are active in the labour market. The needs of children being cared for by a parent who is not active in the labour market were considered to be substantively different and therefore seen as requiring different policies. However, the National Childcare Strategy states that "...*improving the quality and quantity of childcare will also have a positive on parents who choose to care for their child at home since 16% of children with parents who work full-time in the home avail of paid childcare.* (Government of Ireland, 1999b, p.xxv)

The National Development Plan, 2000-2006

The majority of funding for the development of childcare in Ireland is channelled through the National Development Plan 2000-2006 (Government of Ireland, 1999e). This has 5 Operational Programmes, one of which is the Employment and Human Resources Development Operational Programme (EHRDOP). This addresses the labour market and human capital needs of the Irish economy for the period 2000 to 2006. The EHRDOP has 48 measures and sub-measures, of which Early Education is Measure 4. Early interventions are encouraged to improve long-term education participation, to identify and address literacy and numeracy difficulties at an early stage and to prevent subsequent problems giving rise to long-term unemployment, social problems, etc. The Plan aims to target funding at key groups and to provide funding on a devolved basis integrated within area-based interventions in the case of areas with significant concentrations of educational disadvantage.

The NDP has 2 Regional Operation Programmes: (1) the Border, Midlands and West (BMW) Operational Programme and (2) the Southern and Eastern (S&E) Operational Programme. Both of these include 4 priorities, one of which is the Social Inclusion and Childcare Priority. Here, the primary objectives of childcare are seen as overcoming social disadvantage and promoting equality by improving access to education, training and work and reconciling work and family life. For instance, in relation to the EOCP the Regional Operational Programme for the Border, Midlands and Western Region states that

> *The Childcare Measure, which is being promoted as the Equal Opportunities Childcare Programme 2000 to 2006, has both an equal opportunities and a social inclusion focus in that it addresses the needs of men and women generally in reconciling their childcare needs with their participation in the labour force while, at the same time, facilitating access for parents, in particular disadvantaged women, to education, training and employment. The Equal Opportunities Childcare Programme will also cater for the needs of disadvantaged children by initiating play and development opportunities for them.*
> (BWM Regional Assembly, 2000)

While exclusion from the labour market is seen to impact most severely on disadvantaged women and single parent families, the majority of which are headed by lone mothers. However, the interests of men too are to be served as the childcare measures "...*will address the needs of men and women generally in reconciling their childcare needs with their participation in the labour force*" (Government of Ireland, 1999e, p192).

The Social Inclusion and Childcare Priority includes one measure that provides European Structural Funds for capital grants to childcare providers and 2 sub-measures that support staffing and quality improvement grants to childcare providers. These provisions are managed and distributed under what is known as the Equal Opportunities Childcare Programme.

The EOCP 2000-2006 is one of the most important developments in the support and development of childcare in Ireland and is the primary source of funding available to existing childcare providers as well as those seeking to develop new childcare facilities. The details of funding the programme are provided in section 2.5.4 below.

The primary aims of this programme are improving access to education, training and employment and improving equality between men and women in the labour market. This is to be supported through the achievement of three objectives: to enhance the quality of childcare, to increase the number of childcare facilities and childcare places, and to introduce a co-ordinated approach to the delivery of childcare services. While developing services and infrastructure that will help meet the needs of a diverse range of parents, particularly those trying to reconcile work and family life, the EOCP seeks to ensure that the needs of the child are paramount. The NDP allocated €317.4 million to the DJELR for childcare measures. This money has been augmented by an anti-inflationary package agreed with the social partners and the transfer of childcare schemes and their associated funding from other Government Departments to the DJELR. The total funding available to the Department is now €436.7 million for investment in childcare over the period 2000-2006.

The EOCP 2000-2006 is based on the experience of a previous EOCP funded with monies made available following the Mid-Term of the 1994-1999 round of Structural Funds. This earlier programme was much smaller, with expenditure of just €14.6 million, and provided funding for childcare infrastructure projects, a national employer childcare stimulation scheme and core funding for community-based childcare projects (ESF Programme Evaluation Unit, 1999).

A number of structures support the implementation of this programme and the development of the childcare sector more generally. These include the Childcare Directorate of the DJELR, the Inter-Departmental and Inter-Agency Synergies Childcare Group, the National Co-ordinating Childcare Committee and the County/City Childcare Committees. These are returned to in section 1.2.9 below. In addition, ADM provides technical assistance to the EOCP. This involves overseeing the day-to-day implementation and financial management of the programme and appraising applications and making recommendations on foot of these to an appraisals committee. In addition to the DJELR, the NCCC is comprised of representatives of ADM, two Regional Assemblies, the DES, the Department of Social and Family Affairs, the Department of Health and Children, ICTU, IBEC, the Community Pillar, the Farming Pillar, National Voluntary Childcare Organisations, the National Women's Council of Ireland, County/City Childcare Committees, Chambers of Commerce, a number of State agencies and community organisations.

The EOCP provides a range of grants and financial supports to existing and new providers of centre-based childcare facilities and organisations involved in childcare. In line with the Measure and Sub-Measures under which the programme is funded these are:

☐ Capital grants for community/not-for-profit organisations and self-employed and private childcare providers towards the cost of building, renovation, upgrading or equipping childcare facilities;

☐ Staffing grants for community/not-for-profit organisations or a not-for-profit consortium of community organisations and private providers towards the cost of staff for community-based provision in disadvantaged areas;

☐ Improving quality through (i) the provision of finance to support National Voluntary Childcare Organisations (seven organisations are currently being supported to implement a range of measures aimed at up-skilling their members and creating a greater and better informed awareness of quality in relation to childcare), (ii) developing local childcare networks through the County/City Childcare Committees (see 1.2.9 below), (iii) funding innovative projects with the capacity to be replicated, and (iv) the development of a range of supports for childminders, also through the County/City Childcare Committees.

At the end of August 2002, 1,533 applications for funding under the capital and staffing grants had been approved. These will support the creation of 18,206 new childcare places and support 17,710 existing places.

The Social Inclusion and Childcare Priority also includes the Local Development Social Inclusion Programme. Under this, Local Area-Based Partnerships (which have been in existence in disadvantaged areas in Ireland since the early 1990s) and a number of community groups are funded to provide services to the unemployed, develop and deliver community-based youth initiatives and support community development. Within this, a number of Area-Based Partnerships and community groups have supported innovative early education and childcare projects.

The Commission on the Family

The Commission on the Family came into being in 1995 and produced an extensive report, *Strengthening Families for Life* three years later (Government of Ireland, 1998). The Commission comprised 14 experts in the areas of social policy, family law, mediation, marriage and relationship counselling, medicine and psychology, and economic, taxation and income support. Their report was based on the deliberations of these experts, commissioned research and over 500 submissions.

The issue of childcare outside the home, while not central to the report, was addressed by the Commission predominantly from the perspective of supporting families to meet their child rearing responsibilities. The Commission made a number of recommendations in this respect that can be summarised as follows:

☐ A greater role for the State in supporting the care of pre-school children through direct payments that may or may not be used to pay for external care;

☐ The introduction of an Early Years Opportunities Subsidy that would be paid in respect of children attending registered childcare facilities;

☐ The establishment of a national co-ordinating body of childcare provision;

☐ The further development under the auspices of the Department of Social, Community and Family Affairs of a specific out-of-school hours services;

☐ The promotion of the Child Care (Pre-school Services) Regulations 1996 and Child Care (Pre-School Services) (Amendment) Regulations, 1997; and

☐ The development of measures to support childminders and promote the adoption by them of standards of good practice.

Several of these measures coincide with those in other policy documents and most specifically the National Childcare Strategy. As such, a number of these measures have been progressed and are detailed in sections 1.2.7 and 1.2.8 below.

The White Paper on Early Childhood Education

In 1998, a National Forum on Early Childhood Education took place from 23-27th March. This Forum was a first step in meeting the commitment given under the programme for Government, *An Action Plan for the Millennium* (Government of Ireland, 1997) to prioritise early childhood education and care and provide specific funding for pre-school education. During this week, thirty-two agencies involved in early childhood education and care made oral presentations to the Forum

Secretariat, which was comprised of nine experts. Following this week of presentations and discussion, the Secretariat produced the *Report of the National Forum on Early Childhood Education* (The National Forum Secretariat, 1998). This is one of the most comprehensive documents ever produced on early education in Ireland. On foot of this report, the Department of Education and Science produced a White Paper entitled *Ready to Learn: White Paper on Early Childhood Education* in 1999. The overall objective of the White Paper is to

Support the development and educational achievement of children through high quality early education, with particular focus on the target groups of the disadvantaged and those with special needs. (Government of Ireland, 1999c, page 14)

The White Paper examines existing early years provision and, having identified the gaps in this, goes on to propose changes under the headings of improving quality early education in primary schools, meeting the needs of children with special needs, meeting the needs of disadvantaged children, enhancing the involvement of parents, inspection and evaluation, and the establishment of new structures. The National Development Plan allocated €93.98 million (£74 million) to the implementation of the White Paper's recommendations. Of central importance to the present report, this White Paper will be drawn on in many of the following sections.

One of the first steps taken to implement the proposals of the White Paper on early education has been to put in place a centre to develop and co-ordinate early childhood education provision. The *Centre for Early Childhood Development and Education (CECDE)* was established under the joint management of St. Patrick's College, Drumcondra and the Dublin Institute of Technology. The major objectives of this project are

- to develop a quality framework for all aspects of early education, including the development of a Quality in Education Mark for providers,

- to develop targeted pilot interventions for children up to 6 years of age from disadvantaged backgrounds and children with special needs;

- to prepare the ground for the establishment of a Early Childhood Education Agency as envisaged in the White Paper.

In line with these objectives the functions of the CEDCE are

- to develop early education quality standards in relation to all aspects of early education including equipment and materials, staffing, training, qualifications, methodologies and curriculum,

- to develop a support framework to encourage compliance with quality standards,

- to co-ordinate and enhance early education provision, including parental involvement, focusing specifically on provision for children with special needs or at risk of educational disadvantage, and

- to undertake and/or commission research to identify and develop best practice in curriculum, teaching methodologies and parent involvement.

A number of crosscutting themes will underpin the work of the CECDE. These include consultation and networking with the actors involved in the various aspects of early education, bringing international and North/South dimensions to the work of the Centre, the forging of close links with other State bodies with a role in early education and development, consideration of the issues of diversity and equality generally but more specifically when addressing the circumstances and needs of children experiencing disadvantage and those with special needs and the involvement and empowerment of parents in the education of their children. In addition to the management committee made up of representatives of St. Patrick's College and Dublin Institute of Technology, the CECDE also reports to a Steering Committee, which includes a representative of the DES (which acts as chairperson) and an external expert. Although in its early stages of development, the CECDE is responsible for the implementation of much of the work outlined in the White Paper on Early Education.

The National Children's Strategy

Based on extensive consultation with various government departments and agencies, experts in a range of child related disciplines, teachers, parents, children and those involved in the provision of services and supports to families and children, the National Children's Strategy came into being in November 2000. This Strategy takes its perspective from the UN Convention on the Rights of the Child and promotes an approach to children based on this. The vision for children presented in the Strategy is based on the following values:

☐ Children have an innate dignity as human beings deserving respect;

☐ Children enrich the quality of all our lives;

☐ Children are especially vulnerable and need adult protection;

☐ Children thrive through the love and support of a family life;

☐ Children should be supported to explore, enjoy and develop their various talents;

☐ Children need help to learn responsibility as they grow towards adulthood and full citizenship.

The National Children's Strategy has three national goals. These are (i) that children will have a voice, (ii) that children's lives will be better understood and (iii) that children will receive quality supports and services. The operational principles of the Children's Strategy reflect many of those espoused in the National Childcare Strategy. These include the principle that all actions in respect of children should be child-centred, family-oriented, equitable, inclusive, action-oriented and integrated. The Strategy presents an understanding of the children's lives form the 'whole child' perspective, which recognises

☐ the extent of children's own capacities and abilities and their active participation in life;

☐ the mix of formal and informal support that children rely on, most importantly family and including childcare and education and

☐ the nine dimensions of childhood development that must be addressed if children are to enjoy their childhood and make a successful transition to adulthood.

The National Children's Strategy is a wide-ranging policy document that presents a number of objectives that reflect the complexity of the issues it is addressing. Of particular concern to those interested or involved in early education and care is Objective A, which states that "*Children's early education and development needs will be met through quality childcare services and family-friendly employment measures*" (page 50). In respect of this objective, the Strategy identifies placing children's needs at the heart of childcare as one of the key challenges. Objective B of the Strategy is also of direct concern as it relates to the need for a range of educational opportunities that reflect and meet the diversity of needs of children and, as part of meeting this objective, the need for after-school and out-of-school care services.

In relation to early education and care, it is noteworthy that under the goal of giving children a voice in all matters that affect them, in the consultation process undertaken to inform that Strategy some eighty children of approximately 3-4 years gave their assessment of the childcare facility they attended. Their comments reflect the intrinsic value that children themselves place on their playschool experience in terms of play, socialising and learning. Listening to children is seen by the NCO as a critical element of securing quality services, including childcare and one that they are actively promoting in their activities.

While only a small number of the Strategy's objectives are of direct relevance to early education and care, the Strategy proposes a view of children, their rights and their needs that will inform all child related services.

The National Anti-Poverty Strategy (NAPS)

The National Anti-Poverty Strategy was first launched by the Government in 1997. This originally had five key themes: income adequacy, unemployment, educational disadvantage, rural disadvantage and urban deprivation. One of the key features of the NAPS is that it set key targets in a number of these areas, as well as an overall target for poverty reduction. The NAPS was reviewed in 2001 and the revised NAPS, *Building an Inclusive Society* (Government of Ireland, 2002b), included two additional key themes – Health and Housing and Accommodation – as well as specific consideration of particularly vulnerable groups including children and young people, women, older people, Travellers, people with disabilities, and migrants and members of ethnic minority groups. In this revised NAPS a number of commitments are given to combating educational disadvantage by addressing literacy and early school leaving. In the framework document supporting the NAPS (DSCFA, 2001), more explicit measures for the attainment of the NAPS targets are set out. These include an expansion of early education pre-school services, focusing particularly on the disadvantaged areas selected under specific government programmes; making the Early Childhood Education Centre operational by mid 2002; and the incremental build up of pre-school services for children with special needs. Additional measures are funded by the DJELR under the EOCP.

The Programme for Government

The current Programme for Government (2002a) was agreed between the coalition parties (Fianna Fail and the Progressive Democrats) earlier this year. This contains a considerable number of commitments in the areas of childcare and education. Many of these arise under existing agreements and policies including the national agreement and the NDP. With regard to childcare commitments are made to the implementation of existing provisions, such as the county childcare strategies and the EOCP, as well as to the introduction of some new measures including a special working visa scheme for child minders. A general commitment is given to *improving the level and quality of participation and achievement at every level of education, with specific commitments being made in relation to introduce a national early-education, training, support and certification system and expand state-funded early-education places* (p.24). In addition, the Programme for Government prioritises a new national system of funded early-education for particularly vulnerable children, that is, those with intellectual disabilities and children in areas of concentrated disadvantage. Other commitment in relation to the education system more generally, such as continued reductions in the pupil:teacher ratio and the progressive introduction of average size of classes of 20:1 for children under 9.

1.2.7 Types and Coverage of Early Childhood Education and Care Provision

Accepting that early childhood spans from birth to 6 years of age, there is a wide variety of services. One way of looking at these is to separate them into provision funded by the Department of Education and Science (DES) on the one hand, and early education and childcare provision funded by other sources on the other. This coincides with the widely accepted definition of childcare included in the National Childcare Strategy. However, it is important to remember that care and educational components are incorporated in both early education and childcare services, and that both recognise the need for a continuum of care and education that encourages easy transitions for children between early childcare and early education provision. Table 3 below gives a brief overview of the types and amounts of early education and childcare services in Ireland. More detail on these follows.

Table 3
Main Types of Early Childhood Education and Care Services in Ireland, Facilities and Participants

	No. of Facilities	No of Participants
DES Funded Early Childhood Education and Care Provision, 2001		
Early Start	40	1,617
Pre-Schools for Traveller Children	48	512
Primary Schools (children aged up to 6 years)	3,161	126,558
Special Schools (children aged up to 6 years)	125	584
Early Childhood Care and Education Funded from Other Sources, 1999 - 2000		
Centre-based Provision - Full-Time Places	2,029	17,285
Centre-based Childcare Provision – Sessional Places	578	39,518
Naonrai	292	3,359
Parent and Toddler Groups (estimated)	230	not available
Childminders (estimated)	37,900	75,800

Source: *DES, forthcoming 2002, ADM, forthcoming 2002, and Government of Ireland, 1999b.*

DES Funded Early Childhood Education and Care

Early education provided or funded by the DES includes children attending schools exclusively for children with special needs and specific pre-school programmes aimed at children from disadvantaged backgrounds. It includes the following types of provision:

Infant Classes in Primary Schools: These are the first two years of primary school education and are divided into junior (first year) and senior (second year) infants. Typically, these classes are comprised of 4, 5 and 6 year olds. As indicated above, half of 4 year olds and almost all 5 years olds are in infant classes in primary schools.[10] Infant classes are undoubtedly providing for both the education and care needs of this age group. In January 2001 there were 102,820 children aged 3 to 6 years in ordinary infant classes. This category also includes special classes that cater for children with special learning needs that are attached to ordinary primary schools and children in infant classes in special schools. In January 2001 there were 2,335 children in special infant classes attached to primary schools and 584 attending the infant classes in special schools (DES, forthcoming 2002). It is the policy of the DES to integrate children with special needs into ordinary primary classes whenever possible. Unfortunately, the number of children with special learning needs in such classes is not currently available. Table 4 below contains further details on pupils aged up to 6 years who attend primary school.

---

[10] The figures for the number of 4 year olds and 5 year olds in schools are collected in January each year. Many children start school at 4 years of age and then turn 5 before the figures are collected in January (i.e. between September and January) so they are counted as 5 year olds. For this reason, the number of 4 year olds in schools and their participation rate is underestimated.

Table 4

Number of pupils aged 0 – 6 Year in Early Start and Primary Schools by Class Type, 2000/2001

Age on 1st Jan. 2001		National Schools								Total
		Pupils in Ordinary Classes					Pupils with Special Needs in Ordinary N.S.	Pupils in Special Schools	Pupils in Private Primary Schools	
	Early Start	Junior Infants	Senior Infants	1st Class	2nd Class					
3 or under		170	-	-	-		11	59	259	499
4	1,617	24,406	288	-	-		415	91	409	25,609
5		27,341	22,358	296	-		747	181	497	51,420
6		707	27,550	21,030	330		909	253	539	51,318

Note: Private Primary Schools exclude schools/centres not enrolling children aged 6 or over.
Source: DES, forthcoming 2002.

Early Start Programme: this is a programme aimed at pre-school children aged 3 to 4 years in a number of disadvantaged areas. Some 1,617 pre-school aged children were attending Early Start programmes operating in primary schools. A more detailed description of Early Start is included below.

Pre-Schools for Traveller Children: in 2001, the DES grant aided 48 Pre-Schools for Traveller Children. The schools can cater for up to 624 children and aim to provide Traveller children with the opportunity to participate in a secure, stimulating and developmentally appropriate environment.

Although parents have the right to educate their children at home, the vast majority of children start their formal education in the infant classes of State supported primary schools. Statistics on their participation in the formal education system are readily available, predominantly through the DES Annual Statistical Reports. However, a number of gaps exist in this data, some of which have already been alluded to. For example, there are no figures available on the number of children with special needs integrated in ordinary infant classes, no comprehensive data on the number of refugee and asylum-seeking children in such classes and no easily accessible data on infants in Gaelscoileanna.

Early Childhood Education and Care Funded from Other Sources

A wide range of early childhood education and care is funded from sources other than the DES. Funding is obtained from a number of sources including fees paid by parents, support received from the Health Boards and grants secured under the EOCP. The most prominent forms of provision in Ireland include the following.

Play Groups and Pre-schools: these usually provide sessional services (that is, less than three-and-a-half hours per child per day) and children normally attend in the morning or afternoon. Typically these services cater for children aged from 3 to 4 or 5 years and combine education and care through structured play. The majority of Play Groups and Pre-schools are privately owned, with the remainder being community-based. Many are voluntary members of the IPPA - the Early Childhood Organisation (formerly the Irish Pre-school Play-Group Association), which provides training and support to its members. Currently, IPPA - the Early Childhood Organisation has approximately 1,900 members catering for approximately 35,000 children. The majority of these children are under school-going age and some after-school places are also being provided.

Nurseries and Crèches: these typically provide full day services and many cater for children from two to three months up to school-going age. Many provide a structured educational element for children aged 3 to 5 years. These are either privately owned and operated or community–based and run. A small number of drop-in creches operate in shopping centres, leisure centres etc. where irregular and very short-term care is provided. In addition, a small number of workplace crèches are provided by employers, the majority of which are located in the public or civil service. Many creches and nurseries are affiliated to the National Children's Nurseries Association (NCNA). The main aim of this organisation is to promote high quality childcare through the development and dissemination of information to its members. The NCNA also employs a full-time training co-ordinator and provides an advisory service and other resources to its members.

Montessori Schools: there are approximately 500 Montessori schools in Ireland catering for children aged three to 6 years. These are privately owned and managed. Training is provided by the Association Montesorri Internationale (AMI) Teacher Association and St. Nicholas Montessori Society of Ireland.

Naionraí: these are Irish language pre-schools catering for children aged 3 to 6 years. They are financially supported by the Department of Community, Rural and Gaeltacht Affairs. Describing their approach as one of early immersion, there are currently 292 Naionraí in Ireland, 72 of which are located in Gaeltacht (Irish speaking) areas and 220 outside of these areas. This has grown from 26 such playgroups in 1978. In total, 3,359 children are attending Naionraí. These are also privately owned. The umbrella organisation for these Irish-speaking pre-schools is An Comhchoiste Reamhscolaíochta Teo, founded in 1978. This provides training modules on early education and sociological theories for those working in Naionraí as well as providing intensive and in-service courses in Irish and a course in Childcare. In addition, professional counselling support is provided to the Directors of Naionraí.

Parent and Toddler Groups: these offer opportunities for play for children and social interaction and informal support to parents. Typically catering for children from birth to 3 years and attached to other childcare services such as pre-schools or crèches, there were an estimated 230 parent and toddler groups in Ireland in 1998 (Government of Ireland, 1999b).

After-school and Out-of-School Care: this refers to care provided for school-going children outside of school hours, including after-school hours and during school holidays. Some of the providers of other childcare services also offer after-school and/or out-of-school services. However, evidence suggests that this is minimal and after-school and out-of-school provision remains one of the most under-developed and unregulated aspects of childcare for children of all ages in Ireland.

Until recently, relatively little was known about childcare provision and usage in Ireland. A number of studies in recent years have thrown considerable light on these areas. A survey of childcare arrangements was undertaken by the Economic and Social Research Institute (ESRI) for the Commission on the Family. This survey revealed that 38% of all parents with children aged 4 years and under availed of some form of paid childcare. However, this was heavily influenced by the employment status of the mother with just 16% of children with mothers working full-time in the home availing of paid childcare. This is in contrast to 58% of children whose mother was in full-time employment (Government of Ireland, 1999b). Overall, this survey found that the most commonly used forms of childcare were formal and paid provision in crèches, nurseries, pre-schools etc. with 21% of mothers with children aged less than five years using such services. Paid childminders who took care of children in their own (minder's) home is the second most commonly used form of childcare, with 14% of all mothers with children aged 4 years or under availing of such services. However, over one-fifth (22%) of mothers with full-time jobs and 47% of those with part-time jobs used no paid childcare at all, indicating a reliance on informal provision provided either by partners, family, friends or neighbours. This survey also highlighted that many parents relied on a combination of formal and informal childcare arrangements.

In 1998 the DJELR published the results of a study undertaken by Goodbody Economic Consultants on the economics of childcare in Ireland (Department of Justice, Equality and Law Reform, 1998). This report examined the supply of and demand for childcare in Ireland, the economic role such services played in terms of child development and labour market participation and proposed a number of measures to support the demand and supply of services. This study and the ESRI survey outlined above were key in forming the National Childcare Strategy.

In 1999 the Department of Justice, Equality and Law Reform (DJELR), recognising that the lack of information on the number and type of childcare facilities represented a serious data deficit, provided funding for a Childcare Census at county level, in line with developments in the reform of local government and the establishment of County Development Boards and County/City Childcare Committees. This Census was carried out by Area Development Management Ltd (ADM). Drawing on all available lists of childcare services in each area, information was collected from a total of 2,607 centre-based childcare facilities. The National Census Report is currently being drawn up by the Centre for Social and Educational Research (CSER) on behalf of ADM and will be available towards the end of 2002. Advance figures have been supplied for this report and the types of services offered by these providers are shown in Table 5 below.[11]

Table 5
Centre-based Childcare in Ireland 1999 - 2000

	Sessional Service Offered		Full Day Service Offered	
	Number	%	Number	%
Drop-in Crèche	124	5.2	68	6.0%
Playgroup/Pre-school	1,276	53.8	252	22.4%
Montessori School	402	16.9	229	20.4%
Naionra	159	6.7	3	0.3%
Workplace Crèche	22	0.9	40	3.6%
Afterschool Group	97	4.1	-	-
Crèche / DayCare	-	-	414	36.8%
Homework Club	43	1.8	-	-
Parent & Toddler	136	5.7	-	-
Other Service	113	4.8	118	10.5%
Total Services	**2,372**	100	**1,124**	100
Total Facilities	**2,029**		**578**	
Estimated Number of Childminders	37,900[1]			

Note: *The total number of services offered is higher than the total number of facilities as a number of facilities offer more than one type of service.   1. This figure is taken from Government of Ireland , 1999b.*

Source: *ADM, forthcoming 2002 The National Summary of the County Childcare Census 1999/2000.*

---

[11] The author would like to thank ADM and the Centre for Social and Educational Research in Dublin Institute of Technology for providing these advance figures.

Sessional services refer to services that typically last for 3.5 hours or less. What is clear from these figures is the prominence of such sessional services, most typically in the form of play schools, pre-schools and Montessori schools. While these types of provision are also central in the provision of full-day care, crèches and day care centres arise as the most common form of provision.

The Census of Childcare yields much information and represents a significant advance in terms of our knowledge of childcare services in Ireland. However, one of its limitations is that it tells us nothing about one of the most commonly used forms of early childcare in Ireland, that is, formal and, more prevalent, informal childminding. The predominance of informal childminding in the form of regular or irregular paid or unpaid childminding in either the child's or the minder's home is a particular feature of early childhood education and care in Ireland.

Childminders: childminders provide care for children predominantly in their own [minder's] home, although a small number care for children in the child's home. Childminding is usually a year round service and is arranged on a basis to suit both the parent's and the childminder's needs. Therefore childminders may provide full-day and after-school care. While some childminders have notified their local Health Boards of their services, much of this activity is conducted in the informal or black economy. Indeed, only childminders caring for more than three children are required to notify the Health Boards (for more details on exclusion to the Regulations see section 2.1 below). As such, there is little information about childminders in Ireland. However, recent estimates place the number of childminders at close to 40,000. (Government of Ireland, 1999b)

The survey of childcare arrangements undertaken for the Commission on the Family (Government of Ireland, 1998) referred to above reveals that childminders are the second most commonly used form of childcare. In a recent study of the members of 6 of Ireland's main trade unions, the Irish Congress of Trade Unions (ICTU) found that 86.3% of members with children aged 14 years or less relied on some form of childminding arrangement (Irish Congress of Trade Unions, 2002). The main childminding arrangements used were

☐ informally paid [black economy] friend, neighbour or relative minding the child in their own [minder's] home (24.4% of members),

☐ formally paid childminder in the minders home (17.5%), and

☐ unpaid family member or partner in the child's home (12%).

This reveals the heavy reliance by working parents on childminding as a form of care. In addition, this survey illustrates the manner in which childcare arrangements change on entry to the formal school system. Fourteen per cent of all children aged up to 4 years were cared for in centre-based childcare facilities. However, this proportion falls to less that 4% for children aged five years and over, when childcare requirements change from full-time to out-of-school hours.

The prevalence of a large number of childminders operating in the informal or black economy raises a number of concerns. Many of these are believed to be untrained (a belief borne out by the high number of children's relatives filling this role) and are isolated by their informal status from the networks of registered childminders. Informal childminding arrangements are precarious for the minders who have no social protection as they are unregistered for taxation and social security and have no employment rights or protection under the law, and for parents with whom no formal contract is made. Consequently, care arrangements may come to an abrupt and sudden end at the discretion of either the minder or the parents. A recent Childminding Initiative being implemented by the Health Boards aims to address some of these issues (see section 1.2.9, Department of Health and Children below).

1.2.8 Provision for Children in Disadvantaged Areas

It is widely accepted that many children from disadvantaged areas and backgrounds experience educational disadvantage in the school system and the repercussions of this throughout their lives. In order to redress this imbalance, a number of specific early childhood measures have been put in place in recent years. Most of these come under the remit of the DES, whose pre-school responsibility is specific to children from disadvantaged backgrounds and those with special learning needs. Many childcare facilities in disadvantaged area are receiving support through the various measures of the EOCP, while others are receiving support from the Health Boards.

Pre-school Provision

Provision in Community-based Pre-school Facilities

The Childcare Census gives a baseline indication of the number of community-based childcare facilities with there being 1,096 counted in this survey in 1999/2000. Other available figures relate to the involvement of the regional Health Boards in funding pre-school provision for children considered to be at risk of abuse or neglect due to problems and stresses arising in their family. Health Boards provide financial supports to certain pre-school services that cater for children who are regarded as being at-risk or disadvantaged. This function is in keeping with the Boards' overall responsibilities under the Child Care Act, 1991 in regard to the promotion of the welfare of children and the provision of family support services. Funding of approximately €4.9m (£3.9m) (capital and revenue) was provided by the Health Boards towards these services in 1999, supporting roughly 7,000 places in approximately 600 facilities. An additional €2.2m (£1.75m) was provided to the Health Boards for this purpose in 2000. In line with their function regarding the regulation of childcare services (see 2.1.1 below), it is possible to collate the number of notifications of community-based facilities to each individual Health Board and the number of places they offer.

Since 2000, the EOCP has supported childcare in disadvantaged areas, although the Programme is not exclusively concerned with provision in such areas. Staffing grants to community and not-for-profit organisations are only available to services operating in disadvantaged communities, while capital grants for community-based projects prioritise those servicing disadvantaged areas (but do not exclude services outside such areas). Grants made to self-employed/private providers and those made in respect of quality measures are available to all providers irrespective of their location or client group. Although some recipients of these grants serve disadvantaged communities, it is not possible to say how many. As this programme is the main source of state funding directed to such facilities, an accurate account of this can now be achieved. Table 6 below shows expenditure under each grant type of the EOCP from its inception in mid-2000 up to August 2002. In this period, 339 capital grants were made to community/not-for-profit organisations, accounting for expenditure of almost €43 million or 28% of total expenditure. In addition, 604 staffing grants, accounting for expenditure of €70.3 million or 46% of total expenditure, were also approved. It is estimated that the funding approved under the EOCP between mid-2000 and the end of August 2002 will provide support for an additional 6,889 full-time and 11,317 part-time childcare places as well as an additional 1,781 full-time and 978 part-time staff. A more detailed breakdown of applications and expenditure under this programme is provided in Annex 3.

Rutland Street Project

The Rutland Street Pre-School Project began in 1969 as an early education for children living in disadvantaged areas of central Dublin involving Rutland Street Junior National School and Pre-School. It took the form of a special education programme for children between the ages of 3 and 8, with the main focus being on the pre-school level (3-5 years of age). It includes a pre-school centre, a special staff teaching allocation, childcare workers, secretary, cooks and cleaners, together with the provision of school meals. Originally financed jointly by the DES and the Bernard Van Leer Foundation of Holland, since 1974 the DES is the sole funder of the project. The Rutland Street

Table 6
Grant Applications and Expenditure Approved by Sub-Measure of the EOCP, 2000 - 31st August 2002

	No. of Grants Approved	Expenditure Approved €
Staffing Grants to Community-Based Providers	604	70,343,271
Capital Grants to Community-Based Providers	339	42,852,844
Capital Grants to Self-Employed / Private Providers	453	17,128,248
Grants in Respect of Quality Improvement Measures	137	22,600,190
Total	1,533	152,924,553

Source: ADM, unpublished Monitoring and Impact Statistics

Project is now well established and generally well regarded as a positive intervention in meeting the needs of the participating children. This is backed up by evaluations of the Project (see Kellaghan, T. 1977, Kellaghan, T. & Greaney, B. J., 1992). In 2001, the Project employed 6 teachers, 10 non-teaching staff and had 91 children enrolled.

Early Start

The DES introduced the Early Start Programme on a pilot basis in 1994. Its overall aim is to expose children aged 3 and 4 years from disadvantaged areas to a positive pre-school environment to improve their overall development and long-term educational experience and performance. Initially, 8 schools in disadvantaged areas in Cork, Limerick and Dublin were selected and Early Start units were established in vacant classrooms in primary schools. Since 1995, the programme has been expanded and now includes 40 centres, including 16 full and 24 half units. A full unit has two classes of 15 children each morning between 9.00 a.m. and 11.30 a.m., and two classes again in the afternoon from 12 noon to 2.30 p.m.

The educational ethos underlying Early Start is based on a combination of care and education. The programme is informed by the Rutland Street Project and the curricular guidelines for Early Start drew heavily on this earlier intervention (see 2.3.2 below). Early Start aims to provide a programme of structured play that will develop the language, cognitive, personal and social development of the child. This is achieved through intensive, high quality interaction with staff. Each full unit is staffed by two qualified primary school teachers and two trained childcare workers. Therefore, a child to adult ratio of 15:2 applies, with 56 teachers and 56 childcare workers currently employed nationally. Parents may also be involved on a voluntary basis and the programme seeks to devise strategies that actively engage parents in their child's education and development.

Concerns about the displacement of pre-existing local community-based provision and the appropriateness of using primary school teachers in the pre-school setting were raised in relation to Early Start. However, the conclusions of the evaluation of the first three years of Early Start were mixed (Educational Research Centre, 1998). According to this evaluation, positive outcomes include the integration of Early Start into the participating schools and parental satisfaction with and involvement in the programme. However, standardised tests showed no marked increase in the cognitive or scholastic development. This runs contrary to the evaluation of infant teachers who reported that Early Start participants were more developed than non-Early Start children in terms of their cognitive and language skills and their readiness for participation in a classroom setting.

Pre-Schools for Traveller Children

Forty-eight Pre-Schools for Traveller Children are grant-aided by the DES. Their objectives include the provision of educational experiences through play and active learning, to develop the children's cognitive, language and social skills, to prepare children for entry to primary school and to provide a foundation for further learning. These are usually established by voluntary bodies or Traveller support groups with the DES providing 98% of teaching and transport costs plus an annual grant for equipment and materials. Although part funded by the DES, these pre-schools are not considered to be part of the primary school system (unlike Early Start). They are rarely staffed by fully-trained primary teachers and do not come under the auspices of a primary school Board of Management, but they avail of a Visiting Teacher scheme whereby a trained teacher visits the pre-school and then the parents, usually the mother, of each child. An evaluation of the Pre-Schools for Traveller Children has recently been carried out by the Research Unit of the DES and the final report is currently being prepared.

Supported Provision in Further Education Centres

The DES provides for childcare in a number of their training programmes for early school leavers and adult learners, including Youthreach, Vocational Training Opportunities Scheme (VTOS) and Senior Traveller Training Centres. In the academic year 2000/2001, 1,672 childcare places were supported under these programmes in a total of 270 crèches. These crèches include Vocational Education Committee's own crèche facilities, as well as places purchased in community and commercial crèches. Where places on existing community or commercial crèches are purchased a maximum of €63.49 is available per week per child for full time care or on a pro rata basis for part time provision.

Primary School Provision

A number of programmes designed to combat educational disadvantage now operate in primary schools. Although not targeted specifically at early education, infant classes in primary schools benefit from their operation. However, disaggregated statistics on these programmes that would allow for the identification of the proportion of infant pupils or classes benefiting from them, or the amount or proportion of expenditure being directed at these classes and pupils is not available. Nonetheless, different schemes are known to place different emphases on either junior or senior classes. On the basis of this we can say that the two main schemes from which infant classes undoubtedly benefit are Breaking the Cycle and Giving Children an Even Break.

Breaking the Cycle was introduced as a five-year pilot programme in 1996 in schools designated as disadvantaged. The scheme provided for extra staffing, funding, in-career development and a pupil teacher ratio of 15:1. Thirty-two urban schools accounting for 5,652 pupils and 120 rural schools with 6,052 pupils were catered for under this programme. The pilot phase ended in June 2001 and an evaluation of the programme is underway.

Giving Children an Even Break was launched by the DES in 2001. Based on research carried out by the ERC, schools were rank ordered according to their concentration of disadvantaged pupils. Whether or not pupils were disadvantaged was determined on using economic and social criteria associated with educational disadvantage. Using this rank ordering of schools, Giving Children an Even Break targets the schools with the highest concentrations of disadvantaged pupils. Additional resources are made available to schools according to the degree of disadvantage as illustrated by their rank position. In urban areas, where the larger concentrations of disadvantaged pupils were located, these resources resulted in a pupil teacher ratio of no more than 20 to one from junior infants to second class, as well as funding towards additional in-school and out-of-school activities. In rural areas, a teacher / coordinator was appointed to work with clusters of 4 to five schools with high levels of at risk pupils.

Details of these two programmes and other primary school initiatives to combat educational disadvantage are contained in Annex 4.

1.2.9 Institutional Supports for Early Childhood Care and Education

In outlining the main types of early childhood education and care provision above, a number of the key actors have already been identified. These include the DES, the DJELR and the DHC. In addition to these key government departments, other agencies, both statutory and voluntary, play a central role in the development, provision and regulation of early childhood care and education. This section will identify the main actors involved and briefly outline their areas of responsibility.

Department of Education and Science (DES)

This Department provides for all formal primary education. As such, they are the main provider for formal early education as the vast majority of children aged 4 to 6 years attend primary school. In addition the DES also funds a number of pre-school education programmes targeted at children from disadvantaged backgrounds and children with special learning needs. This is achieved through a number of targeted initiatives outlined above. While providing for primary education for all children, this focus on vulnerable groups is also evident in the various supports and programmes operated within the primary schools that benefit infant classes to varying degrees. The objective of these is to combat educational disadvantage from an early age by addressing the needs of those most at risk of educational disadvantage.

A number of additional structures exist that, while not focussed exclusively on early education, consider this area in their work, specifically in respect of children experiencing or at risk of educational disadvantage. The *Social Inclusion Unit* within the DES focuses on the National Anti-Poverty Strategy (NAPS) and, in particular, in co-ordinating the Department's input into the NAPS and monitoring progress towards the achievement of the targets set in relation to educational disadvantage. Clearly, the targeted early education programmes and supports of the DES are considered by this Unit. The *Educational Disadvantage Committee* was established in 2002 to advise the Minister for Education and Science on policies and strategies to identify and address educational disadvantage at all levels. As its remit ranges from 'cradle to grave', early childhood education may be considered within this context of lifelong learning. In order to facilitate participation by a wide range of education partners as well as bodies and agencies active in tackling social exclusion, the *Forum to Address Educational Disadvantage* was also established to inform the work of the Educational Disadvantage Committee.

The Education Act 1998 makes provision for the establishment by regulation of bodies to provide educational services. One such body is the *National Council for Special Education*, which it is anticipated will be put on a legislative footing under forthcoming disabilities legislation. The primary functions of the National Council for Special Education will be

☐ To carry out research and provide expert advice to the Minister for Education and Science in relation to special education issues.

☐ To provide a range of services at local and national level, which will involve ensuring that individual needs are identified and met,

☐ To co-ordinate special needs provision at local and national level.

☐ To put in place an independent appeals mechanism.

It is intended to introduce primary legislation governing the role and duties of the Council in due course. The Council will be appointed by the Minister for Education and Science from among persons who have an interest in or knowledge relating to the education of students with disabilities.

The Council will employ a significant number of Special Needs Organisers (SNOs). Their role will be to act as a single point of contact in respect of a student with special needs with the clear and specific objective of delivering for that student those educational services to which he/she is entitled. The SNO will have a role regarding individual education plans for students with special needs. The SNO will be required to engage in appropriate advance planning in consultation with local schools with a view to meeting the needs of special needs students in his/her area.

In 1999 a review focusing on the operations, systems and staffing of the DES was undertaken. On foot of the recommendations of this report, known as the Cromien Report, a programme of structural reform has been undertaken by the DES. One important aspect of this is the decision by the government to create a regional office structure. This is based on the conclusion that a significant element in the structural difficulties experienced by the Department is that the first point of contact for the majority of some 4,000 primary and second level schools, as well as parents and others seeking information in relation to the vast array of issues arising in education, is the DES itself. A network of 10 *Regional Offices* will be established. These will provide a focal point for schools, parents, teachers and others. The Regional Offices will also have a representative role on local fora such as County Development Boards. Each regional office will have a Head of Office and a small staff. The role of the regional offices will encompass:

☐ acting as a first point of contact for schools, agencies, voluntary organisations and communities with the Department,

☐ information gathering and dissemination,

☐ supporting locally based initiatives to combat disadvantage and provide for special needs,

☐ representing of the Department on local structures, including Drugs Task Forces

☐ co-ordinating across education related services locally (DES Press Release, 15th April 2001).

Department of Justice, Equality and Law Reform (DJELR)

This Department was responsible for convening the Partnership 2000 Expert Working Group on Childcare and the production of its report. The DJELR is now responsible for the implementation of the National Childcare Strategy. It is important to remember here that this strategy covers a wide range of childcare provision, but this does not include primary or special schools, which come under the remit of the DES, or residential centres, which are the remit of the DHC. In 2001, all childcare provision previously under the auspices of other Government Departments was consolidated under the remit of the DJELR.

The DJELR has established a *Childcare Directorate* within its Equality Division. The overall function of this Directorate is to deliver on the Department's childcare commitments. These include:

☐ the provision of grant aid to private and not-for-profit childcare providers to establish and improve childcare facilities;

☐ to support quality improvement in the childcare sector;

☐ to develop new funding initiatives in response to emerging training needs;

☐ to progress and consolidate the County/City Childcare Committees (see below);

☐ to co-ordinate childcare funding policies and programmes at national level.

Much of the work of the Directorate, and particularly that in respect of providing grant aid and the improvement of quality, is achieved under the EOCP described in section 1.2.6 above. Its remaining aims are pursued through various structures in which the Department has a lead or significant role. These structures are included under the provisions of the National Childcare Strategy and include those outlined below.

Chaired by the DJELR, the *Inter-Departmental and Inter-Agency Synergies Group* is comprised of representatives of the various Government Departments and State Agencies with an interest in childcare. Initially, the primary functions of this group were to co-ordinate childcare measures and avoid duplication of effort. However, since the consolidation of childcare provision under the DJELR, this group has become dormant and now needs to revisit its terms of reference. It is intended to reactivate this group in the later half of 2002.

The National Co-ordinating Childcare Committee (NCCC) was established to oversee the co-ordinated development of an integrated childcare infrastructure. It is made up of representatives of the statutory and non-statutory sectors, the social partners and the nine National Voluntary Childcare Organisations (NVCO).[12] The NCCC advises the Minister for Justice, Equality and Law Reform on childcare matters, has a role in the appraisal of grant applications under the EOCP and also provides support to the County/City Childcare Committees (see below). The NCCC is currently pursuing a number of key themes and sub-groups have been developed to undertake this work.

The Certifying Bodies Sub-Group has developed a draft framework to address qualification, accreditation and certification issues (Department of Justice, Equality and Law Reform, 2002). This sub-group has developed a core standard for the occupational role of Childcare Supervisor. This has informed the development of training modules accredited by the Further Educational and Training Awards Council (FETAC) and is currently in pilot phase. In addition, this sub-group is preparing a framework on qualifications in the childcare sector, detailed in section 2.2.1.

The Advisory Group to the NCCC is concerned with the issues of equality and diversity. This sub-group is chaired by a member of the NCCC and is comprised of external experts. The sub-group has commissioned the design of guidelines on these issues for use by childcare providers and parents of children using childcare. When finalised, these will be widely disseminated and, in particular, promoted through the County/City Childcare Committees (see below). It is anticipated that these guidelines will be completed in 2002.

The Working Group on School Age Childcare is an ad hoc group established to examine existing provision for school age children outside of school hours. This group will look at practice in other jurisdictions, develop guidelines for quality in services for school age children and make proposals on provision for school age children on a year round basis. Chaired by the DJELR, it is anticipated that this sub-group will report to the NCCC by the end of 2002.

The National Childcare Strategy proposed the establishment of *County/City Childcare Committees* to promote, develop and support quality childcare at the local level. Thirty-three such Committees have now been established. It is through the County/City Childcare Committees that much of the infrastructure necessary to support childcare will be developed and delivered at local level. Each Committee was required to draw up a five year Strategic Plan to address the particular childcare needs of their county. These contain a detailed action plan for the year 2002 and associated costs. Guidelines were prepared to assist the Committees in developing these plans which were first appraised by ADM. These appraisals were then considered by the Programme Appraisal Committee in the DJELR. All of the County Strategic Plans have now been appraised and approved for funding.

The County/City Childcare Committees are comprised of representatives from a wide range of organisations. Initially chaired by a member of the Health Boards, due to their local structure, they typically include representatives of the childcare providers, parents, County Development Boards, County Enterprise Board, Vocational Education Committees (VECs), FÁS, Local Development

---

12 The members of the NVCO are Barnardos, IPPA - the Early Childhood Organisation, NCNA, An Comhchoiste Reamhscolaíochta, Children in Hospital Ireland, St. Nicholas Montessori Society, Steiner Waldorf Early Childhood Organisation, ISPCC and Childminding Ireland.

Partnership Companies, at least one of the seven National Voluntary Childcare Organisations as well as local community organisations, farming organisations and trade unions. Following their initial establishment, the County Committees will employ a small number of core staff to deliver the County Childcare Plan.

The Guiding Principles of the County Committees mirror those of the National Childcare Strategy. These are the needs and rights of children, equal opportunities and equality of access and participation, diversity, partnership and quality. In addition, a number of key objectives were also identified for all County Committees, which must be reflected in their Strategic Plans. These are set out in the 'County/City Childcare Committee Handbook' as follows:

☐ to maintain and build the local capacity to establish and sustain childcare places/services across all categories of childcare providers/services;

☐ to promote initiatives aimed at the support and inclusion of childminders;

☐ to develop and promote quality standards and targets for the county;

☐ to enhance and develop co-ordination at all levels;

☐ to enhance and develop information sharing and learning systems; and

☐ to lever/attract resources from local and national sources to implement specific actions.

County Childcare Action Plans are only now beginning to be implemented. Each Committee is required to monitor and evaluate its activity and progress towards the goals and targets it has set itself. It will be some time before an overall sense of the success or otherwise of the Committees and Plans will be available.

Department of Health and Children (DHC)

Traditionally, the childcare remit of the DHC was children at risk of neglect or abuse, essentially making their focus one of child protection and welfare rather than care. As part of this function the DHC, through the Health Boards, funds places in community-based childcare facilities primarily as a means of alleviating family stress. The DHC subsequently introduced the Child Care (Pre-School Services) Regulations, 1996 and Child Care (Pre-School Services) (Amendment) Regulations, 1997 (see 2.1.1 below). The Regulations *inter alia* place a statutory duty on Health Boards to secure the health, safety and welfare and promote the development of pre-school children attending pre-school services. This is achieved through inspectors attached to the 10 regional Health Boards.

In 2001, an additional €1.5 million was made available to the Department of Health and Children to introduce a voluntary notification and support system aimed at childminder's looking after three or fewer children in their own home. These are not currently required to notify the Health Boards of their activity or to be inspected under the Child Care (Pre-School Services) Regulations, 1996 (see 2.1.1 below). This funding is to be used towards the cost of employing a childminder's advisory officer in each community care area (sub-divisions of the health board areas) to work specifically with such childminders. Some health boards have already recruited advisory officers, some are currently in the recruitment process. Others have devolved the funding to the relevant County Childcare Committee who will recruit the advisory officer.

This Department also now has responsibility for the National Children's Office (NCO), which in turn has responsibility for the implementation of the National Children's Strategy (see 1.2.6 above). This has brought into being a number of structures through which the National Children's Strategy will be implemented. While not specifically concerned with early education, these structures provide opportunities for all areas of children's needs to be highlighted and discussed. In particular, the wide membership of the *National Children's Advisory Council*, including representatives of the

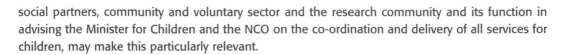
social partners, community and voluntary sector and the research community and its function in advising the Minister for Children and the NCO on the co-ordination and delivery of all services for children, may make this particularly relevant.

The National Children's Office

Reporting to the DHC, the NCO is a cross-departmental office the role of which is to lead and oversee the implementation of the National Children's Strategy (see 1.2.6 above). Individual departments retain responsibility for implementing various aspects of the Strategy and the NCO co-ordinates and monitors their progress in this regard. In addition, the NCO progresses actions under the 3 National Goals of the Strategy in regard to certain key policy areas identified by the Cabinet Sub-Committee as priorities and which require cross-departmental action. The Strategy also provides for a number of new structures through which the National Children's Strategy will be implemented. While not specifically concerned with early education, these structures provide opportunities for all areas of children's needs to be highlighted and discussed. In particular, the wide membership of the *National Children's Advisory Council,* including representatives of the social partners, community and voluntary sector, children and the research community and its function in advising the Minister for Children and the NCO on the co-ordination and delivery of all services for children, may make this particularly relevant.

The Department of Social and Family Affairs (DSFA)[13]

The main supports for children provided by the DSCFA are in the form of various income maintenance payments. The most substantial and relevant of these is Child Benefit. This is a universal payment made in respect of all children aged 16 years or under. Child Benefit is also paid in respect of 16, 17 or 18 years who is in full-time education and attending a FÁS YOUTHREACH course, or is physically or mentally disabled and dependant on their parents / guardians. Although not tied specifically to childcare, in recent years Child Benefit has become the main way in which the State supports parents in meeting the costs of childcare. The main advantage of this approach is seen to be the neutral stance that this allows with regard to labour force status as Child Benefit is paid in respect of all children irrespective of whether their parents work and engage paid childcare or remain at home to care for their children. Child Benefit therefore can be seen either as compensating parents to some extent for the loss of one income should either parent choose to remain in the home to take care of their children, or as being a contribution towards the cost of paid childcare outside the home. Further details on this and other relevant DSFA payments are included in section 2.5.5 below.

Although not specifically concerned with early childhood education and care, the Pilot Family Services Projects of the DSCFA are relevant here. Located in local offices of the Department in Waterford, Cork, Limerick, Mullingar and Finglas in Dublin, these projects adopt a one-stop shop approach with the aim of providing improved access to information for families through the Social Welfare Local Offices. In addition to providing support to families under stress, the service has a particular emphasis on the local support services available for families and provides basic information on local childcare services among a range of other topics. The Government has provided €15.2 million in the National Development Plan for the progressive expansion of the successful elements of the pilot programme.

The Department of Enterprise, Trade and Employment (DETE)

Early education and childcare arises as a concern of the DETE primarily in the context of supporting labour market access by people experiencing social and economic exclusion. In line with this, its main provisions are attached to Community Employment (CE), Ireland's main active labour market

---

[13] Prior to the general election in May 2002, this department's title was the Department of Social, Community and Family Affairs.

programme. Support for early childhood education and care under this programme takes two forms: the allocation of a childcare allowance to participants on CE programmes for the care of their children, and the temporary employment of CE participants as workers in childcare facilities. It is estimated that over 300 childcare facilities are employing staff via CE and this issue is returned to in section 2.2.1 below.

In addition, the DETE provides staffing grants through the City and County Enterprise Boards (CEBs). Established under the NDP, the overall role of the CEBs is to develop indigenous potential and stimulate economic activity at local level, primarily through the provision of financial and technical assistance, as well as ongoing non-financial enterprise supports. The employment grants made available through the CEBs provide a maximum of €6,350 per new employee. In 2001, approximately €2.3 million was approved for employment grants related to childcare services. It is estimated that this will have the potential to support some 450 full-time and 119 part-time jobs.

IDA Ireland, the state body with responsibility for the development of Irish industry through innovation and investment, recently launched a project to develop high quality childcare services for employees in enterprises in 6 of its Business Parks. Tenders were invited from suitable childcare providers for the design, construction, financing and operation of these services.

Under the current national agreement, the *Programme for Prosperity and Fairness* (Government of Ireland, 1999d) the government and the social partners agreed that a *National Framework Committee for Family-Friendly Policies* should be established to support family-friendly policies at the level of the enterprise. The DETE is responsible for the chairing and providing a secretariat to this Committee with, where appropriate, additional support from the DJELR. Comprised of representatives of the Irish Business Employers Confederation (IBEC), public sector employers and ICTU, the Committee is supported by a specific budget within the Human Resources Development Operational Programme of the NDP. The work of this Committee has obvious relevance for early childhood education and care as its considerations cover a range of ways in which family and working life can be reconciled including job-sharing, work sharing, part-time work, flexitime, flexi-place / teleworking and term-time working. Also, the Committee will consider the provisions within existing legislation on Maternity Leave, Adoptive Leave, Parental Leave and Force Majeure Leave (see section 2.4.2 below) and how these are implemented at local or enterprise level.

Department of the Environment and Local Government (DELG)

The principal involvement of the DELG in the early childhood education and care is through the planning authorities, County and City Development Boards (CDBs) and the provision of finance through the Local Authorities for childcare facilities. In 2001, the DELG launched its publication *Childcare Facilities: Guidelines for Planning Authorities* (DELG, 2001). These Guidelines promote the allocation of space for one childcare facility to every 75 dwellings built in new housing developments, with the number of places being determined by the location of existing provision and the emerging demographic profile of the area. The Guidelines also advise planning authorities on suitable sites for childcare facilities and assessment criteria for childcare sites. These Guidelines clearly highlight the need for the planning of childcare facilities to be part of broader County, City and Local Area Development Plans.

Reflecting this planning priority, there is provision made for a community facility in the case of all new Local Authority housing schemes. In many cases this either comprises or contains a childcare facility. This is usually funded by the DELG as part of the capital costs of the building project and the ongoing management and operational costs of such facilities is entirely a matter for the Local Authorities.

In the case of existing Local Authority estates, €6.35 million was made available in 2001 to enable Local Authorities to meet capital costs of providing childcare facilities in Local Authority housing estates and other social housing projects. Eleven projects have been approved for funding in principle under this scheme. These will provide up to 370 additional childcare places. The implementation of the programme, including planning and execution of works, is the responsibility of the relevant Local Authorities. In large remedial projects undertaken in public housing estates, part of the project is allocated to the local community for joint use and again, this is often used for the provision of childcare services.

Under the auspices of the DELG, County/City Development Boards (CDBs) have been established in each of the 29 county councils, and in each of the 5 major cities (Dublin Corporation, Cork Corporation, Limerick Corporation, Galway Corporation and Waterford Corporation). The CDBs comprise representatives of local government, local development bodies, State agencies and the social partners operating locally and have now designed a County/City Strategy for Economic, Social and Cultural Development for their area. This will be the template guiding all public services and local development activities locally, in effect bringing more coherence to delivery of services locally. Each of these Strategies must contain a statement on the provision of childcare and it is envisaged that the CDBs will work with the County/City Childcare Committees (see above) in addressing childcare needs.

Department of Community, Rural and Gaeltacht Affairs (DCRGA)

The DCRGA has responsibility for the Local Development Social Inclusion Programme of the NDP under which Local Area-Based Partnerships and a number of community groups have supported innovative early education and childcare projects. In addition, this Department also has responsibility for two specific development programmes: Revitalising Areas by Planning, Investment and Development (RAPID), which is targeted at disadvantaged urban areas, and Ceantair Laga Ard-Riachanais (CLAR) which focuses on disadvantaged rural areas. Applications for funding under these programmes often include childcare or early education elements. These are subsequently directed to the EOCP if relating to childcare and to the DES if they are educational in focus. Alternatively, childcare projects located in these designated areas may apply directly for funding under the EOCP and schools may apply to the DES for inclusion under their various programmes targeted at combating educational disadvantage.

Chapter 2

POLICY APPROACHES

This section looks at the main policy approaches taken in Ireland to key areas of early childhood education and care. These key areas are regulation, staffing, programme content and implementation, family engagement and support and funding.

2.1 REGULATIONS

2.1.1 Regulating Childcare Provision

Under Part VII of the Child Care Act 1991 the regional Health Boards are given responsibility for the regulation of pre-school provision. Here, 'pre-school service' means any pre-school, play group, day nursery, créche, day-care or other similar service outside of primary schools, which caters for children under the age of 6 years. The Child Care (Pre-School Services) Regulations, 1996 and Child Care (Pre-School Services) (Amendment) Regulations, 1997 give effect to this part of the Child Care Act, 1991. For ease of reading, these regulations are hereafter referred to as the Pre-School Services Regulations.

These Pre-School Services Regulations were drawn up by the DHC in consultation with relevant groups and cover the following main areas:

☐ development of the child (in terms of development and expression through the use of appropriate materials and equipment);

☐ health, safety and welfare of the child;

☐ suitability of premises and facilities;

☐ adult to child ratios;

☐ child to space ratios;

☐ notification, record keeping and provision of information;

☐ notification procedures;

☐ inspection;

☐ insurance;

☐ annual fees.

On notification of the provision of services, or the intention to supply pre-school services, it is considered good practice that the first inspection occurs within 3 months of receipt of the notification and thereafter on an annual basis, but this is highly dependent on the availability of staff and the number of notifications received. In addition, the Health Boards also provide an advisory service to prospective childcare providers on meeting Pre-School Services Regulations as well as advising current providers on how to address deficiencies in their services. Where there are concerns about deficiencies in a service the Health Board arranges more frequent follow up advice visits or inspections as necessary.

Inspectors of childcare facilities come mainly from a public health nursing (PHN) or an environmental health officer background. There is no specific training required for the role of inspector. In individual Health Boards training may be available on relevant issues such as child protection, fire safety, Information Technology, legal issues etc. A number of the inspectors from PHN backgrounds have undertaken a course - Professional Development in Early Childhood Care and Education - provided by the Dublin Institute of Technology (DIT). In the early days of implementing Pre-School Services Regulations, the pre-school officers would have had informal information sharing networks within and across Health Boards. Some of these have since become more formalised.

As not all providers are required to notify the Health Boards, not all childcare provision is covered by Pre-School Services Regulations. Only childcare providers caring for three or more children (excluding their own offspring, offspring of their partner/spouse, other relatives or three children from the same family) are required to notify the Health Boards. While it is believed that Pre-School Services Regulations therefore apply to a large number of childminders caring for children in their (the minder's) home, few of these notify the Health Boards. Childminders looking after three or fewer children in their own home are currently not required to notify the Health Board or be inspected under Pre-School Services Regulations. In attempting to improve the rate of voluntary notification by such childminders, €1.5m was made available to the DHC in 2001 to introduce a voluntary notification and support system.

It should also be noted that these Regulations do not apply to Early Start centres as these are regulated as part of the primary school system. They do, however, apply to Pre-Schools for Traveller Children funded by the DES.

The Explanatory Notes that accompany Pre-School Services Regulations include a proposal to monitor their implementation over three years with a review then taking place with a view to further enhancing pre-school service provision. A review of Pre-School Services Regulations is currently underway and a Review Group has been established comprising representatives of the DHC, the Health Boards and pre-school inspectors, other relevant Government Departments including the DES, DJELR and the DELG, the NCO, the NVCOs, parents representative, ADM and a representative of the CECDE. A public call for submissions was placed in the national and local press in 2002. Health Boards and County Childcare Committees were also invited to make submissions. One hundred and ten submissions were received and are currently being analysed.

The introduction of these Regulations marked a significant development in pre-school services in Ireland. Prior to this, childcare provision was unregulated by the State beyond general regulations relating to health and safety and food safety, if the relevant authorities were aware of the existence or the service of the providers voluntarily notified them. In addition, while not enforceable, many of the umbrella organisations for childcare providers, such as IPPA - the Early Childhood Organisation, the NCNA, An Comhchoiste Reamhscoliochta and the Montessori organisations operated codes of best practice and regulations that providers subscribed to on a voluntary basis.

Anecdotal evidence suggests that while the Pre-School Services Regulations provide for a minimum standard, their introduction and implementation have contributed significantly to the quality of pre-school services. While of importance in the respect that they represent a substantial move forwards and in that they are relatively detailed, the Pre-School Services Regulations are limited in their scope and do not cover many of the less tangible aspects of care, including staff qualifications and training, curriculum and methodology.[14] The proposed approach to these issues is outlined elsewhere in the relevant sections of this report. The Expert Working Group on Childcare (Government of Ireland, 1999b) expressed their concern that Pre-School Services Regulations were not uniformly applied across the Health Boards and that the inspectors were insufficiently trained for this role. This conflict between regulation and quality is an ongoing concern for many providers. Despite this, it is reassuring that almost all (96%) of the facilities included in the National Childcare Census had notified the Health Board of their activities (ADM, forthcoming 2002). Almost 900 facilities identified that they would incur costs in meeting Pre-School Services Regulations, with an estimated required total expenditure of €11.6 million (at 1999 prices). Undoubtedly, many of these facilities are benefiting from grants under the EOCP in supporting their efforts to meet the required standards.

2.1.2 Regulating Primary Education

In addition to the provisions of the Education Act 1998 and the Education (Welfare) Act 2000, primary schools must also comply with 'Rules for National Schools' which cover all aspects of a school's functioning including, among others, the patronage and management of schools, building, improvement and furnishings, repair, heating, cleaning and painting, the school year, timetable, hours, vacations, enrolment, attendance, books, fees, religious and secular instruction, and the qualifications of teachers. These rules were originally published in 1965 and have been amended over the years by Departmental Circular Letters issued to all schools. They are currently under review with a view to their updating and consolidation. In addition, schools must also comply with section 7 of the Equal Status Act, 2000 and existing health and safety legislation.

The evaluation of primary schools falls to the Inspectorate of the Department of Education and Science. The Inspectorate, which was put on a statutory basis by the Education Act, 1998, has the core tasks of inspecting and evaluating the quality of schooling, advising on educational policy, and supporting teachers and school management.

Generally, Inspectors are trained primary or post-primary teachers. Training for the role of Inspector is provided via a formal training programme undertaken within the DES. This mainly involves 'shadowing' an inspector for a period of time and attending training sessions given by outside agencies on specific issues.

Primary schools, and the Early Start units within these, are inspected on a cyclical basis. A report is furnished on each school approximately every 6 years, following a detailed inspection. This inspection examines all aspects of teaching, learning and assessment, as well as school planning, the work of the Board of Management, and the school's accommodation and resources. Inspectors also become familiar with the ongoing work of the school through frequent incidental visits. The work of individual teachers is also inspected, with much of this work relating to the evaluation and support of probationary teachers. In addition, the Evaluation Support and Research Unit of the Inspectorate manages evaluations of key aspects of educational provision in schools through a series of programme or thematic evaluations. For example, an evaluation of 25 Pre-Schools for Traveller Children was carried out in 2001 with individual school reports being furnished to the pre-schools management and with a consolidated report now being finalised by the Evaluation Support and Research Unit. The Inspectorate also has wide linkages with all relevant sections throughout

---

[14] It is noteworthy that teachers, Early Start childcare assistance and childcare workers require Garda (police) clearance to take up employment. This is in contrast to workers in the area of child welfare where Garda clearance in required.

the DES and with external bodies such as the National Council for Curriculum and Assessment (NCCA), the ERC, the NEPS and the Primary Curriculum Support Service. The Inspectorate maintains contacts with international organisations and North/South Bodies in relation to development on regulations and best practice.

Another important regulatory influence on primary education in Ireland is the recently commenced Education (Welfare) Act, 2000. This Act provides a comprehensive new framework for promoting regular school attendance and tackling the problems of absenteeism and early school leaving. A National Educational Welfare Board has been established to develop, co-ordinate and implement school attendance policy so as to ensure that every child in the State attends a recognised school or otherwise receives an appropriate education. In this regard, the Board is currently appointing Education Welfare Officers to work in close co-operation with schools, teachers, parents and community/voluntary bodies. The Board will also maintain a register of children receiving education outside the recognised school structure and will assess the adequacy of such education on an ongoing basis.

2.2 STAFFING

Reflecting the different stages of development of the childcare and formal education sectors in Ireland, different staff issues arise.

2.2.1 Staffing Issues in the Childcare Sector

A number of issues of concern are raised in the relevant policy documents in respect of childcare staff. Among these is the low status and rates of pay attached to positions in childcare, reflecting an almost vocational expectation of those working in this sector. In 1999, it was estimated that, at the higher end of the scale, a junior day nursery teacher in a public sector nursery earned between €12,700 and €17,000 per annum. Senior day nursery teachers earned between €15,800 and €24,000 per annum. At the other end of the scale, a survey of NCNA members revealed that junior staff earned approximately €8,900 per annum and senior staff roughly €11,900. (Government of Ireland, 1999b)

In the current economic climate, which has prompted an increased demand for childcare at the same time as providing childcare workers with more attractive alternative employment opportunities, the availability and retention of staff are central concerns. In particular, the lack of suitably qualified staff and the shortage of accessible accredited training for staff are of ongoing concern. Linked to these issues is the lack of clearly defined occupational profiles and roles for those involved in providing childcare services.

In relation to the childcare sector it is important to contextualise the staffing issues that arise. In particular it should be borne in mind that until recently there was little State involvement in this sector, which was essentially unco-ordinated and unregulated to any significant extent. This manifested itself in the ad hoc development of training for childcare workers, as well as the existence of a large number of 'qualification poor, experience rich' workers. What training existed was largely paid for by individuals, was of variable quality and, in many cases, uncertified. However, it is important to note the range that existed with, for example, Montessori teachers trained to international standards on the one hand and, on the other, childcare workers with no or only extra-mural qualifications in areas such as child development. Accredited childcare training has existed for some time, however. For example, a nationally accredited training course for those working in the early years sector has been running at DIT since 1977. Originally a national certificate course, this has developed and is now offered at degree level. New accredited courses are also currently being developed by third level colleges, including Carlow Institute of Technology and University

College Cork. In addition, while not considered part of the third level system, Post-Leaving Certificate courses in childcare have been developed by FETAC.

The National Childcare Strategy recommended the development of a national qualifications framework. Work on this has been pursued by the Certifying Bodies Sub-Group of the NCCC (see 1.2.9 above). This new *Model Framework for Education, Training and Professional Development in the Early Childhood Care and Education Sector* is based on a process of consultation with childcare providers and training and accreditation providers. It establishes the core values of the childcare and early education sector, including recognition of the value of childhood in its own right, the rights of children who are active agents in their own development and the role of professional development as a central component of good practice. It puts forward 6 key areas of skill and knowledge necessary in childcare. These are Child Development, Education and Play, Social Environment, Health, Hygiene, Nutrition and Safety, Personal Professional Development and Communication, Management and Administration. Five levels of the practitioner occupation profile are presented – Basic, Intermediate, Experienced, Advanced and Expert – along with the intellectual skills and attributes, the processes in which competence should be achieved and the level of accountability relevant to each of these levels. The depth of knowledge as well as the number of hours of supervised practice is clearly set out across the 6 key areas of skill and knowledge. The Framework also addresses the issues of progression through a system of accredited learning, Accredited Prior learning (APL), flexible and work-based learning, as well as the relationship with the various qualification and accreditation structures. This framework was launched in September 2002.

Of importance here is the establishment under the Qualifications (Education and Training) Act, 1999 of the National Qualifications Authority of Ireland (NQAI), which came into being in 2000. The NQAI has been charged with the creation of a national qualification framework, including a framework for the childcare sector. Within this, a clear role is established for sectoral bodies in informing the work of the NQAI and the two principal accrediting bodies – the Higher Educational and Training Awards Council (HETEC) and the Further Education and Training Awards Council (FETAC). The Model Framework outlined above has been submitted to the NQAI and will represent the main submission of the childcare sector to this body.

A related issue here is the reliance on staff employed under the CE Programme. As indicated above, this is Ireland's principal active labour market programme. This programme provides temporary opportunities for persons unemployed for a minimum of 12 months on the Live Register and having being in receipt of any of a number of social welfare payments. Participants on the programme work for an average of 19.5 hours per week. Under the programme, public sector and voluntary organisations are grant-aided by FÁS to carry out worthwhile work that they could not otherwise undertake. Suitable projects must show that they are responding to a clearly identified community need that also develops the work skills of participants, thereby enhancing their prospects of obtaining a mainstream job.

Community and voluntary service providers in disadvantaged areas are the largest group of CE project sponsors. Within this, early education and care services are common with over 300 such services currently participating in the programme. Based on an audit of CE supported services in 2001, FÁS reports that funding was approved under CE for approximately 2,000 childcare workers at a cost of roughly €22 million. The programme has provided many services with much needed staff. However, the reliance of these services on CE staff has distinct disadvantages. These include the temporary nature of the programme, by which the majority of participants may remain on the programme for one year only.[15] Many of the care and education services involved do not have the

---

[15] Following the restructuring of CE in 2001 certain programme participants aged over 35 and 50 years who experience ongoing difficulties in gaining employment may apply to remain on CE schemes for up to three years.

resources to retain individual staff members after this time and move on to recruit new CE workers. This has implications not only for the CE participant in question, but also for the continuity of care for children and works to prevent the facilities from building up their complement of experienced staff. In addition, although CE allows for formal training to be undertaken by participants, the limited duration of participation allows for only short-term participation on training courses. In the wider context, CE has inadvertently but almost undoubtedly contributed to maintaining low salaries within the early childcare and education sector as participants are paid an allowance by FÁS that is commensurate with their previous welfare payments but not in line with salaries.

The formalising and mainstreaming of training, the clear articulation of professional roles and career paths as well as the increasing demand for high quality childcare services are all contributing to the professionalisation of the childcare sector, in centre-based provision at least. Undoubtedly, this will improve both the external perception of, and self-esteem among childcare staff. However, issues remain. Primary among these are the development and adherence to appropriate salary scales and other terms of employment, the untrained nature of the majority of childminding services provided in the home and the gender imbalance among childcare staff that sees almost all staff being women.

2.2.2 Staffing Issues in Primary Education

In contrast to the childcare sector, primary school teachers are trained and qualified through State supported and approved training courses. Such has been the case for over 100 years. In 1974, what had been a two-year course was extended to a three years and 1977 saw the conferral of degrees (Bachelor of Education, B.Ed) on students. These degree courses are now offered by five third level colleges and are conferred by the University of Limerick, Dublin City University and Trinity College.

Although differences exist in the number of hours attributed to each element, all of the B.Ed courses involve a mixture of time spent in lectures or tutorials and time spent on teaching practice in primary schools. Education, as a subject, is the main component of all courses, with components on subjects such as the history of education, philosophies of education and educational psychology, along with a religious studies element. In some cases, a core course on early education is taught with the option of further electives in this area. The colleges differ in their requirements in relation to additional academic subjects. It is important to recognise here that primary school teachers are required to be able to teach at all levels in primary school from junior infants to senior classes. From October 2002, the starting point on the primary teacher's pay scale will be €23,096. The highest point on the scale will be €44,891. This does not take account of the various additional allowances payable in respect of deputy principals and principals and for additional qualifications over and above the B.Ed.

The Irish National Teachers Organisation (INTO, the main trade union for primary school teachers) identified a desire for more pre-service and in-service training among teachers of infant classes (INTO, 1995). The Working Group on Primary Pre-service Teacher Education reported in early 2002 (DES, 2002b). Among its recommendations is the restructuring of B.Ed courses and their extension to 4 years, a rebalancing of the content of courses between education based and academic subjects as well as between various modes of teaching.

The Working Group was also clear in articulating its view that pre-service training cannot prepare graduates with the competencies and skills necessary for a mature teacher and highlighted the importance of induction and in-service training. At present, each teacher is in receipt of 4 days in-service training on the new primary curriculum (see 2.3.1 below). In-service training on this is being phased in at the rate of two subjects per year. Therefore, each teacher receives 2 days in-service training for each subject. This is followed by one-day in-school planning of the implementation of the revised curriculum in the individual school. In addition to this training, the In-Career Development Unit of the DES provides training in a wide range of areas including Information Communication Technologies, Special Education (including remedial teaching), training for involvement in specific programmes including Giving Children an Even Break, Early Start, Refugee Language Support Programmes and Traveller Education, training for newly appointed principals and Relationship and Sexuality Education.

Beyond training, the major staffing issue arising in primary schools and in infant classes is the pupil teacher ratios that exist in many schools. The DES reports an average pupil teacher ratio of 19.2 to 1 in all primary schools, and of 24.5 to 1 in ordinary classes (DES, forthcoming 2002). Some schools have higher ratios. However, the creation of additional teaching posts together with a decline in enrolments has resulted in a significant reduction in the overall pupil-teacher ratio in primary schools in recent years and this will continue to fall over the coming years. For example, the average pupil-teacher ratio in 1996/1997 was 22. By 1998/1999 this had fallen to 21 and in 2000/2001 stood at 19.2. The issue of pupil teacher ratios is returned to in section 3.1.2 below.

Child to adult ratios are more favourable in Early Start, with ratios of 15 to 2 being implemented. In addition, Early Start Teachers and Childcare Workers receive additional training. In the first year of the implementation of Early Start, staff were appointed two to three weeks prior to the commencement of the school year, giving them time to attended a one-week induction course.

2.3 PROGRAMME CONTENT AND IMPLEMENTATION

In the field of early childhood education and care, programme content and implementation are areas in which the distinction between childcare provision and education becomes apparent. Some pre-school settings are clearly informed by a particular approach to learning, such as Montessori and Steiner Nurseries, and Early Start Units have Curricular Guidelines for Good Practice developed by the In-Career Development Team of the DES. However, in the majority of cases the programme content of early childcare provision is not formalised, is outside State regulation and is not informed by education bodies. This is clearly indicated in the National Childcare Census, which shows that, of 2,029 facilities included, over half (1,134) devise their own curriculum for at least some aspects of their services. In more formal early care and educational settings, and in particular in infant classes, a State developed, supported and required curriculum exists. In addition, progress on a voluntary but more structured framework for learning for children aged from birth to 6 years is presently being developed by the NCCA under the Education Act 1998.

2.3.1 The Primary School Curriculum

Until recently, primary schools delivered the Primary School Curriculum (Curaclam na Bunscoile) as revised in 1971. This curriculum built of principles and practice that had emerged over previous years. Central to this development was a child-centred approach that was particularly reflected in the teaching of infant classes. Drawing on this experience, the key aspect of this revised curriculum is that, from 1971 onward, the child was placed at its centre. The Review Body on the Primary Curriculum conducted a critique of the 1971 curriculum. Based on the report of this Review Body, the National Council for Curriculum and Assessment (NCCA) was charged with the revision of the primary school curriculum, and the revised curriculum was launched in 1999.

The curriculum is child centred, concentrates on children as active agents in their own learning and details what and how the child can learn most effectively. Its two key principles are the uniqueness of each child and the development of each child's potential to the full. The following are the Primary Curriculum's defining features:

☐ a focus on learning that recognises different kinds and ways of learning as well as approaches to teaching;

☐ a relevant curriculum that meets the developmental and education needs of the child in the context of their immediate needs and their functioning in wider society;

☐ learning through guided activity and discovery;

☐ a balanced approach that reflects the breadth of human experience and expression and flexible implementation of the curriculum at school level;

☐ a developmental approach to learning that recognises the integration of the various subject areas covered in order to create a harmonious learning experience for the child;

☐ a detailed statement of content that supports flexibility in teaching approach;

☐ a balanced approach to the acquisition and use of knowledge, concepts and skills;

☐ assessment as an integral part of teaching and learning;

☐ planning as an important tool in the implementation of the curriculum to maximum positive effect in individual schools. (DES, 1999a)

The curriculum has 6 curriculum areas covering 11 subjects. These 6 areas are (i) Language (encompassing the subjects of English and Irish) (ii) Mathematics, (iii) Social, Environmental and Scientific Education (covering History, Geography and Science), (iv) Arts Education (encompassing Visual Arts, Music and Drama), (v) Physical Education, and (vi) Social, Personal and Health Education. Religious education is to be determined by the individual Churches. It is envisaged that the curriculum will be implemented on a phased basis over a seven-year period, in line with the in-service training exercises outlined in 2.2.2 above. This is organised by the In-Career Development Unit of the DES through a Primary Curriculum Support Programme (PCSP) Although this implementation programme will proceed on a subject-by-subject basis, schools may introduce subject areas as they see fit, taking account of the expertise and interests of their staff. However, it is anticipated by the NCCA, supported by experience to date, that most schools will choose to follow the in-career development programme from year to year.

A number of points in relation to the new national curriculum have been raised. The first concerns the issue of flexibility in delivery. While the content of the curriculum is very detailed according to each subject and each level within the school, there is an emphasis on allowing schools to deliver this according to their particular circumstances, the needs of individual classes and the learning needs of individual children. The second is recognition of the role of families in the education of their children and the need for parental information on the revised curriculum. To this end, the NCCA produced an introductory booklet for parents for the DES entitled *Primary School Curriculum: Your Child's Learning – A Guide for Parents* (DES, 1999b) outlining the content of the curriculum, how parents can help their children learn before and when they start school, how they can help implement the curriculum and how they can help the children in the various subject areas. Finally, the curriculum is designed in such a way that, through effective curriculum differentiation, children may have access to learning experiences appropriate to their learning needs. This facilitates the DES policy of, in so far as possible, integrating children with specific learning needs within the ordinary primary school classroom. These issues are dealt with in more detail below.

2.3.2 Curricular Guidelines for Good Practice in Early Start

While there is no defined curriculum for Early Start, the In-Career Development Unit of the DES has developed guidelines for good practice (DES, 1998), which have been informed by the Rutland Street project (see 1.2.8 above). These guidelines emphasises the following:

☐ the provision of developmentally appropriate learning opportunities;

☐ a view of learning as an interdependent and continuous process the elements of which cannot be compartmentalised;

☐ the active involvement of the child in their own learning;

☐ recognition of the value of child-initiated, self-directed learning;

☐ recognition of play as the main medium through which children learn;

☐ the need for adults to structure the learning contexts of children;

☐ the active involvement of the adult in collaborative learning;

☐ the necessity of parental involvement in the child's education and learning. (Byrne, 1999)

These curricular guidelines have been available since 1998 and were updated again in 1999 and 2000. It is intended that these guidelines will be continuously updated in light of best practice and research. The guidelines have both a practical and theoretical emphasis. Considerable attention is given to the identification of learning outcomes for the four main elements of the curriculum: cognitive development, language development, personal emotional and social development, and creative and aesthetic development. Principles of good practice, including assessment and record keeping, adult-child interaction, the teacher-childcare worker relationship, and parent and community partnership are highlighted. Finally, the guidelines provide a series of developmental assessment profiles for each of the curriculum areas (excluding creative and aesthetic development), a set of exemplars for planning small group activity, and lists of additional educational resources.

2.3.3 A New Framework for Early Childhood Learning

Both the Report of the Forum on Early Childhood Education and the White Paper on Early Education (Government of Ireland, 1999c) raise the absence of a curriculum for children aged 0 to 3 years. The need for a range of methodologies and flexibility in curricula to allow for the various developmental needs of young children to be met is central to the development of such a curriculum. The White Paper does not recommend one curriculum over another and proposes that guidelines on the broad principles that should underlie early childhood curricula be developed rather than a specific curriculum being recommended or imposed. However, the White Paper also recognises that many providers may have difficulty in identifying or selecting an appropriate curriculum and, in light of this, recommends the development of a specimen curriculum that providers may use if they wish. It is also suggested that this will be of use to parents in helping them with the early development of their children.

In pursuing this objective, the NCCA is currently preparing a working paper on Learning Framework for Early Childhood Learning. The Framework will identify (i) children's needs at different ages and (ii) the learning and development experience that will meet those needs. It will not be prescriptive so that diversity of need and provision on the ground can be accommodated. It will contain some broad approaches/learning principles but there will be no compulsion for practitioners to adhere to it. Nonetheless, it is anticipated that should a Quality in Education Mark be developed (see 3.1 below), implementation of the Framework will be an important assessment criteria. While the achievement of a Quality in Education Mark will not be obligatory for service providers, it will be desirable, thereby introducing an incentive to adopt the Framework.

The proposed Framework for Early Childhood Learning will recognise and draw on the existing and on-going work of early childhood services in the development of learning programmes for very young children, including the work on the Early Start curriculum as well as the work of the various third level colleges and educational institutions delivering training for pre-school and primary school staff. Through this consultative approach, the NCCA aims to develop a framework with clear linkages between provision and needs of the different age groups within the birth to 6 years age bracket. The educational philosophies and principles of other types of early childhood education will be recognised within the framework, thereby making it of relevance to a broad range of provision and providers. The overall aim here is to provide a framework that will recognise the continuum between overlapping stages of development of the child from birth to the age of 6. This will ease the transition of the child from the home or childcare setting to the formal educational system.

Work on the discussion paper on the Framework for Early Childhood Learning is ongoing. When this is finalised, formal consultation on the Framework will commence. It is anticipated that this will happen in the autumn of 2002. This consultation process will involve the establishment of a number of enabling structures that will consult with parents, early childhood education and care providers, professionals and experts in areas relevant to early childhood education and care, relevant Government Departments, third level colleges and training institutions and other concerned and interested organisations. It is expected that this entire process will take 12 – 18 months, giving an estimated completion time of spring to summer 2004.

2.3.4 A Curriculum for Children with Special Needs

Section 1.2.6 above outlines much of the State provision for children with special needs in early childhood education and care. Government policy in respect of children with special needs is to provide them with an education appropriate to their needs. This is legislated for in the Education Act, 1998 and is the subject of pending legislation under the Education for Persons with Disabilities Bill, 2002. The broad policy proposed by these pieces of legislation reflects current practice to a large degree. With regard to young children this focuses on the integration of children with special needs in ordinary classes in primary schools whenever possible or to establish special classes in ordinary primary schools. Where the degree of disability makes neither of these options appropriate to the child's needs they are educated in special schools that cater for the specific disability in question. This policy is well summarised in the Report of the Special Education Review Committee (Department of Education, 1993) which states that it favours *'as much integration as is appropriate and feasible with as little segregation as possible'* (p. 22).

No specific curricula exist for the education of children with special needs. In cases where such children are educated in an ordinary primary school, teachers adapt the national curriculum as necessary to meet the needs of the child. The NCCA is addressing this issue and has developed draft guidelines specifically aimed at children with mild, moderate, severe and profound general learning disabilities. This work will be furthered through a process of consultation. In reinforcing the philosophy of integration, these guidelines will be based on the areas covered in the Primary Curriculum and include enabling skills (attending, responding, interacting) and life skills (communication, personal and social skills, aesthetic and creative skills, physical skills and mathematical skills). The guidelines also uphold the principles of the Primary Curriculum with respect to the uniqueness of each child and the development of their full potential. The key areas covered in these guidelines are as follows:

☐ broad principles and aims of education for children with general learning disabilities;

☐ the identification and use of realistic, time-referenced targets;

☐ the development and use of individual education programmes for each child;

☐ the use of a variety of appropriate assessment tools;

☐ lines of development in the skill areas, with short exemplars illustrating how these can be developed;

☐ new content and linkage points with the national curricula;

☐ whole-school and classroom planning approaches;

☐ a range of multi-disciplinary approaches in the education of students with special needs.

While the curriculum for children with learning disabilities has been the area of priority in recent years, the NCCA is also now beginning to examine the adaptation of the Primary Curriculum for specific use with children from disadvantaged backgrounds who are at risk of educational disadvantage. This work is at a very early stage.

2.4 FAMILY ENGAGEMENT AND SUPPORT

2.4.1 The Involvement of Parents in Early Education and Childcare

The White Paper on Early Childhood Education highlights the importance of involving parents in their children's education, taking the perspective that, as parents are enshrined in the Constitution as the natural and primary educators of their children, their involvement is of particular importance.

In the primary school sector, this key role of parents is given specific recognition in the Education Act, 1998. Section 26 of this Act provides that parents of students in a school may establish a parents association to promote the interests of students in co-operation with the Board of Management. In addition, the Board of Management, on which parents are represented, is required to promote contact between the school and parents and to give all reasonable assistance to a parents association.

The advancement of partnership with parents in the formal education sector can be seen in the work of the National Parents Council – Primary, the nationwide organisation of parents of primary school children. This represents parents' views on educational issues such as curriculum, class size and school transport as well as supporting the process of building partnership in education. The Council also provides a number of services to parents:

☐ an advocacy service for parents taking a formal complaint to the Board of Management of their child's school;

☐ a parents programme to improve and enrich the education of children by supporting the involvement of parents in their children's education;

☐ a help-line to provide support, encouragement and information to assist parents in responding to their children's educational needs;

☐ training courses and workshops funded by the DES and the European Social Fund.

The National Parents Council – Primary has representatives on the NCCA, the National Educational Welfare Board and various other education bodies.

Many of the initiatives of the DES targeted at children at risk of educational disadvantage seek to encourage parental involvement in education. For instance, some of the main aims of the Home/School/Community Liaison Scheme (see section 1.2.6) are to promote active co-operation between home, school and relevant community agencies in advancing the educational interests of the participating children, raise awareness in parents of their own capacities to enhance their children's progress and to assist them in developing relevant skills. Another example of this is the Visiting Teacher Scheme, which works to involve Traveller parents in their children's early education in Pre-Schools for Traveller Children.

The White Paper on Early Childhood Education discusses a strategy to facilitate and encourage parental involvement. It suggests that parents should be provided with advice and support regarding the learning process; be supplied with information and recommendations on how they may best assist their children's education and development; and be facilitated and encouraged to get involved in the provision of early childhood education. Responsibility for progressing this strategy and for co-ordinating and enhancing parental involvement in early education has been given to the recently established CECDE. The Centre will also undertake and/or commission research and development through which best practice in regard to parental involvement may be implemented and evaluated.

In the area of childcare, each County Childcare Committee has at least one parent's representative and parental involvement in the management of community-based facilities is common. However, evidence would suggest that many services are still struggling with the idea and practice of parental involvement and a partnership approach. In the National Childcare Census, only 40% of facilities had a policy on parental involvement and only 19% had a written policy on this area. Where parents were involved, this most commonly took the form of providing parents with information, holding open days for parents and involving parents in outings.

2.4.2 Family Friendly Policies: Reconciling Work and Family Life

Increasing employment among women and the need to attract and retain women in the work force have led to a greater emphasis on family-friendly policies that assist parents, and particularly mothers, in reconciling work and family responsibilities. The Programme for Prosperity and Fairness (PPF) recognises that policies to support childcare and family life are a cornerstone of future social and economic progress in Ireland. In meeting the challenges this presents, the PPF aims not only to increase the quality and quantity of childcare provision but also to further policy measures to reconcile work and family life, including family-friendly employment policies.

In Ireland, family-friendly policies have a primarily labour market focus. They are considered to be policies that (i) help workers to combine employment with their family lives, caring responsibilities and personal and social lives and (ii) facilitate equality of opportunity for men and women in the workplace. This definition includes statutory entitlements such as Maternity Leave, Adoptive Leave, 'Force Majeure' Leave, Parental Leave and Carer's Leave as well as the provision of non-statutory atypical working arrangements. Obviously, all employers must honour the statutory entitlements of their employees. Other non-statutory arrangements, however, are at the discretion of the individual employer.

Statutory Entitlements

Maternity Leave: Following a review of the maternity protection legislation in 2000, the period of maternity leave attracting a social welfare payment was increased by 4 weeks to 18 weeks and the period of unpaid maternity leave was increased by 4 weeks to 8 weeks with effect from March 2001. In essence, therefore, expectant women and new mothers may avail of up to 26 weeks leave. This is highly dependent on the individual's financial situation, which, in turn, is heavily influenced by the practice of employers in relation to pay. Maternity Leave is calculated by dividing gross income in the Relevant Tax Year by the number of weeks worked in that year. Seventy per cent of this amount is payable, subject to minimum payment of €135.60 and a maximum payment of €232.40 per week (rates applicable from January 2002). However, in many instances, and particularly among large employers, women are paid their salary for 18 weeks and in turn they give their welfare payments to their employer to off set this cost. This obviously makes longer maternity leave and unpaid leave more attractive.

Adoptive Leave: With effect from 8th March 2001, an adopting mother or sole male adopter is entitled to 14 weeks paid and 8 weeks unpaid adoptive leave.

Parental Leave and Force Majeure Leave: The Parental Leave Act, 1998, which gives effect to the EU Parental Leave Directive (96/34/EC), introduced for the first time in Ireland a statutory right to Parental Leave. The Act entitles parents to 14 weeks (per child) unpaid Parental Leave from work to take care of children under 5 years of age. Its unpaid nature has meant that there has been limited take up of Parental Leave and it can reasonably be expected that this has been particularly low among lower paid workers.

This Parental Leave Act also provides an entitlement to limited paid 'Force Majeure' leave for urgent family reasons owing to injury or illness of an immediate family member. The employee may not be absent for more than 3 days in any period of 12 consecutive months or 5 days in any period of 36 consecutive months.

Carer's Leave: The Carer's Leave Act, 2001 entitles employees to take unpaid leave from employment for the purpose of providing full-time care and attention to a 'relevant person' for a period not exceeding 65 weeks. Again, the unpaid nature of this leave has restricted its uptake. Its advantage, as with Parental Leave, is that employment must be held open for those taking leave.

Non-Statutory Atypical Working Arrangements

Atypical working arrangements are the way in which many parents meet their long-term family responsibilities. The provision or availability of these is not subject to legislation and is dependent on the positive perspective of employers towards such arrangements. It is also the case that the majority of those availing of atypical work arrangements are women. The following are among the most common forms of atypical work arrangements in Ireland.

Part-time Working: Part-time working means working fewer hours than a comparable full-time worker in the same organisation. Typically, this involves working a half-week of approximately 18 to 20 hours. The number of people working part-time in Ireland has soared in recent years. According to the Quarterly National Household Survey, 17% of those in employment are in part-time employment. However, this is true of almost 31% of women in employment, compared to 7% of men (CSO, 2002b).

Job-Sharing: This is an arrangement where one full-time job is divided or the work is shared between two people. The responsibilities and benefits of the job are shared between the holders. The job can be shared in a number of ways, for example, on the basis of a split week; (alternating 2 and 3 day weeks), on the basis of a split day; or on a week on-week off basis.

Work sharing: Work sharing is a development of the job-sharing concept. It attempts to achieve business tasks while allowing for a wider range of attendance patterns. It requires a high level of employer / employee co-operation with a view to achieving the tasks that make up the job. It is important that the tasks are clearly defined, targets identified and the level of service decided upon before the workload is divided up. At this stage, the manager and jobholders can agree on a system of work attendance to complete the work that best accommodates the staff.

Flexitime: This is an arrangement whereby employers and employees negotiate hours of work that are of advantage to both. It usually involves defining 'peak' hours when all employees must be in work. Starting and finishing times, on the other hand, are normally flexible and there is usually provision for taking leave in lieu of additional hours worked.

Other non-statutory leave and atypical work arrangements are becoming increasingly common in Ireland as the need for a flexible approach to recruiting and retaining staff emerges. These include the following.

☐ *Paternity Leave:* There is currently no entitlement to paid or unpaid paternity leave. However, a number of employers are recognising the importance of making some provision for such leave.

☐ *Compassionate or emergency leave:* Most employers recognise the need for leave in emergency situations. Arrangements vary from organisation to organisation and are frequently informal.

☐ *Term-time working:* This system means that the employee works during school terms but not during the school holidays. It appeals, in particular, to parents of school going children. Operational in a number of Government Departments, this has yet to be taken up by many private sector employers.

☐ *Employment or career break:* A growing number of organisations provide such breaks on either a formal or less structured basis. The facilitating of such breaks for study / travel / child rearing can assist in retaining valued staff.

☐ *Sabbaticals:* This is a period of absence from work, which may or may not be on full pay, and duration is normally related to length of service. They provide an opportunity for employees to take a break from or reflect on their work, or engage in new activities.

☐ *Alternative work arrangements:* Innovative ways of working are no longer confined to the workplace. Models that have been developed include such concepts as teleworking or e-working. This means working at a distance, or even a remote location, and using technology to ease communications. It can also include a combination of e-working and office-based work. It is well suited to performing information technology tasks and works well in certain situations where the employee has a high degree of autonomy, e.g. architecture or journalism. Difficulties to be overcome can include issues of control, lack of face-to-face contact and consistency of service provision.

2.5 FUNDING

The current and capital costs of a small number of specific pre-school initiatives targeted at disadvantaged children and primary schools, including the full cost of teachers' salaries, are funded by the State through the DES. Total expenditure on primary education amounted to some €1,407 million in 2000. While it would be useful to be able to disaggregate expenditure by class for the purposes of this report, such disaggregated statistics are not currently available.

The primary source of funding for childcare is the EOCP. This has been detailed above and the financial element is covered in 2.5.4 below.

2.5.1 DES Funded Pre-School Education

As already indicated above, the DES main pre-school intervention in through the Early Start Programme. Each full Early Start unit receives a start-up grant of €11,428 (€5,714 for a half unit) for the purchase of a range of suitable equipment and €2,539 per annum (€1,524 for a half unit) for the purchase of materials/equipment. In addition, each full unit receives €1,905 per annum (€952 for a half unit) for the development of parental involvement. The Board of Management of the school also receives an annual capitation grant of €95.23 per Early Start participant to meet the day-to-day running costs of the unit. A total current per capita cost of the programme is not available due to the provision by both the DES and FÁS of teaching assistants to the programme. However, an estimate based on teacher salaries, capitation grants, Start up and annual grants towards teaching materials and equipment, and grants for the development of parental involvement places the minimum per capita cost at €2,330 in the school year 2000/2001.

The DES provided a total of €1.11 million in 2001 to Pre-Schools for Traveller Children and also provided funding of €203,979 to the Rutland Street Pre-School Project.

2.5.2 Core Funding for Primary Education

Teachers' salaries constitute the State's main financial support to primary education. In 2000, this amounted to €855 million. This level of expenditure reflects not only the level of teachers' salaries, but also the number of primary teachers which in the school year 2000/2001 was 22,850. Capitation grants constitute the second main form of government funding for primary schools and are intended to contribute towards the cost of such items as heating, lighting, cleaning, insurance, general up-keep and general teaching aids required in the schools. The rate of this grant has been steadily increased in recent years and currently stands at a rate of €111.58 per pupil. Special enhanced capitation rates are paid in respect of children with special needs who attend special schools or special classes dedicated to children with particular special needs, although not to children with special needs who are in ordinary primary school classes. Higher capitation rates are also paid for children in schools with designated disadvantaged status and for children benefiting from the Giving Children an Even Break programme (see 1.2.8 above). This rate is currently €38.09 - €20.31 towards general running costs, €11.43 for classroom materials and equipment and €6.35 for home school liaison activities. In addition, grants are provided to primary schools for secretarial and caretaking services, with the rates currently standing at €102 per pupil.

Prior to the school year 2001/2002, primary schools were required to raise a local contribution towards their operating costs. While this traditionally amounted to at least 25% of the State grant, the local contribution has now been abolished with 100% of funding now arising from the State.

A grant scheme to enable minor works to be carried out to primary school properties is also in place. Payment is made every school year at a rate of €3,809 per school plus €12.70 per pupil. The scheme is intended to cover minor improvements to school buildings and grounds, replacement of mechanical and electrical services, the purchase of furniture and the provision of floor coverings and blinds.

2.5.3 Additional Funding for Primary Education

As indicated in 1.2.8 above, in addition to the core funding the DES provides additional support to schools with pupils encountering or at risk of educational disadvantage through a range of programmes. These supports take the form of enhanced capitation grants to designated schools for the purpose of assisting them in meeting management costs, purchasing teaching and learning materials and developing home/school links. Other supports include concessionary or ex-quota staffing.

Furthermore, over the past 4 years, the State has provided primary schools with a number of additional grants to assist them with the purchase of various resources and materials. They include:

☐ An annual physical education grant. This is made available to all primary schools. Schools designated as disadvantaged and schools in the rural phase of the Breaking the Cycle scheme receive an annual grant of €1,270 per school while all other schools will receive €635 per school.

☐ Schoolbooks for Needy Pupils Grant Scheme. These grants are paid to school principals to assist with the purchase of textbooks for children who come from needy homes. Funding provision for these grants in 2002 is in excess of €3.6 million.

☐ The School Transport Scheme was established in 1967 and it currently carries about 130,000 pupils each school day, 50,000 of which are primary school pupils. The total cost of the scheme is approximately €90 million per year, about 5% of which is covered by parental contributions.

❑ A grant for schools enrolling refugee children. Schools with between 3 and 8 such pupils receive grant assistance to the amount of €6,349 and schools with between 9 and 13 such pupils receive €9,523. This grant aid is designed to enable schools to take appropriate measures to improve the standard of English of the non-national pupils. Schools with 14 or more non-English speaking non-nationals are entitled to an additional full time temporary teacher.

❑ Grants available under the Schools IT Initiative. Funding of €108 million is being made available over three years (2001-2003) to build upon the achievements made in the Schools IT2000 Programme.   Schools are empowered to allocate funds available for Information and Communications Technology within the context of their own IT planning process.

❑ Once-off grants such as a Library Grant, a Science Grant, an Equipment Grant for infant classes and a National Reading Initiative Grant.

2.5.4 Funding for Childcare

The main source of funding for childcare providers is the EOCP administered by the DJELR. As outlined above, the NDP allocated €317.4 million to the DJELR for childcare measures, with this subsequently augmented by an anti-inflationary package and the transfer of childcare schemes and their associated funding from other Government Departments to the DJELR. The total funding available to the Department is now €436.7 million for investment in childcare over the period 2000-2006. This is made up of a combination of exchequer funds (€119.93 million or 27% of the total) and European Funds (€318.86 million of 73%).

As indicated above, the EOCP provides a range of grants and financial supports to existing and new providers of centre-based childcare facilities and organisations involved in childcare for capital, staffing and quality improvement. The level of grant provided varies as follows:

❑ Capital Grants for Community-Based/Not-For-Profit Groups: there is no upper limit to the amount that can be awarded here.

❑ Capital Grants for Self-Employed Childcare Providers: the maximum grant available is €50,790. In addition, 35% of the total cost of the project must be secured by the applicant from private sources.

❑ Staffing Grant for Community-Based/Not-For-Profit Groups: these are not made in respect of individual staff members but are awarded towards the overall staff costs of the facility. The maximum grant for facilities providing full-time services is €63,487 per annum and €31,743 per annum for sessional services.

❑ Sub-Measure 3/Quality Improvement Grants: there is no limit to the amount of funding available under this Sub-Measure and the amounts awarded vary in accordance with the quality of the application and the anticipated impact on quality.

At the end of August 2002, 1,533 grant applications had been approved for funding under the EOCP. In total, just over €152.9 million was allocated through these grants (see Annex 3 for further details).

Other smaller sources of funding for childcare providers include contributions by the DHC for facilities delivering services for children at risk due to family stress. These are delivered via the regional Health Boards. In 1999, approximately €4.9 million was made available in grants by the Health Boards, supporting roughly 7,000 in approximately 600 facilities. An additional €2.2 million was provided in 2000.

The DETE also provides funding for childcare providers via employment grants administered by the CEBs.   In 2001, approximately €2.3 million has been made available through these grants. In addition, as outlined above, Community Employment supports roughly 300 childcare facilities through the provision of staff. In May 2001, FÁS estimated that approval had been given for 2,000 CE workers in childcare facilities at an average cost of €11,000 per place.

In 2002, the DELG made €2.5 million available to Local Authorities for projects associated with the provision of childcare facilities connected with Local Authority housing estates and other social housing projects.

Finally, the capital costs of constructing, refurbishing or extending a premises for the provision of childcare services are eligible for tax relief at 100% for the first year of operation.

2.5.5 Supports to Parents

The main child-related payment in Ireland is universal Child Benefit (see 1.2.9 above). The rate of Child Benefit was increased by over 50% in 2001 and by over 37% in 2002. These increases are part of a three year strategy to substantially increase child income support in real terms. Currently, the rates of payment are €117.60 per month in respect of the first and second child and €147.30 per month in respect of the third and subsequent children. The final step in this programme is expected to raise these rates to €149 and €185 respectively in 2003. This will bring total expenditure on Child Benefit to an estimated €1.27 billion, up from approximately €0.6 billion in 2000. While undoubtedly contributing to childcare expenses in many households, it is also important to note that Child Benefit is also a key instrument in addressing child poverty. (DSFA, 2002, unpublished).

The other major payment related to early childhood education and care is Maternity Benefit which is payable to mothers for 18 weeks – 4 weeks prior to birth and 14 weeks following birth. Adoptive Benefit is paid on the same basis to women who have adopted a child. The Homemaker's scheme is also worth noting here. This allows men or women to give up work to care for a child aged under 12 years (or an incapacitated person aged over 12 years) and maintain a social insurance record for the purposes of qualifying for an Old Age (Contributory Pension). Time spent on this scheme is disregarded when assessing average annual social insurance payments that determine eligibility for this Pension. Prior to the introduction of this scheme in 1994 women in particular lost out in respect of such pensions due to time spend in child rearing.

In addition, other payments by the Department that are explicitly linked to people in receipt of social welfare payments target support at children at risk of educational disadvantage. The main scheme of relevance here is the Back to School Clothing and Footwear Allowance designed to help low income families with the costs of school uniforms. The scheme is administered by the Health Boards as part of the Supplementary Welfare Allowance (SWA) Scheme and, generally, Community Welfare Officers determine entitlement to this Allowance. The value of this Back to School payment currently stands at €80 per annum for each child aged 2 to 11. Covering both primary and second-level pupils, in 2001 the DSCFA spent just under €13 million on this allowance and made payments in respect of 143,029 children. (DSCFA, 2002)

Although primary education is provided for by the DES, a number of costs arise in attending schools, such as the costs of book and uniforms. A number of supports are available to families experiencing socio-economic disadvantage to help meet such costs. These include the DES School Books for Needy Pupils Grant Scheme outlined above in section 2.5.3.

In community-based care a number of places may be provided free of charge and fees tend to be very low in order to allow families experiencing poverty or disadvantage to access them. This is made possible, by-and-large, through State grants and subsidies. Parents experiencing disadvantage and seeking to return to education or the labour market may receive childcare supports under the various employment, training and adult education programmes aimed at increasing employability. In such cases, the DETE provides specific subsidies for childcare costs or, in some instances, makes crèche facilities available. In addition, lone parents in receipt of a Lone Parent payment and in employment receive an additional top up payment to contribute to the costs of childcare in the absence of a partner.

Parents who use private sector childcare facilities or childminders are largely responsible for meeting the fees charged by the providers for these services. Had childcare fees remained static at 1999/2000 prices, they would now average approximately €83 per week per child for full-time care in centre-based provision. In a recent survey of their members the NCNA found that average costs of services in their centres ranged from €94 to €137 for children and between €107 and €145 per week for babies (usually defined as under 1 year) depending on location (NCNA, 2002). The only direct State payment to assist such parents is Child Benefit (see section 1.2.9 above). While intended to contribute to the overall cost of raising children, the substantial increases in Child Benefit in recent years have been closely connected with assisting parents meet the costs of childcare. At current levels, Child Benefit would pay for between 1 and 1.5 weeks of care per month.

Chapter 3

POLICY CONCERNS

3.1 QUALITY

3.1.1 Conceptualising Quality: Indicators and Criteria

It would be true to say that the issue of quality in childcare and early education has been to the fore in recent policy debates in Ireland. Virtually all documents concerned with such policy and provision use 'quality' as an indicator of good rather than bad or poor services and the attainment of 'quality' is almost always embedded in statements relating to the provision or development of early childhood education and care. Informed by research and wide consultation exercises, some of the most important conceptualisations of quality are contained in the Report of the Forum on Early Childhood Education, the White Paper of Early Education and the National Childcare Strategy.

The Report of the National Forum on Early Childhood Education (National Forum Secretariat, 1998) identified a range of quality indicators that can be grouped under five key areas. These are

☐ Child Indicators - developmentally appropriate programmes, child progress assessments, programme assessment and the size of the group;

☐ Staff Indicators - appropriately trained staff, appropriate pay and conditions, continuity of care and child staff ratios;

☐ Physical Environmental Indicators - health and safety standards, quality of space and physical resources;

☐ Social Indicators – affordability, accessibility and parental and community involvement;

☐ National Indicators – a national policy provision for regulation, provision and supervision, co-ordination of responsibility for services (p. 55-56).

These indicators are reflective of the work and articulated position of the European Commission Network on Childcare. The National Childcare Strategy, in which quality is a key concern, adheres to the work of this European Network and in line with this defines quality as a dynamic, continuous open-ended process that should be subject to regular review. The Strategy goes on to identify the key components of a quality service that are closely related to the indicators outlined above. These key components deem a quality service to be one that:

☐ offers both appropriate care and play-based opportunities based on the age and stage of development of the child;

☐ provides a quality environment with appropriate equipment, materials, activities and interactions;

☐ has a high adult to child ratio;

☐ has suitably trained staff that are registered with the relevant lead agency;

☐ offers continuity of relationships with adults and other children;

- ☐ works in partnership with parents;
- ☐ listens to and gives due consideration to the views and wishes of the children;
- ☐ provides equal opportunities for all children attending as well as for staff;
- ☐ recognises and promotes the cultural needs of children;
- ☐ provides adequate remuneration for staff;
- ☐ provides opportunities and support for in-service training of staff;
- ☐ through a partnership approach with parents, links in with other community activities and services;
- ☐ positively asserts the value of diversity;
- ☐ is accessible for all (p. 49).

The National Childcare Strategy states that removing the obstacles to attaining these indicators, key amongst which are a lack of information and insecure funding, is central to the recommendations of Strategy. Nonetheless, in the work that informed the National Childcare Strategy, the National Forum of Early Childhood Education, and the White Paper on Early Childhood Education the need for a wide range of areas to be recognised and addressed in quality assurance was an issue of paramount importance.

The White Paper on Early Childhood Education raises a number of important and universal concerns in respect of the concept of quality. These include the fact that quality means different things to different people and can be defined by children, parents, teachers or care workers. The White Paper also recognises that no one standard of quality can exist for all children in all types of services. Instead, the White Paper conceptualises quality as a set of core criteria to which services can progress and against which their progress can be measured. These include tangible criteria, such as staff-child ratios, space and equipment, as well as non-tangible criteria such as staff-child interaction and appropriate activities for the age and developmental stage of the child. In going on to identify a programme of work in developing quality standards in these less tangible areas, the White Paper focuses on curriculum and methodology, qualifications and training, staff retention and equipment and materials.

Progress on a number of areas related to the quality indicators identified above has been made under a number of the areas of work outlined in this report. These include the introduction of the Pre-School Services Regulations (see 2.1.1), the development of an Early Childhood Learning Framework (see 2.3.3) and the development of a Model Framework for Education, Training and Professional Development in the Early Childhood Care and Education Sector (see 2.2.1). In addition, the development of new institutional structures, as promoted in the National Childcare Strategy and the White Paper, in itself marks progress towards a national policy framework and co-ordinated provision viewed as central to the development of quality services.

3.1.2 Measuring Quality

The measurement of quality and the regulation of services are closely related. In Ireland, quality is currently measured or regulated through the Child Care (Pre-School Services) Regulations, 1996 and Child Care (Pre-School Services) (Amendment) Regulations 1997 (see 2.1.1) and the Inspectorate of the DES (see 2.1.2). It is important here to remember that much of the work identified throughout Section 2 above is inherently concerned with quality measurement, control and improvement. In addition, further ongoing and proposed work will add considerably to this arena. One of the measures proposed in the White Paper on Early Childhood Education concerns the development of minimum standards for some of the areas not covered by the Child Care (Pre-School) Regulation and the establishment of best practice in others. Meeting these standards will be obligatory for those receiving State funding for the provision of developmental/educational places. Non-State funded providers may voluntarily adopt these standards and apply for the Quality in Education (QE) Mark. The QE Mark or its equivalent is to be devised by the CECDE and will cover curricula, methodologies, staff qualifications and training. It is hoped that this development will lead to an increased recognition of the need for quality standards both to improve services and to guide parents in their choices. It was proposed that attaining of a quality standard would be based on inspection and evaluation visits.

Work on the development of quality standards is being progressed by the CECDE. The programme of work for the Centre proposes the development of a conceptual framework describing how children from birth to 6 years learn and identifying appropriate learning goals and objectives. Consultation with all relevant stakeholders will be a key aspect of this work. This framework will be developed into a set of guidelines that will aim to be adaptable enough for application across the diverse range of early years provision. These guidelines will be extensively piloted over a 15 to 18 month period.

In order that providers do not have to submit to two separate inspections, one from the Health Boards and one from the DES, the White Paper on Early Education proposed the development of a system of single inspections that would cover both the health and safety aspects of provision and the educational input. This would apply to all services outside the primary schools. The development of such a system will require significant time. In recognising this, the CECDE will undertake work to encourage compliance with quality standards in the interim. This will involve work on the development of the proposed inspection system and the provision of support to State-funded services seeking to meet new educational standards as they are phased in. The CECDE will also work to put in place a monitoring infrastructure.

The DES Inspectorate, in consultation with the education partners, is currently working on objectively defined evaluation and quality criteria for use in the evaluation of primary school, including the early education components of this. These criteria will help schools in conducting self-evaluations and assist the Inspectorate in external evaluations. The criteria will cover areas already addressed by the Inspectorate, including curriculum and teaching methodologies, and are based on definitions and common understandings to be agreed between schools and the Inspectorate. A final draft of these is currently being prepared and will be circulated to teachers for final comments in autumn 2002. These will contribute to an increased awareness of the concept and measurement of quality services among schools.

Adult child ratios are a central factor that impact on quality. These ratios are known to have an impact on the quality of early years experience and outcomes, and are frequently one of the visible and discussed indicators of quality. The following are the ratios that apply to children in childcare and early education settings.

- **Centre-based Childcare Full-Day Services**
  - ☐ Babies (under 1 year):   1 care staff to every 3 babies
  - ☐ Toddlers (1-3 years):   1 care staff to every 6 children
  - ☐ Infants (3 – 6 years):   1 care staff to every 8 children

- **Centre-based Childcare Sessional Services**
  - ☐ Children aged 0 to 6 years: 1 care staff to 10 children

- **Primary School**
  Ordinary Classes
  - ☐ Infants (ages 4-6)   1 teacher to a maximum of 30 pupils

  Classes in Disadvantaged Programmes
  - ☐ Infants (ages 4-6)   1 teacher to 20 pupils

However, despite progress in recent years, DES figures show that a significant proportion of infant pupils are in classes above the recommended maximum size. Table 7 shows that in 2000/2001, 24,661 infant pupils, accounting for 24% of all such pupils, were in classes of 30 pupils or above. It is important to note that progress is being made in this area. The proportion of children in infant classes of 30 or more has fallen from 36.7% in 1996/1997. It is also encouraging to see that the current Programme for Government (Government of Ireland, 2002a) contains a commitment to *'reduce the pupil / teacher ratio in our schools....which will ensure that the average size of classes for children under 9 will be below the international best-practice guideline of 20:1* (p.24).

Table 7
Proportion of Pupils in Junior and Senior Infant Classes by Class Size, School Year 2000/2001

	Class Size						
	0 - 19	20 - 24	25 - 29	30 - 34	35 - 39	40+	Total
Junior Infants	17%	28%	37%	17.1%	1.9%	0%	100%
Senior Infants	14.5%	26.4%	34.2%	22.8%	2%	0.1%	100%
Total	15.7%	27.3%	34.8%	20.1%	2%	0.1%	100%
N	16,349	28,319	36,120	20,932	2,072	40	103,832

Source: Department of Education and Science, forthcoming 2002,Table 2.5.

3.1.3 Quality Initiatives Under the EOCP

While quality remains a national issue, as reflected in the various national policy documents, this is also an issue being addressed by organisations involved in the delivery of childcare services or their umbrella organisations. Under Sub-measure 3 of the EOCP 137 quality initiatives are being funded in August 2002. This includes

☐ funding for specific quality actions under the County Childcare Committees' Strategic Plans;

☐ the provision of development support for the National Voluntary Childcare Organisations;

☐ a number of nationally or regionally focussed innovative quality improvement initiatives. Here, a small sample of these initiatives is presented to highlight some of the ways in which quality is being addressed on a day-to-day basis.[16]

The IPPA - the Early Childhood Organisation Quality Initiative holds that the biggest single indicator of a quality service is the ability of staff to reflect on how they work and to use this to effectively plan and implement their curriculum. For staff to become reflective practitioners, they must develop their understanding of how children learn and how they support children's strengths and interests. This then has implications for how they organise each dimension of the service. In supporting practitioners in this practice, this quality initiative provides intensive support to: (i) evaluate their services and implement quality improvement plans; (ii) develop a curriculum framework for each particular services and their clients; (iii) to become reflective practitioners through, observation, listening and reflection; (iv) to safeguard the child's right to play; and (v) to document their work and share this with families, funders and inspectors. The programme is based

---

[16] The author would like to thank IPPA - the Early Childhood Organisation, Barnardos and the Border Counties Childcare Network for providing materials and text used here to describe their quality initiatives.

on an extensive review of relevant international research. Training and support is delivered through workshops that focus on a range of areas including values, aims and objectives of individual services, the physical educare environment, working with parents, interactions with children and staff and management. Participants are supported to develop action plans to improve quality in these areas. The further development of the work undertaken in these workshops and the implementation of action plans is supported through onsite support visits by Quality Officers.

The aim of the *FÁS/Barnardos Quality Assurance Programme* is to introduce the concept of self-assessed quality assurance into FÁS childcare projects. This is organised as a three-staged process, based on the three basic elements of quality assurance systems - standards, assessment /monitoring and response mechanisms. The process involves a series of training days accompanied by an assessment/resource manual and ongoing support. The philosophy guiding the process is based on community development principles. The project is targeted at FÁS childcare projects. These differ from each other in many ways including the type of premises they operate from, training/experience of team members, numbers of children, indoor and outdoor activities, systems for recording, cleaning etc. Quality Assurance Programme so as to respect these differences. It allows for the identification of project specific standards, assessment of each projects own strengths and areas for improvement (using the accompanying manual) and then returning for guidance on what is and how to make the next step.

Stage 1 – Standards
Participants are assisted in the development of standards for their individual projects. Training is delivered on each of the topics identified as key criteria for a quality service. These are Service Details, Aims and Objectives, Policy and Procedures, Management and Administration Systems, Planning, Monitoring and Reviewing Systems, Human Resources, Relationships and Communications, Child Centred Environment, Curriculum to Include Child Development and Play, Child Observation and Assessment Systems, Equal Opportunities, Accessibility, Parental, Community and Statutory Involvement, and Health and Safety.

Stage 2 – Assessment/Monitoring
Participants assess their own projects in situ with the aid of questionnaires included in the manual and ongoing telephone support. Participants return for a further five days training to review their completed assessments and identify elements of their projects which are working well and elements which require alteration or enhancement.

Stage 3 – Implementation/Response
Having identified areas for change in Stage 2, participants return for a further four days training to generate development plans, which will bring about that change. The final stage of training is followed by a site visit by the trainer(s) to consult with the project team.

The Border Counties Childcare Network - Quality Assurance Programme (BCCN QAP) aims to support the development of a co-ordinated approach to the delivery of high quality early years services in the border counties of Louth, Meath, Donegal, Monaghan, Cavan, Sligo and Leitrim. Based on research carried out in 1998, the programme has developed an efficient, effective, user-friendly, and consumer-led process of Quality Improvement. This involved the development of a two pronged approach based on the Service Evaluation System (checklists) and Performance Indicators of Good Practice (evidence gathering procedures). Assessment of quality is concerned with 6 key areas or units: premises; the learning environment; legislation and management, safety health and hygiene; partnership with parents; and, the pre-school curriculum. Support and Development workers from the County Childcare Committees and other relevant workers are issued with BCCN QAP Service Evaluation Systems for each of the 6 units and use these to work with all service providers. Participation by services in the QAP is voluntary. For those who join the programme the Support and Development workers continue to support and advise as the service providers gather the evidence to demonstrate how they are meeting each of the performance indicators of quality. Assessments are carried out at three levels: first, by an assessor from the BCCN Assessor Team; second, by the BCCN Quality Officer; and, third, by the accreditation board.

NCNA Centre of Excellence Award members have always recognised and promoted the value of providing quality day care for each child in their care, based on the premise that high quality provision positively influences children's earliest experiences in day care and plays a vital role in their future development. Prior to the spring of 2002, the achievement of excellence in day care in Ireland had not been formally recognised by an awards scheme. As part of the NCNA's commitment to its members, the organisation developed the Centre of Excellence Award. This mark of distinction acknowledges member services that are providing excellent standards of care for children throughout Ireland.

The Centre of Excellence Award has several criteria, which forms the basis of the Self Evaluation Profile (SEP). The SEP's enables members to assess their own services under the following headings:

☐ Activities and Programmes for Children

☐ Relationships in the Nursery

☐ Partnerships with Families

☐ Health, Safety and Hygiene

☐ Staff Conditions and Professional Development

☐ Physical Environment

☐ Food and Nutrition

☐ Management and Administration

☐ Implementation of Policies and Procedures

☐ Evaluation and Review of Nursery

This self-evaluation process takes approximately five months for participating members to complete.

Each member service returns a completed SEP for appraisal by the NCNA. This appraisal stage involves a validation process, in which the NCNA staff review each SEP received and arrange validation visits to the childcare services, enabling the NCNA to assess the services.

3.2 ACCESS

It is clear from the discussion of quality above that access to early childhood education and care services is seen as a quality issue. However, access is a multi-dimensional concept in itself and encompasses physical access as determined by the location and design of premises, financial access in terms of affordability, equality of access in terms of appropriate services for various groups of children, including children of different ages, religions, cultural and ethnic backgrounds and of different physical and intellectual capabilities.

3.2.1 Availability of Places: Supply and Demand

In many senses, access to childcare and education depends on the supply of, and demand for services. The first point to be made here is in respect of the right to such services. As stated above, under the Irish Constitution and the Education Act 1998 every child in the State is entitled to an education appropriate to their needs within the school system. Therefore, access to infant classes in primary schools is universal and the obligation of the State to provide access to appropriate education for children is clear. In relation to childcare, however, and to provision outside the education system, there are no established rights to provision. Access, therefore, remains highly market driven and is determined, at least in part, by the available supply of and demand for childcare places.

The most comprehensive data on supply and demand in respect of childcare is the National Childcare Census. Table 8 below shows the number of 0 – 6 year olds attending a childcare facility and the number on the waiting lists of these facilities. This clearly indicates the particular shortage of available places for babies aged under one year and the impact of primary school attendance at 4, 5 and 6 years. The high number of 3 to 6 year olds availing of childcare services is an indication of the prevalence of pre-school and play school provision in Ireland that primarily caters for children in the year(s) immediately before primary school. It should be noted here, however, that these figures relate to 1999/2000, before the provision of large scale funding under the EOCP.

Early Start has provided access to pre-school services and illustrated that there is a demand for such services in disadvantaged communities in particular. However, the number of places provided is limited. However, the framework document that supports the revised NAPS proposes the creation of a more widespread pre-school initiative and the expansion of early childhood education to all children in designated disadvantaged areas. (Department of Social, Community and Family Affairs, 2001).

Table 8
Number of Children Attending and on Waiting Lists for Centre-Based Childcare Services, 1999/2000

AGE	Children Attending	Children on Waiting List	Children on Waiting List as a Percentage of those Attending
Under 1 Year	1,471	1,137	77.3
1 to 3 Years	7,590	1,992	26.2
3 to 6 Years	23,065	4,313	18.7
Total Places	32,126	7,442	23.2

Source: ADM, forthcoming 2002 The National Summary of the County Childcare Census 1999/2000.

3.2.2 Location of Services

The issue of the location of services has a number of dimensions. Key among these in the Irish debate is the provision and location of services for children in disadvantaged areas, and, more broadly, the availability of suitable premises. It is important in the first instance to acknowledge the existence of high quality early years services in disadvantaged urban and rural areas, including those provided under Early Start and those provided by private and community-based not-for-profit organisations. However, issues remain and the National Childcare Strategy clearly recognised that there are substantively different issues arising in urban, primarily disadvantaged, areas and rural areas. In addition, many of these issues also arose in an evaluation of the Community Support Childcare Initiative of the previous EOCP that ran from 1998 to 2000. (ADM, 2002).

In urban disadvantaged areas, the pertinent issues include the dependence on voluntary services that are largely under resourced, the inability of these services to attract and retain trained staff, a reliance on CE staff, poor physical facilities and premises and the difficulty experienced by parents in meeting even minimal childcare costs. In rural areas, problems arise due to low population densities and scattered populations. In many cases this makes typical centre-based care unsuitable. Additional issues concerning limited public transport, the fragmented nature of many services in rural areas, high staff costs due to the existence of small services and shortage of appropriate premises also impact substantially on childcare provision in rural areas. In both urban disadvantaged and rural situations, these issues become even more significant when addressing questions of access for specific groups of children such as those with physical and intellectual disabilities or from minority ethnic and cultural backgrounds. The National Childcare Strategy identifies measures and supports necessary to address these problems including information strategies and suitably flexible training provision for staff. Ultimately, the development of appropriate strategies is left to the County/City Childcare Committees, the membership of which is seen as vested with the necessary local knowledge to develop measures tailored to the needs of their own areas.

The issues raised in the National Childcare Strategy are also pertinent to access to primary schools. Many primary schools in disadvantaged urban areas experience difficulty in attracting and retaining teachers and in meeting the needs of disadvantaged children. Similar staffing problems are experienced in rural areas due to their physical isolation. In addition, in rural areas, dwindling populations result in children having to travel and be transported over long distances, adding another dimension to the question of access and quality of education experience. The DES programmes aimed at addressing educational disadvantage outlined in section 1.2.8 above are working to counter some of these difficulties.

Although not representative of all childcare facilities the county and regional location of childcare facilities that have secured funding under the EOCP is available. This is included in the information presented in Annex 3 below.

A concern that arises in both urban and rural areas is the recognised shortage of suitable premises for pre-school and after-school provision. One way in which this could be addressed is through making the spare capacity in primary schools (arising due to falling school enrolments by virtue of falling fertility rates) available for the delivery of pre-school and out-of-school care and education. This approach, recommended by both the Commission on the Family and the White Paper on Early Childhood Education, has a number of advantages. These include the establishment of a close relationship between pre-school and school services, ease of transition for children between these services and the improved quality of premises in which pre-school and out-of-school services are delivered. Concerns have been expressed about the longer term effects of placing very young children in classroom and school environments. It has also been suggested that should negative effects arise, these can be minimised or eradicated by locating pre-school services in classrooms not used by primary school classes and by creating a physical environment in these that is substantially different to primary classrooms. The Early Start Programme has taken this approach. The use of schools as premises for after-schools provision comes with similar caveats that children should not remain in the same classroom for in-school and out-of-school hours and that there should be a clear shift in the type of activities pursued so that out-of-school activities do not simply represent an extension of the school day and year.

3.2.3 Affordability

In policy debates in Ireland the issue of affordability is closely linked to quality, access and equal participation in early childhood education and care. Affordability is generally only discussed in relation to pre-school provision in Ireland due to the universal availability of free primary education. However, as is illustrated in section 2.5.5 above, parents still incur costs in relation to books, uniforms, transport to and from school, etc. The significance of these costs will be relative to the economic position of families but for low income families they may be considerable and a number of supports are available to help them meet these costs.

Affordable childcare is like many other areas to which the concept of affordability is attached. These, by-and-large, result in general statements in respect of an average cost for a typical service. However, in a situation such as Ireland's, where the supply of and demand for childcare is predominantly market-led and there is no universal or widespread State provision, affordability in childcare as in all such areas is a relative concept and will depend on the financial position of individual families. The difficulty of determining a definition of affordability in such circumstances is reflected in the lack of attention paid to this area in the various policy documents. While these contain assertions of affordability as a key aspect of quality and access, none has determined what the term means either in real terms or as a proportion of family income.

3.2.4 Equality of Access: Reflecting Diversity

The need for children of all religious denominations, physical and intellectual abilities and from varying socio-economic backgrounds to have access to appropriate early years care and education is widely accepted among policy makers and providers of such services. In addition to having its own indigenous ethnic group in the Traveller Community, Ireland is now becoming an increasingly multi-ethnic, multi-racial society through immigration from a range of countries.

This cultural and racial diversity is a challenge to the providers of early years care and education services. It is reassuring to note that the National Childcare Census shows that over three-quarters of facilities (78%) included in the Census claim to operate an equal opportunities policy. Less encouraging, and perhaps more realistic in terms of practice, is the finding that less than one quarter (24%) have a written policy on equal opportunities. As indicated above, in relation to pre-school and out-of-school provision, the Advisory Group to the NCCC is concerned with the issues of equality and diversity and is commissioning the design of guidelines on these issues for use by childcare providers and parents of children using childcare services. The DES supported Pre-Schools for Traveller Children, Early Start, special programmes to support children at risk of educational disadvantage, provisions for non national children in primary schools and services for children with special needs are all part of an overall policy to cater for children with diverse needs and from diverse backgrounds. In addition, the INTO has produced and widely disseminated its *Intercultural Guidelines for Schools: Valuing Difference, Combating Racism, Promoting Inclusiveness and Equality* (INTO, undated). Produced in English and Irish, these cover areas such as enrolment policy, inclusive strategies for parents, whole school and classroom guidelines, bilingualism in the classroom and dealing with racist incidents.

However, this is an area in which much remains to be done. In particular, recognising the ability of children to recognise and deal with diversity is an issue of some concern. Adults, including many of those involved in the provision of early childhood education and care, frequently do not realise that children are not insensitive to such issues. This is captured by the following quote that appears in a recent report entitled *Éist – Respecting Diversity in Early Childhood Care, Education and Training* (Pavée Point, 2001).

> '*I treat all children the same in my group; children accept everyone and see no difference. Why can't we leave well enough alone and not burden children with all this stuff about difference.' Anonymous*

This report goes on to make recommendations targeted at the Government, at training, accrediting and certification bodies and at providers of early childhood education and care services and will be instrumental in informing the work of the Advisory Group to the NCCC. It is clear, however, that there is a need and a demand for specific training to help providers cope with the increasingly common issue of diversity. A diversity training course has been developed as part of the Éist project in Pavee Point and this will be included in the Degree course in Early Childhood Care and Education in DIT in the academic year 2002/2003. This pilot course consists of ten training sessions in which students will be encouraged to explore their attitudes, assumptions, experiences and feelings regarding diversity. There are five themes that will shape the course (i) an introduction to the concepts of diversity and equality: (ii) personal identity and group identity; (iii) the value of policies and their implementation; (iv) approaches to diversity education and the anti-bias approach; and (v) evaluation and reflection.

An important development in this area is the proposed work programme of the CECDE. One of the functions of the CECDE is to co-ordinate and enhance provision for disadvantaged children and children with special needs. The Centre has taken a wide interpretation of this function and includes consideration of inequalities, such as those based on gender or ethnicity, which result in educational disadvantage. The Centre proposes to undertake an audit of all existing provision relating to disadvantage and special needs and use this to consider how existing provision could be improved or extended and to identify innovative means by which gaps in provision can be filled. In addition, the CECDE sees an implementation role for itself in these innovative measures. All of this work will be undertaken in consultation with relevant structures and stakeholders, including parents.

3.3 CO-ORDINATION

3.3.1 Co-ordination Structures

As indicated in section 3.1.1 above, a co-ordinated national strategy on early childhood education and care, as well as co-ordinated services, are considered to be key aspects of a high quality system of provision. In Ireland, there are a number of structures specifically concerned with the co-ordination of services. These have been identified in section 1.2.9 above. In relation to childcare, the main structures are

☐ the Inter-Departmental and Inter-Agency Synergies Group - this aims to co-ordinate relevant provision and policy across Government Departments and Agencies;

☐ the Childcare Directorate of the DJELR – this draws together the work of the DJELR in their roles as the implementing agent for the childcare measures under the NDP, primarily the EOCP, and their function as the chair of the NCCC;

☐ the National Co-ordinating Childcare Committee – this aims to co-ordinate the measures being undertaken to implement the National Childcare Strategy and acts as a support to the County/City Childcare Committees;

☐ the County/City Childcare Committees – these are responsible for the co-ordination of local childcare services.

The main co-ordination structures in the education field are:

☐ the DES – this is responsible for the co-ordination of all educational measures nationally and is represented on the Inter-Departmental and Inter-Agency Synergies Group identified above. Its remit covers but is obviously not exclusive to early childhood education;

☐ the CECDE, which has responsibility for co-ordinating early education provision, including parental involvement, with a particular emphasis on children experiencing disadvantage and those with special needs.

Other relevant co-ordinating structures include the NCO, which is responsible for the implementation of the National Children's Strategy and the National Children's Advisory Council.

3.3.2 Effective Co-ordination: Progress and Challenges

On a positive note, it must be recognised that there has been very substantial progress made in relation to co-ordination in recent years. This is particularly the case in relation to childcare policy and services. Prior to the National Childcare Strategy, there was relatively little State involvement in this area. This applied to services on the ground as well as management and policy structures. In less than 4 years this situation has changed dramatically to one where there is significant State investment in this area, primarily through the EOCP, the creation and operation of national and local co-ordinating structures, as well as a consolidation of initiatives under the auspices of the DJELR.

A brief survey of the list of co-ordinating structures listed above may suggest that the co-ordinating structures are themselves in need of co-ordination. In the interviews with key actors to inform this report, the issue of co-ordination was the one raised most frequently and with the greatest sense of frustration. In the main, the issues raised related to a perceived lack of co-ordination between the main structures and initiatives concerned with 'childcare' on the one hand and 'education' on the other. In essence, while the actors in these two sectors profess to a philosophy of a continuum of child development in which care and education are inseparable, essentially these are separated into 'out-of-school' childcare according to the definition applied by the National Childcare Strategy and primarily now under the remit of the DJELR, and 'in school' provision, primarily the services funded, managed and administered by the DES. To further add to the picture, the NCO was ascribed the role of *ensuring inter-departmental co-operation and the integration of activities on children's issues.* (Government of Ireland, 2000, p.85) Presumably this includes early childhood education and childcare services.

The need for still greater co-ordination and for the articulation of how this is to be achieved is clear. One example of this is in relation to the proposed work of the CECDE in respect of establishing quality standards. As of yet, it remains somewhat unclear how these will relate to and interface with the Child Care (Pre-School) Regulations 1996 and (Amendment) 1997. The recent Programme for Government (Government of Ireland, 2002a) promises to *'introduce a national early-education, training, support and certification system and expand state-funded early-education places. Priority will be given to a new national system of funded early-education for children with intellectual disabilities and children in areas of concentrated disadvantage'* (p.24). Implementation of this aspect of the Programme for Government raises the issues and challenges of co-ordination with existing provision.

A number of co-ordination structures have been suggested in the various policy documents that underpin early childhood education and care. In relation to childcare provision, almost all of the structures proposed in the National Childcare Strategy are now in place. With regard to early education, both the Report of the National Forum for Early Education and the White Paper which followed on from this identify potential co-ordination structures. In the Forum discussions, a number of options were considered, but these centred on the creation of a central Early Years Development Unit that would have responsibility for the co-ordination of all services. While the establishment of such a Unit received unanimous support its location within the government structures was less easily resolved. Possible locations considered were the Department of the Taoiseach, the DES and the DHC. The difficulties of establishing and ensuring the effective operation of the Unit was not overlooked and it was suggested that, if created, its operations should be reviewed after 3 years.

In its consideration of co-ordination structures, the White Paper on Early Education recommended the creation of two structures. The first is an inter-departmental committee, comprised of the DES, the DJELR, the DHC, the DSFA and the Department of Arts, Sport and Tourism, as well as the relevant agencies that act on behalf of these departments, including the Health Boards. The purpose of this committee was seen to be the co-ordination of policy and provision at a high level. The second structure proposed was an advisory expert group, comprised of representatives of parents, providers of services, trainers, researchers, academics, staff organisations, national early childhood organisations, relevant Government Departments and agencies and other interested parties. The overall role of this group was seen as promoting co-ordination and understanding between the various stakeholders in order to minimise duplication and overlap of effort. More specifically, it was anticipated that this group would provide advice to the proposed Early Years Development Unit and the Early Childhood Education Agency, evaluate and select research and development projects, oversee the evaluation and inspection function of the Early Childhood Education Agency and assist in the development of early childhood curricula and methodologies.

Given recent developments and the creation of a number of agencies and structures concerned with co-ordination another possibility that might be considered here is the creation of a co-ordination mechanism that would draw on the experience and work of the CECDE, the NCO and the National Co-ordinating Childcare Committee. Such an approach would allow for the combination of early education expertise, childcare expertise and the location of this within a broader framework of children's lives.

Chapter 4

RESEARCH AND EVALUATION

There are two main sources of data available on early childhood education and care. These are administrative data that arise from the management and administration of various services and programmes and which is primarily held by Government Departments or agencies, and data arising from research and evaluation studies.

4.1 Administrative Data

Most frequently, the core function of administrative data collected by statutory and other bodies is the planning, administration and management of services and financial management. Nonetheless, much of this data has been drawn on for research, monitoring and evaluation purposes.

The DES is clearly one of the main sources of administrative data on early childhood education and care. Data is regularly maintained by the Department on staffing, pupils and funding in relation to their services. Much of this data appears in the annual statistical reports of the DES. The following are examples of the data reported in relation to pre-school and primary education:

☐ the number of schools, pupils, teachers and childcare assistants in Early Start programmes by county;

☐ the number of pupils in primary schools by age and gender;

☐ the number of pupils by age and grade by type of school (ordinary primary school, special schools and private primary schools);

☐ the number of new entrants to ordinary classes and the origin of these (previously not at school, entrants from Early Start, entrants from other national schools within the State, entrants from schools in Northern Ireland, entrants from schools outside Ireland);

☐ a statement of annual expenditure of public funds on primary education.

It is noteworthy in the context of administrative data that no central primary pupil database currently exists, as is the case for second-level pupils through which the participation of students can be tracked using their Personal Public Services Number (Corrigan, forthcoming 2002). Consideration is being given to the creation of a new primary pupil database in conjunction with the tighter monitoring of participation and absenteeism under the Education Welfare Act, 2000.

Central administrative data on childcare is predominantly held in relation to the EOCP. This is collected and managed by ADM on behalf of the DJELR as part of their Technical Assistance remit.

The primary function of the data collected is the management and monitoring of expenditure and financial reporting to the Department of Finance. Examples of the data collected and included on the ADM database include:

☐ the number of applications received, approved and declined,

☐ the amount of funding awarded to each approved applicant,

☐ the location (county) of each applicant and approved grant;

☐ the type of grant awarded (capital, staff or quality development);

☐ the number and type of new employment posts created and maintained;

☐ the number and type of childcare places created and maintained;

☐ expenditure by measure.

This information is essential to the ongoing monitoring and evaluation of the EOCP and will be central to consideration of the programme in the forthcoming ESF Mid-Term review of the NDP.

The Health Boards maintain data on the number of childcare facilities notified to them, inspections carried out and the outcome of these inspections, but this data is not regularly collated on a national basis. In order to determine the number of facilities notified, the number of inspections carried out and their outcomes at a national level, each of the 10 Health Boards must be contacted separately.

The DHC and the Health Boards have identified the need to develop and improve management information to facilitate the provision of accurate and timely information in the child care area. Chief Executive Officers of the Health Boards have recently begun to develop of an agreed suite of Performance Indicators for each of the care group areas. Among the Performance Indicators for Child Care are (i) the number of operational pre-school centres, which were notified in accordance with the Pre-school Regulations 1996 and (ii) the percentage of operational pre-school centres, which were notified in accordance with the Pre-School Regulations 1996 and were inspected in accordance with the Regulations. Once a system for the regular reporting on these indicators is in place in each of the Health Boards, the collation of data at national level should be more easily achieved. In addition, a major review of child care information is currently reaching conclusion and is likely to recommend that the DHC and Health Boards conjointly commission the development of a single national child care information system, which defines the core operational requirements for child care and the management information to be derived from those requirements. If such an information system is developed it will include information on pre-school services.

4.2 Research and Evaluation Studies

A number of major research projects have been undertaken or are ongoing that are of significance in this area. Some of these have been referred to above and include the National Childcare Census undertaken by ADM on behalf of the DJELR and the first evaluation of Early Start. Also, some of the structures identified above have burgeoning research programmes, as in the case of the Educational Disadvantage Committee, which will contribute to our knowledge. Research by post-graduate students in a number of third-level colleges including the DIT, the Early Years Unit of the Department of Education in University College Cork and the various teacher training colleges are also a valuable source of research material.

In addition, evaluation is an inherent component of the work of other structures and this has the capacity to increase greatly our knowledge and understanding of the working of these structures. A particular case in point here is the County/City Childcare Committees, which are charged with the ongoing monitoring and evaluation of their work. Finally, Government Departments conduct or commission evaluations of many of their programmes and schemes. Relevant examples here include the evaluation of Early Start and the evaluation of a number of Pre-Schools for Traveller Children.

Research and evaluation also forms a key element of the work of many early childhood education and care projects and organisations. Some of this work, particularly in the area of evaluation, has been undertaken in line with funding requirements. At present, for example, each project funded under the EOCP completes an annual evaluative questionnaire for analysis by ADM. This is in addition to ongoing monitoring and reporting requirements. Many organisations have also conducted more detailed evaluations of their projects and services. For example, Barnardos has undertaken and published an evaluation of their work and services in the Dun Laoghaire and Loughlinstown/Ballybrack areas of Dublin. (Barnardos, 2000a) This evaluation, which involved interviews and group discussions with relevant Barnardos staff, the children attending the services, parents, support agencies and members of the local community. It also involved observation of the activities and documentary analysis. In addition, Barnardos also commissioned a broader evaluation of their early years services, based on a representative sample of their services. This focused on issues such as the structure of the services, their curriculum, resources, user profiles, staff profiles and training needs. (Centre for Social and Educational Research, 2000) Another example is that of County Wexford Partnership, which commissioned an evaluation of their Childcare Programme 1996-1999 in order to assess the impact of this programme and to inform the Strategic Plan of the Wexford County Childcare Committee. This evaluation involved interviews with the Childcare Sub-Committee and Childcare network, childcare providers, parents and other relevant agencies. (County Wexford Partnership, 2000)

There are now a number of bodies in Ireland that are specifically concerned with research and evaluation in respect of early childhood education and care. For some, this is their sole area of research and evaluation activities, while others locate their work in the wider context of social, economic and educational research.

The Centre for Early Childhood Development and Education (CECDE)

The White Paper on Early Childhood Education (Government of Ireland, 1999c) clearly recognises the need for policy and provision that is underpinned by research and the importance of evaluation in determining and improving the effectiveness of these in meeting the needs of children. Much of the research and evaluation work highlighted in the White Paper now falls within the remit of the CECDE. While there is a research component to all areas of its work, the Centre will also develop a programme of relevant research. This research will focus on identifying best practice in curriculum, teaching methodologies and parental involvement and longitudinal studies that examine long-term impact of early education interventions, with a particular emphasis on the experience of children from disadvantaged backgrounds and children with special needs. In its first year of operation (2002/2003), the CECDE plans to carry out a comprehensive review of relevant national and international research with a view to establishing where significant gaps in this lie. Following this, the Centre will design a research programme aimed at filling at least some of these gaps.

The Centre for Social and Educational Research (CSER)

The Centre for Social and Educational Research (CSER) was established in 1997. Located in the Dublin Institute of Technology, the CSER is an independent research and policy analysis body carrying out applied social research studies and evaluations. The Centre has three research units: the Families Research Unit; the Early Childhood Care and Education Research Unit and the Residential Child Care and Juvenile Justice Research Unit. In addition, projects dealing with transversal themes are also undertaken from time to time. The Centre has links with a range of international bodies, European academic institutions and national research centres, third-level institutions and voluntary organisations.

The work of the Early Childhood Care and Education Research Unit is of particular significance here. One key area of the work of this Centre is the ongoing International Association for the Evaluation of Early Education Achievement (IEA) Pre-primary project. This is a cross-national study that examines education and care in the pre-primary years, the transition into formal education and the experience of the early years of school. Starting from a position where there was little or no information on these areas, the study has yielded valuable information on the development of Irish children in these early years (see Hayes and O'Flaherty, (1997), and Hayes and Kernan (2001)). The CSER has also conducted a number of evaluations of childcare provision in a number of local areas, including Tallaght (Dublin) and Loch Gorman (Wexford). This Unit is responsible for drawing together the ADM National Childcare Census on the basis of county reports and also for the OMNA project, which has prepared the Model Framework for Education, Training and Professional Development in the Early Childhood Care and Education Sector on behalf of the NCCC.

The Education Research Centre (ERC)

The Education Research Centre (ERC) is located in St. Patrick's College, Drumcondra. Established in 1966, the ERC has been involved in many national international research and evaluation projects. Some of the areas involved have been:

☐ programme evaluations, including that of Early Start,

☐ educational policy, including that relevant to early education;

☐ national assessments of educational achievement

☐ the functioning of the education system

☐ research in curriculum areas (e.g., reading)

☐ educational disadvantage.

The current programme of work includes a number of projects that are of particular relevance here, including an evaluation of the Breaking the Cycle Programme, a review of the Home/School/Community Liaison Scheme and the further evaluation of Early Start. The ERC has been involved in a major survey of all primary schools in Ireland in order to establish the number of disadvantaged pupils in each. This survey was instrumental in developing the Giving Children an Even Break programme of the DES. All primary schools were requested to participate in a comprehensive survey that was designed to identify the level of concentration in each school of pupils with characteristics that are associated with educational disadvantage and early school leaving. Approximately 75% of schools responded, making this the most comprehensive survey of primary schools available.

The Quarterly National Household Survey: Module on Childcare

The Quarterly National Household Survey replaced Ireland's National Labour Force Survey in September 1997. Based on a total sample of 39,000 households in each quarter, data are collected by interviewers and are entered directly onto laptop computers. The principal purpose of the QNHS is to collect up-to-date information on the labour force.

However, the QNHS also carries occasional or regular additional modules covering a range of supplementary issues. In September 2002, the QNHS will contain such an occasional module on childcare. Distinguishing between pre-school children and children attending primary school, this module will collect information on the types and combination of childcare arrangements used during the day and school term, during school holidays and after-school hours, the number of hours spent in care, the main reason why parents are availing of childcare, distance to the childcare service and principal means of transport there, the cost of such services, the preferred type of childcare and whether or not this is currently available. A copy of the Childcare Module is contained in Annex 6.

This module will provide valuable and up-to-date information on a number of issues central to the provision of childcare services and address a number of gaps in current knowledge. In addition, as it is collected as part of the QNHS, this information can be cross-tabulated with labour market information that will increase the depth of our knowledge in how these two facets of life are related. To be carried in the September – November 2002 quarter, results from this module can be expected in mid-2003.

Research and Evaluation under the EOCP

ADM has commissioned a review of the beneficiaries of grants to Small Scale Private Childcare Providers funded under the EOCP in 2000 – 2001. The terms of reference for this review states the following aims to:

☐ document the impact, progress and experience of the first round EOCP beneficiaries;

☐ identify benefits to children/families using the services provided by projects;

☐ record the number of childcare places (full and sessional), total capacity of all projects and the number of additional places as a result of this funding;

☐ document the employment and training opportunities created directly (number of staff employed by projects);

☐ document the employment and training opportunities created indirectly (parents returning to work/education due to crèche facilities being available);

☐ document (via a case study overview) the variety of childcare models funded, e.g. new/existing/upgrade, urban/rural;

☐ comment on the value for money emanating from the investment;

☐ review the differentials in projected project costs and actual project costs;

☐ recommend any policy implications which could impact on future development of the EOCP;

☐ make recommendations on the future development of the EOCP in terms of administrative procedures.

This review is now underway and it is expected to be completed in early 2003.

The NDP/CSF Evaluation Unit has responsibility for the evaluation of activity and expenditure under the various Operational Programmes of the NDP, including the Human Resources Operation Programme, which includes early education, and the two Regional Operation Programmes under which the EOCP is funded. At present, this Unit has drafted terms of reference for the evaluation of these Operational Programmes. The relevant monitoring committees will discuss these in September 2002. Assuming their approval, evaluation of these Operational Programmes will commence before the end of the year.

In addition, the Unit is undertaking an evaluation of the EOCP. According to the agreed terms of reference for this evaluation, its overall aim is to determine *whether the Childcare Programme is likely to achieve the objective of increasing both the quantity and quality of childcare places and support greater social inclusion by facilitating women and men to participate in/return to, education, training and employment.* The objectives of this evaluation are to establish:

☐ how the Childcare Programme is progressing and whether any adjustments are needed to ensure its objectives are fulfilled;

☐ more specifically, is the Programme meeting the key objectives of:
   → increasing the number and the quality of childcare facilities and places;
   → addressing staffing issues with a particular focus on increasing the number of trained staff, and up-skilling existing staff, in the childcare sector;

→ promoting equal opportunities and social inclusion;

→ improving the quality of childcare provision.

☐ is the Programme being managed and delivered in an efficient and effective way?

The evaluation is being carried out by staff of the NDP/CSF Evaluation Unit and overseen by the NDP/CSF Evaluation Steering Committee. It involves desk research, a survey of a sample of funded projects, in-depth interviews with key stakeholders involved in programme management and delivery and focus groups. It is anticipated that the evaluation will be complete by April 2003.

Research under the National Children's Strategy

One of the goals of the National Children's Strategy is that *Children's lives will be better understood; their lives will benefit from evaluation, research and information on their needs, rights and effectiveness of services.* (Government of Ireland, 2000), p38) Under this goal, several research studies are planned. Two of the most significant of these are the Longitudinal Study on Children and the *State of the Nation's Children Report.*

The National Children's Strategy and the Report of the Commission on the Family both proposed a longitudinal study of children in Ireland. In April 2002, the Minister for Social, Community and Family Affairs and the Minister for Children announced the decision of the Government to establish Ireland's first long-term study of children growing up in this country. This study will be jointly managed by the National Children's Office and the Department of Social, Community and Family Affairs, and is a key mechanism in implementing the second goal of the National Children's Strategy that children's lives will be better understood..

The study will monitor the development of 18,000 children from different backgrounds from two age cohorts. It will follow 10,000 children from birth and 8,000 from nine years to adulthood, yielding important information about each significant transition throughout their young lives. It will seek to identify the circumstances which allow children to thrive and those which hinder children's development. Information on three main areas will be collected in the course of this study: (i) social, economic and demographics, (ii) education and psychology and (iii) health. By looking at factors that contribute to or undermine the well-being of children in contemporary Irish families the study will contribute to formulation of policy and the design of services for children and their families.

A consortium of 117 experts from 20 different organisations produced a design for the study. Preparations for a request for tender are currently underway and it is anticipated that this will be issued in autumn 2002. It is expected that the contract will be awarded before the end of 2002 with a 12 to 18 month lead-in period before the study is fully operational. The Government has allocated €1.27 million to the study in 2002 to cover the start up costs of the study.

The *State of the Nation's Children Report* will be produced on a bi-annual basis and will provide a regularly updated and easily accessible statement on children's well being as this is reflected in a number of indicators. These indicators of child wellbeing will relate to the three national goals of the Children's Strategy – Children will have a voice, children's lives will be better understood and children will receive quality supports and services. Other work, including an EU wide feasibility study on the development of a system for sharing information on an inter-agency basis to support children in crisis will be drawn on in the development of an appropriate set of child wellbeing indicators for Ireland. International examples of data, such as that of the UNICEF, WHO and Federal Interagency Forum on Child and Family Statistics, will also inform this work. The work will also pay due attention to the goals on combating child poverty identified in the NAPS. Work on these indicators and the first *State of the Nations' Children Report* has not yet begun.

Chapter 5

CONCLUDING COMMENTS AND ASSESSMENTS

The issues of early childhood education and care have been central concerns of many organisations in Ireland for many years, most particularly those concerned with the needs and rights of children and women. It is, however, only in more recent years that these issues have come to the fore of national policy discussion and provision. This is particularly true of childcare. The factors encouraging this have been outlined earlier, and various weights can be, and have been attributed to these. Whatever the principal driving forces, it is important to acknowledge that much progress has been made in this area in recent years. Again, this is particularly the case in relation to non-school based early education and care. This sector has moved from being unco-ordinated and virtually unfunded by the State to one that has inter-connected structures to support its development at various levels and very considerable State funding through the NDP. In relation to early school-based education much has also been achieved in recent years with the introduction of Early Start and a range of primary school schemes targeted at those children most vulnerable to educational disadvantage and the problems that this brings in later life. These developments have been made possible due to the commitment and vision of those involved.

This report aims to provide an overview of the context and background to early childhood education and care in Ireland, the main policies in this area, the principal types of provision and the policy concerns arising. Throughout, a number of issues have been flagged. These are returned to here as it is considered that they warrant further comment. It is without doubt that not all of the relevant issues will be addressed, and the intention is not to be exhaustive in this regard. To do so would require significantly more analysis than is possible here. However, the following are a number of issues and concerns that arise in the early childhood education and care arena in Ireland.

The Focus of Early Childhood Education and Care

Having acknowledged progress in recent years, it is important to highlight some of the issues that remain outstanding in the early childhood education and care arena in Ireland. One such issue relates to the different rationales underlying State provision in these areas: combating educational disadvantage, promoting social inclusion and facilitating labour force participation by parents, and mothers in particular.

While a number of factors have influenced the increased concern with childcare, primary among them has been the growing economy and its adherent demand for female labour. This has generated an unprecedented demand for early childhood education and care services. Recognition of this is clearly stated in the National Childcare Strategy. While the EOCP seeks to develop high quality provision and ensure that the needs of children are paramount, to promote greater gender equality and to attain greater social inclusion, it also emphases the provision of services for parents trying to reconcile work and family life and the achievement of gender equality in the labour market. The other main source of support to this sector has been through the Community Employment Programme aimed at easing the transition to employment for the long-term unemployed. In this regard, while the development of early childhood services may well be critical in addressing the needs of the labour market and promoting participation, it is unlikely that such provision alone will address the many and diverse needs of those experiencing labour market disadvantage and long-term unemployment.

Where the labour market needs of parents are referenced in terms of early childhood care and education, it is not uncommon to find a negative tone. However, a growing economy, increased employment, and greater gender equality in the work force are, generally, positive developments in a society. In Ireland, they have coincided and provided a context for the development of quality early childcare and education services that work to the benefit of children. The contribution of the EOCP to this development is considerable as it is through this Programme that many of the recommendations of the National Childcare Strategy have been implemented and substantial financial support has been channelled to providers. Using a partnership approach that has built on existing provision and tapped into existing experience and expertise, this Programme has contributed significantly to the development of the childcare sector.

The aims and immediate policy context of early education services in the school system are often articulated in terms of the education and development of the child in order to allow them to participate fully in their communities and society. Specific measures to combat educational disadvantage have been introduced, which also have a social inclusion function.

These different approaches and underlying rationales have implications for the development of co-ordinated policies and services and this issue is returned to below. It is important here to also note the absence of universal pre-school provision in Ireland. This key issue was debated in the policy fora identified above, with the government of the day making a decision that the needs of the most vulnerable should be given priority through targeted interventions. However, the debate on universal provision is now beginning to re-emerge in Ireland in the context of the debate on the rights of the child.

Continuum of Education and Care

It has already been stated above that almost every policy document concerning early childhood education and care in Ireland professes a view that care and education cannot be separated but must be viewed as part of a learning continuum that starts at birth. Despite this, in looking at education and care in Ireland, it is difficult not to conclude that these two concepts separate into the two main categories identified earlier in this report: childcare on the one hand and early education on the other. In essence, this is an administrative divide and separates provision into non-school based childcare and school-based early education, even though childcare services embrace education components, and early school-based education provides elements of care.

In the course of meetings to inform this report this administrative separation was referred to repeatedly and was often seen as the result of so-called 'turf wars' or competition over the control of resources or policy areas. However, this does not appear to be the case. Instead, there appears to be a genuine lack of understanding of how and where 'care' and 'education' overlap, a lack of opportunities to discuss this and the absence of clear channels of communication between those responsible for relevant policies and programmes. This issue was also clearly identified in discussions relating to co-ordination where there is seen to be little correspondence between the principal policy actors in the 'care' and 'education' sectors, despite the clear overlap of care and education in provision on the ground.

The historical context is vital here. School-based early education provision in the form of infant classes has existed for many years and has long established policy development, management and administration structures. Childcare on the other hand has come to the fore only in recent years and is at the stage of developing as a national sector and putting in place national and local structures for the co-ordination and management of policy and delivery of services. It will take time for these two systems to come to an accommodation of each other that serves the integrated needs of children, parents and society more generally. On a positive note, however, a number of moves were identified as addressing this gap on the ground if not in the policy echelons. These include the emergence of accredited courses that emphasise a combination of childcare and education that will better enable workers to address the care, education and developmental needs of young children.

Quality, Access and Co-ordination

Quality, access and co-ordination are intrinsically linked and, in many cases, it is difficult to clearly separate the issues arising in each area. However, the relationship between these three areas is one of ongoing tensions such as that between accessibility in terms of affordability and quality as defined by the Child Care (Pre-School) Regulations. Predominantly, these issues tend to be discussed from the perspective of parents. However, they should also be considered from the provider's perspective. For parents, the issues of affordability, access and quality are not separate. The relationship between these issues is not a simple linear one where high cost services lead to ready access (defined in either physical or other terms) and high quality. Due to the rapid increases in the demand for services and the time-lag experienced in meeting these demands due to the low base position from which Ireland started in the mid-1990s, the relationship tends to be one of high cost, low accessibility and variable quality.

From the provider's perspective, the relationship between these is equally if not more complex. In attempting to meet Pre-School Services Regulations, many have to update their facilities at a minimum and in some cases undertake renovations and refurbishments. The cost of this alone may be sufficient to result in a price increase to parents. The demands for additional staff required by expansion also impacts on quality and linked to this is a need for innovative approaches to training. In addition, many providers are now concerned with quality beyond the Child Care (Pre-School) Regulations in terms of employing trained staff, maintaining voluntary standards in respect of materials, equipment, etc. Again, adherence to these quality standards may result in price increases that parents may be unwilling or unable to pay. The EOCP is providing valuable support to some providers in this regard through the provision of capital and staffing, as well as support to specific initiatives targeted at improving the quality of provision.

The relationship between access, quality and co-ordination is not a simple one. Wider access to early childhood education and care through the provision of additional places is a key quality concern and also a stated commitment of the current Government. However, given the current situation regarding co-ordination outlined above, it is difficult to determine which Government Department or Departments or agencies should have central responsibility for the co-ordinated creation, regulation and support of such expanded provision.

The Future: Key Challenges

Early childhood education and care has seen substantial development and improvement in recent years that is to be welcomed. Nonetheless, key challenges remain in many areas. The issues of improving and assuring quality services is one in which further policy and support is needed. Forthcoming work in this area has been identified above. This work should draw on the experience of current quality initiatives and measures as well as regulatory mechanisms.

In the area of access, how wider access is provided to disadvantaged or vulnerable children and families is of primary importance and, following this, if and how more widespread or universal access to pre-school education and care can be achieved.

Co-ordination remains one of the key challenges facing policy-makers in particular. The creation of effective and efficient co-ordination mechanisms or structures that address the needs and concerns of the various stakeholders – children, parents, providers, funders - involved in early education and care and that recognises the contribution and expertise of both the 'education' and 'care' sectors would be a substantial advance in this arena.

In research and evaluation, the substantial body of work already achieved as well as that planned will contribute to our growing knowledge of the needs of young children and how these can be addressed though early education and care. However, gaps remain. In particular, there is a need for additional statistics on early childhood services provided for by the DES and for the further disaggregation of those that are currently collected. For example, disaggregated statistics on participation in infant classes and the funding these attract from core and additional sources would be a useful addition to our knowledge. There is also a need for the regular collection and analysis of data on childcare services that builds on the experience of the National Childcare Census and on national surveys carried out to inform the various policy makers. Regularly collated information on childcare services notified to the various Health Boards would also prove useful, as would further research into the early childhood education and care experiences and needs of particularly vulnerable groups of children.

Ensuring that children are placed and remain at the centre of all policies and services aimed at them is a key challenge in every relevant area of policy and provision. In addressing this and other challenges, one option is to adopt, or adapt, an approach underpinned by the principles that guide existing government policy in the National Children's Strategy. Central here are the six operational principles on which the implementation of the Strategy is based. These are that all actions will be child-centred, family oriented, equitable, inclusive, action oriented and integrated. Such an approach allows aspiration of meeting the needs of all children and for targeted interventions to address the needs of children at risk of exclusion and disadvantage as a priority.

REFERENCES

ARCHER, P., HANNAN, D.F., DENNY, K. AND HARMON, C. (2000), *Features of the Irish Education System – Report for the United Kingdom Department of Employment and Education,* Dublin, Educational Research Centre.

AREA DEVELOMENT MANAGEMENT LIMITED (2000), *Targeting Disadvantage and Exclusion, Annual Report 2000,* Dublin, ADM Ltd.

AREA DEVELOMENT MANAGEMENT LIMITED (2002), *Staffing, Quality and Childcare Provision: An Evaluation of the Community Support Childcare Initiative of the Equal Opportunities Childcare Programme 1998-2000,* Dublin, ADM.

AREA DEVELOMENT MANAGEMENT LIMITED (forthcoming, 2002), *The National Summary of the County Childcare Census 1999/2000,* Dublin, ADM.

BARNARDOS (2000a)' *Evaluation of Work and Services in Dun Laoghaire and Loughlinstown/Ballybrack 1989 – 1999,* Dublin, Barnardos.

BEST HEALTH FOR CHILDREN (2000), *Investing In Parenthood to Achieve Best Health for Children: The Supporting Parents Strategy,* Dublin, Best Health for Children.

BMW REGIONAL ASSEMBLY (2000), *Ireland: Border, Midlands and West Regional Operational Programme 2000-2006,* Ballaghaderreen, BMW Regional Assembly.

BYRNE, C. (1999), "Education for Early Years Teachers", paper presented to the "Enhancing Quality in the Early Years" international conference, November 1999.

CENTRAL STATISTICS OFFICE (1990-1997), *Annual Labour Force Surveys,* Dublin, The Stationery Office.

CENTRAL STATISTICS OFFICE (2002a), *Census 2002 Preliminary Report,* Dublin, The Stationery Office.

CENTRAL STATISTICS OFFICE (2002b), *Quarterly National Household Survey, Second Quarter 2002,* Dublin, The Stationery Office.

CENTRE FOR SOCIAL AND EDUCATIONAL RESEARCH (2000), *An Evaluation of Barnardos Early Years Services,* Dublin, CSER.

COMBAT POVERTY AGENCY (2002), *Combat Poverty Agency Annual Report 2001,* Dublin, Combat Poverty Agency.

CORRIGAN, C. (ed.) (forthcoming 2002), *Sources of Data on Poverty,* Dublin, Combat Poverty Agency.

COUNTY WEXFORD PARTNERSHIP (2000), *Report of the Evaluation of the County Wexford Partnership Childcare Programme 1996-1999 and Recommendations for a County Childcare Strategy for County Wexford Partnership,* Wexford, County Wexford Partnership.

DEPARTMENT OF EDUCATION (1992), *Education for a Changing World - Green Paper on Education,* Dublin, The Stationery Office.

DEPARTMENT OF EDUCATION (1993), *Report of the Special Education Review Committee,* Dublin, The Stationery Office.

DEPARTMENT OF EDUCATION (1995), *Charting Our Education Future - White Paper on Education,* Dublin, The Stationery Office.

DEPARTMENT OF EDUCATION AND SCIENCE (1998), "Early Start Pre-School Intervention Project Curricular Guidelines for Good Practice", Unpublished.

DEPARTMENT OF EDUCATION AND SCIENCE (1999a), *Primary School Curriculum: Introduction,* Dublin, The Stationery Office.

DEPARTMENT OF EDUCATION AND SCIENCE (1999b), *Primary School Curriculum: Your Child's Learning – Guidelines for Parents,* Dublin, The Stationery Office.

DEPARTMENT OF EDUCATION AND SCIENCE (1999c), Annual Report 1999, Dublin, Department of Education and Science.

DEPARTMENT OF EDUCATION AND SCIENCE (2000), *Boards of Management of National Schools – Constitution of Boards and Rules of Procedure,* Dublin, The Stationery Office.

DEPARTMENT OF EDUCATION AND SCIENCE (2001a), *Statistical Report 1999/2000,* Dublin, The Stationery Office.

DEPARTMENT OF EDUCATION AND SCIENCE (2001b), "Woods Establishes Regional Education Office Network", Press Release, 15th April, 2001.

DEPARTMENT OF EDUCATION AND SCIENCE (2002a), *Guidelines on Traveller Education in Primary Schools,* Dublin, The Stationery Office.

DEPARTMENT OF EDUCATION AND SCIENCE (2002), *Preparing Teachers for the 21st Century: Report of the Working Group on Primary Preservice Teacher Education,* Dublin, The Stationery Office.

DEPARTMENT OF EDUCATION AND SCIENCE (forthcoming 2002), *Statistical Report 2000/2001,* Dublin, The Stationery Office.

DEPARTMENT OF THE ENVIRONMENT AND LOCAL GOVERNMENT (2001), *Childcare Facilities Guidelines for Planning Authorities,* Dublin, The Stationery Office.

DEPARTMENT OF THE ENVIRONMENT AND LOCAL GOVERNMENT (2002), *Annual Housing Statistics Bulletin 2001,* Dublin, The Stationery Office.

DEPARTMENT OF FINANCE (2002), *Economic Review and Outlook 2002,* Dublin, The Stationery Office.

DEPARTMENT OF FOREIGN AFFAIRS (1996), *United Nations Convention on the Rights of the Child: First National Report of Ireland,* Dublin: Department of Foreign Affairs.

DEPARTMENT OF HEALTH AND CHILDREN (1997), *Child Care (Pre-School Services) Regulations 1996 and Child Care (Pre-School Services) (Amendment) Regulations 1997 and Explanatory Guide to Requirements and Procedures for Notification and Inspection,* Dublin, The Stationery Office.

DEPARTMENT OF HEALTH AND CHILDREN (2001), *Progress Report on the Statement of Strategy: Working for health and Wellbeing 1998-2001,* Dublin, Department of Health and Children.

DEPARTMENT OF JUSTICE, EQUALITY AND LAW REFORM (1998) *Study of the Economics of Childcare in Ireland,* Dublin, The Stationery Office.

DEPARTMENT OF JUSTICE, EQUALITY AND LAW REFORM (2000), *Childcare Funding in Ireland,* Dublin, Department of Justice, Equality and Law Reform

DEPARTMENT OF JUSTICE, EQUALITY AND LAW REFORM (2001), 'County Childcare Committee Handbook', unpublished.

DEPARTMENT OF JUSTICE, EQUALITY AND LAW REFORM (2001b), *Statement of Strategy 2001-2004,* Dublin, Department of Justice, Equality and Law Reform.

DEPARTMENT OF JUSTICE, EQUALITY AND LAW REFORM (2002), *Quality Childcare and Lifelong Learning: Model Framework for Education, Training and Professional Development in the Early Childhood Care and Education Sector,* Dublin, Department of Justice, Equality and Law Reform.

DEPARTMENT OF SOCIAL AND FAMILY AFFAIRS (2002), *National Report for the OECD Review of Family Friendly Policies – The Reconciliation of Work and Family Life,* Department of Social and Family Affairs, unpublished.

DEPARTMENT OF SOCIAL, COMMUNITY AND FAMILY AFFAIRS, (2001), *Review of the National Anti-Poverty Strategy, Framework Document 2001,* unpublished, available on request from the Department of Social and Family Affairs.

DEPARTMENT OF SOCIAL, COMMUNITY AND FAMILY AFFAIRS (2002), *Statistical Information on Social Welfare Services 2001,* Dublin: The Stationery Office.

DEPARTMENT OF AN TAOISEACH (2002), *Programme for Prosperity and Fairness: Eight Progress Report,* Dublin, Department of An Taoiseach.

DUBLIN INSTITUTE OF TECHNOLOGY (2001), *Research and Training Centres Report of Activities 2000,* Dublin, Dublin Institute of Technology.

DUFFY, D., FITZGERALD J., KEARNEY, I. AND SMYTH, D. (1999), *The Medium-Term review 1999 – 2005,* Dublin: Economic and Social Research Institute.

DRUDY, P.J. AND PUNCH (2000), "Housing and Inequality in Ireland", in S. Cantillon, C. Corrigan, P. Kirby and J. O'Flynn (Eds.), *Rich and Poor: Perspectives on Tackling Inequality in Ireland,* Dublin, Oak Tree Press.

EDUCATIONAL RESEARCH CENTRE (1998), *Early Start Pre-school Programme: Final Evaluation Report,* Dublin, Educational Research Centre.

EUROPEAN SOCIAL FUND PROGRAMME EVALUATION UNIT (1999), *Preliminary Evaluation of the Equal Opportunities Childcare Programme,* Dublin, ESF Programme Evaluation Unit.

FAHEY, T. AND RUSSELL, H. (2001), *Family Formation in Ireland: Trends, Data Needs and Implications,* Policy Research Series No. 43, Dublin, Economic and Social Research Institute.

FANNING, B, VEALE, A. AND O'CONNOR, D. (2001), *Beyond the Pale: Asylum-Seeking Children and Social Exclusion in Ireland,* Dublin, The Irish Refugee Council.

FINE-DAVIS, M., CLARKE, H. & BERRY, M. (ED.S) (2002), *Fathers and Mothers: Dilemmas of the Work-Life Balance, Conference Proceedings,* Dublin, Centre for Gender and Women's Studies, Trinity College.

FINNEGAN, R.B. AND MCCARRON, E.T. (2000), *Ireland: Historical Echoes, Contemporary Politics,* Oxford, Westview Press.

GOVERNMENT OF IRELAND (1990), *Report of the Primary Education Review Body,* Dublin, Stationery Office)

GOVERNMENT OF IRELAND, (1997), *An Action Plan for the Millennium,* Dublin, The Stationery Office.

GOVERNMENT OF IRELAND (1998), *Strengthening Families for Life: Final Report of the Commission on the Family to the Minister for Social, Community and Family Affairs,* Dublin, The Stationery Office.

GOVERNMENT OF IRELAND (1999a), *The Constitution of Ireland / Bunreacht na hEireann,* Dublin, The Stationery Office.

GOVERNMENT OF IRELAND (1999b), *National Childcare Strategy: Report of the Partnership 2000 Expert Working Group on Childcare,* Dublin, The Stationery Office.

GOVERNMENT OF IRELAND (1999c), *Ready to Learn: White Paper on Early Childhood Education,* Dublin, The Stationery Office.

GOVERNMENT OF IRELAND (1999d), *Programme for Prosperity and Fairness,* Dublin, The Stationery Office.

GOVERNMENT OF IRELAND (1999e), *Ireland's National Development Plan, 2000-2006,* Dublin, The Stationery Office.

GOVERNMENT OF IRELAND (2000) *The National Children's Strategy, Our Children – Their Lives,* Dublin: The Stationery Office.

GOVERNMENT OF IRELAND (2002a), *An Agreed Programme for Government Between Fianna Fáil and The Progressive Democrats,* Dublin, The Stationery Office.

GOVERNMENT OF IRELAND (2002b), *Building an Inclusive Society: Review of the National Anti-Poverty Strategy under the Programme for Prosperity and Fairness,* Dublin, The Stationery Office.

HAYES, N. and O'FLAHERTY, J., with KERNAN, M. (1997), *A Window on Early Education in Ireland: The First National Report of the IEA Preprimary Project,* Dublin, Dublin Institute of Technology.

HAYES, N. and KERNAN, M. (2001), *Seven Years Old – School Experience in Ireland: National Report of the IEA Preprimary Project (II),* Dublin, Centre for Social and Educational Research.

HAYES, N. (2001), "Cherishing all the Children of the Nation Equally": State Provision and Respinsibility for Children in Ireland", in Cleary A, Nic Ghiolla Phadraig, M. and Quin, S. *Understanding Children, Volume 1: State, Education and Economy,* Dublin, Oak Tree Press.

HAYES, N. (2002) *Children's Rights – Whose Right? A Review of Child Policy Development in Ireland,* Dublin: The Policy Institute at Trinity College Dublin.

HUMPHRIES, P., FLEMING, S. AND O'DONNELL, O. (2000), *Balancing Work and Family Life: The Role of Flexible Working Arrangements,* Dublin, Department of Social, Community and Family Affairs with the Institute for Public Administration.

IPPA, THE QUALITY CHILDCARE ORGANISATION (2001), 'Quality - a Discussion Paper' , Presented to the National Coordinating Childcare Committee, March 2001.

IRISH CONGRESS OF TRADE UNIONS (2002), *Identifying Member's Childcare Needs,* Dublin: Irish Congress of Trade Unions.

IRISH NATIONAL TEACHERS ORGANISATION (1995) *Early Childhood Education: Issues and Concerns,* Dublin, INTO.

IRISH NATIONAL TEACHERS ORGANISATION (2000) *Early Years Learning, Proceedings of an Early Education Conference, St. Patrick's College of Education Drumcondra, February 2000* Dublin, INTO.

IRISH NATIONAL TEACHERS ORGANISATION (undated) *Intercultural Guidelines for Schools: Valuing Difference, Combating Racism, Promoting Inclusiveness and Equality,* Dublin, INTO.

KELLAGHAN, T. (1977), *The evaluation of an intervention programme for disadvantaged children,* Slough, NFER Publishing Company.

KELLAGHAN, T. & GREANEY, B. J. (1992), *The educational development of students following participation in a preschool programme in a disadvantaged area,* Dublin, Educational Research Centre, St. Patrick's College.

KENNEDY, F. (2001), *Cottage to Crèche: Family Change in Ireland,* Dublin, The Institute for Public Administration.

MURPHY, B. (2000), *Support for the Educationally and Socially Disadvantaged: An Introductory Guide to Government Funded Initiatives in Ireland,* Cork, Education Department, University College Cork.

MURRAY, C. and O'DOHERTY, A. (2001), *Eist – Respecting Diversity in Early Childhood Care, Eduation and Training,* Dublin, Pavee Point.

NATIONAL CHILDREN'S NURSERIES ASSOCIATION (2002) NCNA Members Survey, August 2002

NATIONAL ECONOMIC AND SOCIAL COUNCIL (1999), *Opportunities, Challenges and Capacity for Choice,* Dublin, National Economic and Social Council.

NATIONAL EDUCATION CONVENTION SECRETARIAT (1994), *Report of the National Education Convention,* Dublin, National Education Convention Secretariat.

NATIONAL FORUM SECRETARIAT (1998), *Report on the National Forum for Early Childhood Education,* Dublin, The Stationery Office.

NOLAN, B. (2000), *Child Poverty in Ireland,* Dublin, Oak Tree Press in association with the Combat Poverty Agency.

PAVEE POINT (2002a), *Fact Sheets: Traveller Children,* Dublin, Pavee Point.

PAVEE POINT (2002b), *Fact Sheets: Education and Training,* Dublin, Pavee Point.

UNITED NATIONS (1998), *Concluding observations of the Committee on the Rights of the Child: Ireland. 04/02/98. CRC/C/15/Add.85. (Concluding Observations/Comments),* Geneva: United Nations.

Annex 1

THE IRISH EDUCATION SYSTEM

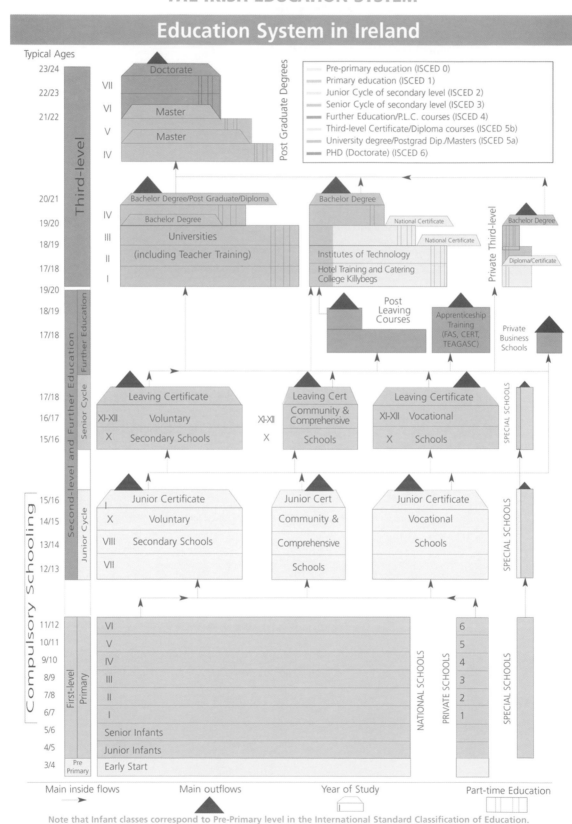

Education System in Ireland

Note that Infant classes correspond to Pre-Primary level in the International Standard Classification of Education.

Annex 2

PRINCIPAL TYPES OF EARLY CHILDHOOD EDUCATION AND CARE PROVISION

Type of Care Catered For	Typical Age Range	Typical Duration of Service	Ownership
Pre-schools / Play Schools	3 to 6 years	Sessional – morning or afternoon	Mainly privately owned, with some community-based not-for-profit
Nurseries / Crèches	Birth to 6 years	Full day, although some accept children on a part-time basis. Small number of drop-in facilities	Mainly privately owned, with some community-owned
Montessori Schools	3 to 6 years	Sessional, usually mornings	Privately owned
Naionrai	3 to 6 years	Sessional, usually mornings	Privately owned
Parent and Toddler Groups	Birth to 3 years	Sessional	Attached to both privately owned and community-based not-for-profit services
Early Start	3 to 4 years	Sessional, usually mornings	Supported by the Dept. of Education and Science
Pre-Schools for Traveller Children	3 to 6 years	Sessional, usually mornings	Supported by the Dept. of Education and Science
Infant Classes	4 to 8 years	Shortened school day – mainly mornings	Supported by the Dept. of Education and Science
Childminders	Birth to late childhood	Various – full day and part-time	Private individuals
After-School and Out-of School Care	From 4 years upwards	Various – after-school and school holidays	Privately owned facilities as well as some community-based not-for-profit

THE EOCP: SUMMARY TABLES

Table 12 Summary by Region and County of the Original and Projected number of childcare places (full-time and part-time) and number of paid staff (full-time and part-time) in facilities supported under the EOCP, 2000 – 31 August 2002[1]

Border, Midlands, and West Region / County	Childcare Places Full Time		Childcare Places Part Time		Paid Staff Full Time		Paid Staff Part Time	
	At Time of First Successful Application	Projected with EOCP Support[2]	At Time of First Successful Application	Projected with EOCP Support	At Time of First Successful Application	Projected with EOCP Support	At Time of First Successful Application	Projected with EOCP Support
Cavan	43	97	316	800	17	44	27	63
Donegal	50	319	521	964	11	78	60	123
Galway County	87	290	575	1282	35	104	54	86
Galway City	70	147	420	639	23	56	32	35
Longford	37	219	142	357	4	48	12	33
Louth	86	418	340	730	27	112	13	48
Leitrim	15	92	307	567	9	33	27	50
Laois	62	252	278	606	13	52	22	67
Monaghan	41	180	397	639	7	47	24	38
Mayo	45	172	457	889	13	40	39	72
Offaly	10	53	287	621	4	23	20	42
Roscommon	44	149	217	356	10	42	25	39
Sligo	6	85	118	190	2	12	13	41
Westmeath	130	282	655	862	34	64	36	70
TOTAL BMW	726	2755	5030	9502	209	755	404	807

[1] In these two tables *it is essential here to note that these figures relate only to facilities funded under the EOCP and are not an exhaustive or representative account of the number of childcare services, places or staff at county, regional or national level.*

[2] In all cases 'Projected with EOCP Support' are impact figures. These refer to the total number of childcare places or staff the facilities are anticipated to have following receipt and use of funding. This includes the original number of places and staff facilities had at the time of their first successful application to the EOCP.

Source: ADM Monitoring Statistics for the EOCP Programme

Summary by Region and County of the Original and Projected number of childcare places (full-time and part-time) and number of paid staff (full-time and part-time) in facilities supported under the EOCP, 2000 – 31 August 2002

Southern and Eastern Region	Childcare Places Full Time		Childcare Places Part Time		Paid Staff Full Time		Paid Staff Part Time	
County	At Time of First Successful Application	Projected with EOCP Support[2]	At Time of First Successful Application	Projected with EOCP Support	At Time of First Successful Application	Projected with EOCP Support	At Time of First Successful Application	Projected with EOCP Support
Cork County	126	659	1027	1633	51	191	86	129
Cork City	152	353	885	1175	37	110	58	84
Clare	91	284	259	709	24	87	21	40
Carlow	34	122	122	246	11	25	12	17
Dublin County Borough	547	1494	2049	3216	133	366	114	210
Fingal	175	522	187	590	45	132	19	44
DunLaoghaire Rathdown	291	749	398	744	90	193	46	70
South County Dublin	212	587	496	917	67	140	45	105
Kildare	108	244	147	527	27	68	19	57
Kilkenny	52	197	361	649	14	60	30	39
Kerry	104	367	607	1473	25	121	54	117
Limerick County	38	149	195	356	13	44	18	24
Limerick City	108	214	525	663	29	50	30	67
Meath	77	191	377	652	34	59	36	68
Tipperary North	27	195	156	330	9	44	13	33
Tipperary South	7	150	381	541	5	36	25	40
Waterford County	38	81	101	195	6	13	7	13
Waterford City	128	263	275	267	22	49	36	45
Wicklow	44	110	424	706	12	39	25	41
Wexford	141	429	484	710	27	89	39	65
TOTAL SAE	**2,500**	**7,360**	**9,454**	**16,299**	**681**	**1,916**	**733**	**1,308**
CUMULATIVE TOTAL	**3,226**	**10,115**	**14,434**	**25,801**	**890**	**2,671**	**1,137**	**2,115**

Source: ADM Monitoring Statistics for the EOCP Programme

Grants Approved Under the EOCP by Grant Type, Region and County – 2000 to 31 August 2002

County	Staffing Grants		Capital Grants – Community-Based Facilities		Capital Grants – Self-Employed		Sub-measure 3 – Quality Improvement		Total Approved	
	No.	€	No.	€	No.	€	No.	€	No.	€
Cavan	19	1,384,313	9	772,721	9	225,153	3	338,726	40	2,720,913
Donegal	28	1,926,276	19	1,874,662	12	469,526	7	694,441	66	4,964,905
Galway County	29	1,868,289	7	203,161	31	855,585	3	123,262	70	3,050,297
Galway City	17	1,748,446	11	1,083,154	8	290,841	2	451,158	38	3,573,599
Longford	11	1,138,245	7	616,724	11	457,036	2	169,100	31	2,381,105
Louth	12	2,537,976	6	328,829	24	742,176	5	421,931	47	4,030,912
Leitrim	19	1,743,708	12	950,611	4	79,290	3	323,873	38	3,097,482
Laois	12	989,388	5	1,752,065	14	324,733	3	216,975	34	3,283,161
Monaghan	16	1,430,709	15	1,643,766	1	57,816	3	831,844	35	3,964,135
Mayo	29	2,743,800	9	676,646	10	311,740	3	321,589	51	4,053,775
Offaly	9	1,047,889	2	77,981	9	130,950	3	314,368	23	1,571,188
Roscommon	13	985,029	8	371,477	5	162,501	2	186,907	28	1,705,914
Sligo	10	1,036,753	5	431,347	2	37,777	2	261,777	19	1,767,654
Westmeath	15	1,396,656	9	913,210	15	488,771	3	540,325	42	3,338,962
TOTAL BMW	**239**	**21,977,477**	**124**	**11,696,354**	**155**	**4,633,895**	**44**	**5,196,276**	**562**	**43,504,002**
Cork County	35	3,161,577	23	1,615,746	35	1,113,032	6	248,449	99	6,138,804
Cork City	33	4,754,203	21	159,249	8	3,312,201	3	567,931	65	8,793,584
Clare	11	1,690,580	7	1,584,835	11	466,524	5	476,287	34	4,218,226
Carlow	7	1,086,408	8	878,518	4	41,995	3	212,296	22	2,219,217
Dublin County Borough	94	12,963,773	51	11,472,459	22	824,917	18	6,266,147	185	31,527,296
Fingal	9	1,300,559	9	766,395	25	906,754	4	171,700	47	3,145,408
South County Dublin	10	1,068,442	7	1,224,251	25	683,333	4	505,986	46	3,482,012
DunLaoghaire Rathdown	30	3,621,984	15	3,417,661	17	642,136	3	3,818,297	65	11,500,078
Kildare	4	457,433	4	126,730	12	775,914	3	330,595	23	1,690,672
Kilkenny	14	1,797,694	6	639,265	9	288,670	4	305,561	33	3,031,190
Kerry	38	5,200,095	16	3,037,660	19	569,292	7	436,081	80	9,243,128
Limerick City	6	648,430	3	303,320	30	283,778	4	403,432	43	1,638,960
Limerick County	13	2,990,949	2	454,193	5	160,807	1	167,418	21	3,773,367
Meath	5	541,312	1	4,444	18	668,395	4	219,248	28	1,433,399
Tipperary North	7	1,654,465	2	1,054,472	9	224,537	5	536,324	23	3,469,798
Tipperary South	16	1,011,516	9	937,687	3	13,374	2	268,492	30	2,231,069
Waterford County	1	82,450	3	195,907	8	211,684	2	236,267	14	726,308
Waterford City	4	1,132,814	5	894,573	3	90,191	5	178,571	17	2,296,149
Wicklow	9	1,015,781	8	190,338	13	378,916	5	1,623,311	35	3,208,346
Wexford	19	2,185,329	15	2,198,787	22	837,903	5	431,521	61	5,653,540
TOTAL SAE	**365**	**48,365,794**	**215**	**31,156,490**	**298**	**12,494,353**	**93**	**17,403,914**	**971**	**109,420,551**
CUMULATIVE TOTAL	**604**	**70,343,271**	**339**	**42,852,844**	**453**	**17,128,248**	**137**	**22,600,190**	**1533**	**152,924,553**

Source: *ADM Monitoring Statistics for the EOCP Programme*

Annex 4

PRIMARY SCHOOL PROGRAMMES
TO COMBAT EDUCATIONAL DISADVANTAGE

Breaking the Cycle

Breaking the Cycle was introduced as a five-year pilot programme in 1996 in schools designated as disadvantaged. Based on research conducted by the Combat Poverty Agency and the ERC on selection criteria, schools were designated as disadvantaged according to a number of social and economic characteristics. These included the proportion of pupils from homes in which the main breadwinner was unemployed for more than one year, the proportion of pupils living in lone parent households and the proportion of pupils whose father and/or mother had, at most, basic educational qualifications. The scheme provided for extra staffing, funding, in-career development and a pupil teacher ratio of 15:1. The purpose of these additional resources was to support each participating school to develop improvement strategies, which are designed to break the cycle of intergenerational educational disadvantage. The pilot phase ended in June 2001 and the future of the scheme will be considered in light of an evaluation report being prepared by the ERC. Thirty-two urban schools accounting for 5,652 pupils and 120 rural schools with 6,052 pupils were catered for under this programme.

Giving Children an Even Break

This initiative was launched by the DES in 2001 following a survey of primary schools by the ERC. This survey provided an objective basis for the identification of pupils at risk of educational disadvantage and early school leaving and is the most comprehensive survey of the incidence of educational disadvantage in primary schools in Ireland. Based on the concentration of disadvantaged pupils, schools were ranked on the basis of economic and social criteria associated with educational disadvantage. Additional resources were then made available to schools according to the degree of disadvantage as illustrated by their rank position. In urban areas, where the larger concentrations of disadvantaged pupils were located, these resources resulted in a pupil teacher ratio of no more than 20 to one in the infant classes and the following two classes, as well as funding towards additional in-school and out-of-school activities. In rural areas, a teacher / coordinator was appointed to work with clusters of 4 to five schools with high levels of at risk pupils. These coordinators will support schools and teachers in developing ways of meeting the needs of pupils experiencing disadvantage. Individual schools that could not be clustered received additional funding for in-school and out-of-school activities.

Teachers and schools are supported in adapting their teaching styles and strategies to derive maximum benefit from significantly reduced pupil/teacher ratios. Schools and their staff, including new local coordinators, will be supported in the effective use of the new teaching supports and financial allocations in providing enhanced services that meet the needs of at risk young people in school and out-of-school.

A key condition of participation in this programme is that the school subscribes to a holistic interpretation of the child's development. Other conditions of participation include the development of a specific school retention policy, the preparation of a three-year developmental plan for policy and practice in the school, collaborative planning with the representatives of local statutory and voluntary agencies for the integrated delivery of in-school and out-of-school supports for the targeted pupils and their families, targeting of new in and out-of-school supports at the pupils whose enrolment qualified the school for the additional supports through the survey, the identification of the needs of the individual targeted pupils – curricular and learning needs and social and personal needs – and the development of strategies that best meet those needs, and the development of strategies that encourage and enable parents to become involved in their children's education.

The DES has given a commitment to external formative and summative evaluation of this programme. In this, a sample of schools given assistance will be selected for intensive examination of a number of issues including matters related to the concentration and dispersal of disadvantage, possible anomalies highlighted in the survey analyses and an evaluation of criteria and methods used for pupil identification and school selection in the current and in possible future processes. This work will provide an estimate of the accuracy of the information supplied in the original survey undertaken by the ERC and will inform future exercises of this kind.

The full implementation of this new programme has yet to be achieved. Costing €33 million, it will benefit 2,144 primary schools around the country, with initiatives targeted at over 80,000 pupils considered to be risk of educational disadvantage. In total it is expected that 204 extra teachers will be employed over a three-year period, 150 of which will be in urban areas and 54 of which will be in rural areas. Training will be provided for teachers to help them gain an understanding of educational disadvantage and to help them in the delivery of targeted supports.

Scheme of Assistance to Schools in Designated Areas of Disadvantage (Primary)

Until recently, the primary mechanism for addressing the effects of socio-economic deprivation in primary schools was the Disadvantaged Areas Scheme. Under this DES funded scheme, special teaching assistance and extra funding was provided to schools in areas designated as disadvantaged. Schools seeking disadvantaged status were assessed and prioritised on the basis of socio-economic and educational indicators such as unemployment levels, housing, medical card holders, information on basic literacy and numeracy and pupil teacher ratios. In the school year 2001/2002, 314 primary schools serving 68,565 pupils received support under the Disadvantaged Areas Scheme. There are 293 additional over-quota teaching posts in 250 of these schools.

For the 2001/2002 school year, a capitation supplement of €38.09 is paid per pupil to schools designated under this scheme. This is to cover general running costs, classroom materials and equipment and home / school liaison activities. In addition to these supports, schools also received a refund of their television licence fee, a 95% Building Grant for approved building projects, and financial assistance to alleviate serious current financial difficulty.

Home/School/Community Liaison Scheme (HSCL)

The HSCL is a key aspect of the DES's strategy to address educational disadvantage at both primary and second level. Under the HSCL, a co-ordinator (teacher) is assigned to a school or group of schools and works with school staff, parents and community agencies to address the educational needs of children at risk of or experiencing educational disadvantage. In September 1999, all primary and second level schools with disadvantaged status that were not already part of the HSCL scheme were invited to join and most have taken up this invitation. There are currently 176 whole time equivalent posts at primary level. A National Co-ordinator oversees the day-to-day operation of the Scheme. In 2000, almost €9 million was spent on this scheme which serves over 70,000 pupils at primary level.

Traveller Children

Support is provided for an estimated 5,000 Traveller children at primary level, approximately 4,600 of which attend ordinary primary schools. These are supported by 465 resource teachers for Travellers. The remaining children are attending one of the 4 special schools dedicated to Traveller children. These special schools for Travellers operate at a pupil teacher ratio of 14:1. A special capitation rate of €249.50 is paid in respect of Traveller children under 12 years, irrespective of where they are attending school.

Children with Special Needs

Education policy in respect of children with special needs seeks to secure the maximum possible level of integration of these children into the mainstream school system. Where this is not possible due to the level of disability, dedicated specialist facilities continue to be made available in a special dedicated class attached to an ordinary school or in a special dedicated school.

Under the Education Act 1998, all children with disabilities within the primary system have an automatic entitlement to a response to their needs, irrespective of their level of need or location. This has resulted in the number of resource teachers supporting children with general learning disabilities in integrated settings in the primary system increasing from 104 in October 1998 to approximately 2,000 in 2002. In addition, the number of special needs assistants supporting children with learning disabilities in the primary system has grown from less than 300 to 3,000 over the same period. Approximately 13,000 children with special needs attend ordinary primary schools on a fully integrated basis.

Where a child has a learning disability that prevents them from attending integrated primary school classes they may attend special classes attached to ordinary primary schools or special schools. There are 465 special classes catering for approximately 3,700 children. There are 108 special schools dedicated to children with special needs, serving the needs of some 6,600 children. These special schools employ 1,089 teachers and 940 full-time equivalent special needs assistants.

All special classes and schools operate significantly reduced pupil teacher ratios with, for instance, an eight to one ratio applying in special classes and special schools catering for children with moderate learning disabilities. Special rates of capitation apply to all children attending special classes and special schools. In addition, all children attending such classes or schools are entitled to avail of the Special School Transport Service where an escort accompanies them on bus services.

Special provision is made for addressing the educational needs of children with autism. Autistic children are now provided for in dedicated special classes with a maximum of 6 children. Each class has the support of a teacher and two special needs assistants. The DES has sanctioned the establishment of approximately 90 such classes and the number of classes is increasing on an ongoing basis in response to assessed needs. The DES has also allocated funding to the extension of education programmes through the month of July for pupils attending dedicated units for children with autism. This is in addition to funding a number of special pilot projects delivering a dedicated Applied Behavioural Analysis (ABA) model of response to children with autism. Finally, a special Task Force on Autism was established in November 2000 to review current approaches and make recommendations for the future development of education services for children on the autistic spectrum. The Task Force has presented its report to the Minister and its recommendations are currently being considered within the DES.

Learning Support/Remedial Teachers

The Learning Support Scheme provides assistance for primary school children experiencing learning difficulties, particularly in the core areas of literacy and numeracy. Although the development of this service was closely linked to the Disadvantaged Areas Scheme outlined above, all schools in need of this service now have access to it. Just short of 1,500 teacher posts are currently funded by the DES.

Education of Non-English Speaking Pupils

Ireland has seen an increasing number of non-English speaking immigrants in recent years. In order to cater for the children of such imigrants the DES has put in place supports for the teaching of English in primary schools. Schools with an enrolment of fourteen or more non-nationals with English language deficits are entitled to an additional temporary teacher, appointed on a year by year basis, to provide language support for such pupils. In the case of a school having twenty-eight or more non-English speaking non-nationals, the school is entitled to a second additional teacher. Where the number of eligible pupils is less than fourteen, grants are paid to enable the school authorities acquire the services of a suitable qualified person to teach these pupils English. Such grants are available to any school with between three and 13 relevant pupils. In the school year 2001/2002, approximately 144 posts were sanctioned at primary level and grant assistance in excess of €1.3 million was paid.

School Development Planning

Introduced in the school year 1999/2000, the School Development Planning Initiative aims to facilitate schools in devising and implementing strategies to achieve maximum school effectiveness. It is targeted specifically at schools with designated disadvantage status, including those participating in the Breaking the Cycle initiative. At the core of this initiative is the belief that combating educational disadvantage involves a 'whole school' philosophy that encompasses the home-school-community approach. A National Co-ordinator, 4 Regional Co-ordinators and 40 facilitators assist schools in implementing this initiative.

The first phase of the School Development Planning Initiative involved 1,775 schools, of which 442 were designated as disadvantaged. The budget for 1999/2000 was €616,775 which was increased to €1.3 million in 2001. From September 2001 this initiative was further extended to all schools within the education system. Schools catering for disadvantaged communities will continue to receive special assistance. Guidelines for Primary Schools on Developing a School Plan have been developed and circulated by the DES.

National Educational Psychological Service (NEPS)

The National Educational Psychological Service (NEPS) Agency was established in September 1999 as an executive Agency of the DES. This has the delegated authority to develop and provide an educational psychological service to all students in primary and post-primary schools and in certain other centres supported by the DES, with particular attention paid to those with special educational needs. Currently, some 86 psychologists are employed in the NEPS. Following a recruitment drive in 2001, just over 60 additional psychologists have been placed on a panel and will join the NEPS by the end of 2002. In addition, pending the expansion of NEPS to all schools, the Minister for Education and Science approved the commissioning of psychological assessments from private practitioners. All of these psychologists work with individual pupils with specific problems, identify learning difficulties, and work with teachers on how to address these. In short, they aim to co-ordinate the efforts of teachers, parents and school management in meeting the needs of the pupils.

The NEPS service is now available to approximately 1,950 primary schools serving over 200,000 pupils. NEPS psychologists are located throughout the country in 10 regions corresponding to the Health Board regions in order to facilitate co-operation with the psychological services provided by the Health Boards and Voluntary Bodies. It is intended that there will be offices in approximately 20 locations around the country so that each team of psychologists will be located near the schools it serves. In 2002, €11.26m has been committed to the provision of the NEPS.

School Completion Programme

Incorporating the elements of best practice from previous pilot schemes (specifically the 8-15 Year Old Early School Leaver Initiative (ESLI) and the Stay-in-School Retention Initiative at Second Level (SSRI)), the School Completion Programme focuses on young people between the ages of 4 and 18 years who are educationally disadvantaged and at risk of leaving school early. The Programme is designed to address the issues of both concentrated and regionally dispersed disadvantage. This Programme is now considered a key component of the DES strategy to address early school leaving. The Programme is operating in 273 primary schools and the second-level schools to which pupils progress.

Annex 5

DEPARTMENTAL RESPONSIBILITY FOR ECEC

Department	Principal Responsibility	ECEC Sections/Structures	Principal ECEC Programmes
Dept. of Education and Science	□ Funding, managing and inspection of pre-school education measures for children at risk of educational disadvantage □ Funding, managing and inspection of infant classes in primary schools. □ Funding, managing and inspection of specific measures to address educational disadvantage in primary schools.	□ Primary Section(s) □ Inspectorate □ Social Inclusion Unit Educational Disadvantaged Committee □ Educational Disadvantaged Forum □ Centre for Early Childhood Development and Education	□ Rutland Street Project □ Early Start □ Pre-Schools for Traveller Children □ Provision in Training / Further Education Centres □ Primary School Infant Classes, including Special Classes for Children with Learning Disabilities □ Special Schools for Children with Learning Disabilities □ Giving Children and Even Break □ Designated Disadvantaged Areas Scheme □ Support Teacher Scheme □ Home/School/Community Liaison Scheme □ Learning Support/Resource Teachers □ English language provision for Non-Nationals □ School Development Planning □ National Educational Psychology Scheme
Dept. of Justice, Equality and Law Reform	□ Chair and Co-ordinate the National Childcare Strategy □ Management and Administration of the Equal Opportunities Childcare Programme	□ Equality Division □ Childcare Directorate □ Inter-Departmental and Inter-Agency Synergies Group □ National Co-ordinating Childcare Committee □ Certifying Bodies Sub-Group □ Advisory Sub-Group □ Working Group on School Age Children □ County Childcare Committees	□ Equal Opportunities Childcare Programme

Department	Principal Responsibility	ECEC Sections/Structures	Principal ECEC Programmes
Dept. of Health	☐ Regulation of pre-school facilities ☐ Provision of childcare places for children from families under stress ☐ Delivery of the National Children's Strategy	☐ Child Care Policy Unit ☐ Child Care Legislation Unit ☐ National Children's Office	☐ No specific programmes
Dept. of Social and Family Affairs	☐ Payment of child-related income support	☐ None	☐ Child Benefit ☐ Back-to-School Clothing and Footwear Scheme
Dept. of the Environment and Local Government	☐ Regulation of the planning and building of childcare facilities	☐ None	☐ Programme of building new public and social housing ☐ Programme of renovation of existing public and social housing
Dept. of Enterprise, Trade and Employment	☐ Provision of childcare support to those on labour market programmes	☐ None	☐ Community Employment Programme
Dept. of Community, Rural and Gaeltacht Affairs	☐ Provision of support under the Local Development Social Inclusion Programme	☐ None	☐ Local Development Social Inclusion Programme ☐ RAPID ☐ CLAR

Annex 6

QNHS MODULE ON CHILDCARE ARRANGEMENTS

Childcare Module[17]

Introduction

A Childcare module for inclusion on the QNHS in Q4 2002 has been designed by the Central Statistics Office, at the behest of the Department of Justice, Equality and Law Reform in association with a Liaison Group of interested parties drawn from the public and private sectors (See LG members below). The module is designed to supply data on the use, cost and availability of childcare throughout the State.

Members of Liaison Group
Department of Justice, Equality and Law Reform
National Voluntary Childcare Organisations
Area Development Management Ltd.
Irish Congress of Trade Unions
Department of Health and Children
Central Statistics Office

The Department of Enterprise, Trade and Employment also provided some comment on an early draft of the questionnaire.

Technical Notes

For the purposes of this survey *Childcare* is to be distinguished from babysitting, and arrangements made during holiday periods and days off unless referred to explicitly by the questions. It refers to arrangements that are usually made by parents/guardians on a regular weekly basis during the working day (e.g. Mon-Fri 7am – 7pm… or whatever constitutes same) for the care of their children.

NOTE: The usual care of children by their parents in the early morning or early evening should not be coded as 'Children minded at home by me / partner'. This response option is aimed at capturing parents who mind their children for a period *during* what might be considered typical working hours. For example, a parent collecting a child at noon or mid-afternoon from a childcare facility and looking after him/her for the rest of the day would be considered to be minding him/her at home for the purposes of this survey, whereas someone collecting a child after work at 6pm would not.

A distinction is made in this questionnaire between children attending primary school and younger children who are not attending primary school.

---

[17] Please note that all coding references have been removed here for ease of presentation.

SHOW CARD: The list of childcare options will not apply in all cases, but the list is the same for all questions to facilitate responses.

[Q1.]

Will someone answer the childcare questions now?

1. Yes
2. No

Note: The Childcare module is only to be asked in households where there are children currently attending primary school or younger non-school going children

[Q2.]

[List of persons in household]
Please enter the line number of the person who is answering the Childcare module.
Note: The person who answers this module must be 15 or over and a guardian of the child in question

---

Interviewer Note: This refers to any child(ren) within the household for whom the responding adult has direct responsibility

---

How many children currently attending primary school do you have?   ___

[Q3.]

How many younger non-school going children do you have?   ___

[Q4.]

[Q1.] Can I ask you which of the following types of childcare you usually avail of on a weekly basis for your <u>school-going</u> child(ren), outside of holiday periods and weekends? [SHOW CARD]

1. Children minded at home by me
2. Children minded at home by partner
3. Unpaid relative (or family friend) in your own home
4. Unpaid relative (or family friend) in his/her own home
5. Paid relative (or family friend) in your own home
6. Paid relative (or family friend) in his/her own home
7. Paid childminder in your own home
8. Paid childminder in his/her own home
9. Au Pair / Nanny
10. Work-based crèche
11. Naíonra
12. Crèche / Nursery
13. Montessori school
14. Playgroup / pre-school / sessional childcare
15. Homework club
16. After-school activity-based facility
17. Special needs facility
18. Activity Camps (Sports, recreation, arts & crafts etc.)
19. Other

Allow multiple responses

> **Interviewer Notes:**
> 1. **Childcare for school-going children is the care they receive on weekdays outside of school hours in the morning and/or afternoon.**
> 2. **Parents caring for children directly before they go to school should not be recorded here, but if the child is cared for by someone else before they go to school then this should be recorded here.**
> 3. **Relatives/friends are considered to be paid if this is a regular arrangement, and not an ad hoc or occasional payment.**

[Q1.]

You have just mentioned some different types of childcare that you use. Can you say which is the main type of childcare that you use for your <u>school-going</u> child(ren)? [SHOW CARD]

1. Children minded at home by me
2. Children minded at home by partner
3. Unpaid relative (or family friend) in your own home
4. Unpaid relative (or family friend) in his/her own home
5. Paid relative (or family friend) in your own home
6. Paid relative (or family friend) in his/her own home
7. Paid childminder in your own home
8. Paid childminder in his/her own home
9. Au Pair / Nanny
10. Work-based crèche
11. Naíonra
12. Crèche / Nursery
13. Montessori school
14. Playgroup / pre-school / sessional childcare
15. Homework club
16. After-school activity-based facility
17. Special needs facility
18. Activity Camps (Sports, recreation, arts & crafts etc.)
19. Other

Multiple responses not allowed

> **Interviewer Note: Use time spent in care and then if necessary cost of care to determine primary source of care.**

Do you use the same types of childcare arrangements during the holidays for you school-going children?

1. Yes
2. No
3. Not applicable (Child just started school)

[Q2.]

> **Interviewer Note: The holiday period refers to primary school holidays and runs from July to August only.**

What type of childcare arrangements did you make during the school holiday period? [SHOW CARD]

[Q3.]

1. Children minded at home by me
2. Children minded at home by partner
3. Unpaid relative (or family friend) in your own home
4. Unpaid relative (or family friend) in his/her own home
5. Paid relative (or family friend) in your own home
6. Paid relative (or family friend) in his/her own home
7. Paid childminder in your own home
8. Paid childminder in his/her own home
9. Au Pair / Nanny
10. Work-based crèche
11. Naíonra
12. Crèche / Nursery
13. Montessori school
14. Playgroup / pre-school / sessional childcare
15. Homework club
16. After-school activity-based facility
17. Special needs facility
18. Activity Camps (Sports, recreation, arts & crafts etc.)
19. Other

Allow multiple responses

[Q4.]

Can I ask you which of the following childcare arrangements you usually avail of on a weekly basis for your non school-going child(ren), outside of holiday periods and weekends (or days off)? [SHOW CARD]

1. Children minded at home by me
2. Children minded at home by partner
3. Unpaid relative (or family friend) in your own home
4. Unpaid relative (or family friend) in his/her own home
5. Paid relative (or family friend) in your own home
6. Paid relative (or family friend) in his/her own home
7. Paid childminder in your own home
8. Paid childminder in his/her own home
9. Au Pair / Nanny
10. Work-based crèche
11. Naíonra
12. Crèche / Nursery
13. Montessori school
14. Playgroup / pre-school / sessional childcare
15. Homework club
16. After-school activity-based facility
17. Special needs facility
18. Activity Camps (Sports, recreation, arts & crafts etc.)
19. Other

Allow multiple responses

Interviewer Notes:
1. **Childcare for non school-going children is the care they receive on weekdays during the working day. For example, if a child is in childcare and returns to the care of their parents at the end of the working day, this is considered to be the termination of childcare for that day.**
2. **Parents caring for children directly before they go to childcare should not be recorded here, but if the child is cared for by someone else before they go to the childcare facility then this should be recorded here.**
3. **Relatives/friends are considered to be paid if this is a regular arrangement, and not an ad hoc or occasional payment.**

[Q5.]

You have just mentioned some different types of childcare that you use. Can you say which is the main type of childcare that you use for your non school-going child(ren)? [SHOW CARD]

1. Children minded at home by me
2. Children minded at home by partner
3. Unpaid relative (or family friend) in your own home
4. Unpaid relative (or family friend) in his/her own home
5. Paid relative (or family friend) in your own home
6. Paid relative (or family friend) in his/her own home
7. Paid childminder in your own home
8. Paid childminder in his/her own home
9. Au Pair / Nanny
10. Work-based crèche
11. Naíonra
12. Crèche / Nursery
13. Montessori school
14. Playgroup / pre-school / sessional childcare
15. Homework club
16. After-school activity-based facility
17. Special needs facility
18. Activity Camps (Sports, recreation, arts & crafts etc.)
19. Other

Multiple responses not allowed

Interviewer Note: Use time spent in care and then cost of care to determine primary source of care.

[Q6.]

Can I ask you how many hours per week your school-going child(ren) spend(s) in your <u>main</u> form of childcare? _____

Note: If more than one child enter the total number of hours spent by all children in childcare

Example: If two school-going children spend 40 hours each per week in a Crèche then record 80 hours for HOURPRIM.

[Q7.]

You previously indicated that your childcare arrangements differ during the school holidays. Can I ask you how many hours childcare per week for your school-going child(ren) did you avail of during the school holiday period? _____

Note: If more than one child enter the total number of hours spent by all children in childcare

Example: If two school-going children spend 30 hours each per week in a *Activity Camp* then record 60 hours for HOLHOURS.

[Q8.]

Can I ask you how many hours per week your non school-going child(ren) spend(s) in your <u>main</u> form of childcare? _____

Note: If more than one child enter the total number of hours spent by all children in childcare

Example: If three non school-going children spend 20 hours each per week with a paid childminder then record 60 hours for HOURPREP.

[Q9.]

What is your <u>main</u> reason for using childcare on a weekly basis?

1. To enable me to work
2. To enable me to avail of education/training
3. To provide a social/educational outlet for the child
4. Other

Multiple responses not allowed

[Q10.]

*You have indicated that you avail of childcare outside of your home. Is **this** childcare within walking distance of your home?*

1. Yes
2. No, I have to travel with my child(ren)
3. No, but child is collected from my home by someone else.
4. Yes and No (some care within walking distance and some care not within walking distance)

[Q11.]

How far from your home is this childcare facility? (miles) _____

Note: If more than one childcare facility, record total distance travelled to reach last childcare facility.

Note: Record distance <u>from</u> home only

[Q12.]

How long does it usually take to get there?

_____ (mins)

Note: If more than one childcare facility, record total time travelled to reach last childcare facility.

Note: Record time taken to drop children off (e.g. in the morning) <u>not</u> collect them

---

[Q13.]

How do you usually take your child(ren) to your childcare facility?

1. Car
2. Bus
3. Train
4. Minibus
5. Taxi
6. Car Pool

Multiple responses not allowed

Interviewer Notes for Travel questions:
1. The travel questions refer to the entire journey from someone's home to their childcare facility, for <u>both</u> their schoolgoing and non-schoolgoing children.
2. If someone has a number of stops at different childcare facilities, for children of different ages then record the <u>total distance travelled up to the last facility</u>.
3. Distance and time questions generally refer to the <u>one-way</u> journey from home to childcare <u>in the morning.</u>
4. Enter distances less than 1 mile as '1' and all other distances to the nearest mile
5. In a situation where the child is collected by someone else and taken out of the home to childcare enter 3 for TRAVCARE

Can I ask you, how much in total does your [MAIN TYPE OF CARE FOR SCHOOL GOING CHILDREN] typically cost you per week for your school going children?

EUR _ _ _   **[Q14.]**

Interviewer Notes:
1. The cost of childcare is for the main source of childcare identified in MAINCAR1.
2. The cost of care is the total cost for all children in this type of care per week.
   E.g Two children in a crèche @ €150 each = €300 per week for COSTPRIM
3. Cost should be recorded against all care types where money is paid on a regular basis, regardless of whether this is a formal or informal arrangement

---

Can I ask you, how much in total does your [MAIN TYPE OF CARE FOR NON-SCHOOL GOING CHILDREN] typically cost you per week for your non-school going children?

EUR _ _ _   **[Q15.]**

> **Interviewer Notes:**
> 1. **The cost of childcare is for the main source of childcare identified in MAINCAR2.**
> 2. **The cost of care is the total cost for all children in this type of care per week.**
>   **E.g Two children in a crèche @ €150 each = €300 per week for COSTPREP**
> 3. **Cost should be recorded against all care types where money is paid on a regular basis, regardless of whether this is a formal or informal arrangement**

[Q16.]

Is there any type of childcare arrangement that you would like to use for your school-going children but which you are not using at the moment?

1. Yes
2. No

> *Note:* If respondent has previously indicated multiple options that are used for the care of the school-going child and now indicates that they would prefer to adopt one of the same options exclusively then accept this as a response to NEEDTYP1
>
> *Example:* The respondent might mind the children themselves at home and also use a crèche, but that as an 'alternative' arrangement they would prefer to look after their children at home full-time themselves. In this case accept 'Children minded at home by me' as a response to NEEDTYP1, even though this is not strictly speaking an 'alternative' form of childcare.

[Q17.]

What type of alternative arrangement would you like to use for your school-going children? [SHOW CARD]

1. Children minded at home by me
2. Children minded at home by partner
3. Unpaid relative (or family friend) in your own home
4. Unpaid relative (or family friend) in his/her own home
5. Paid relative (or family friend) in your own home
6. Paid relative (or family friend) in his/her own home
7. Paid childminder in your own home
8. Paid childminder in his/her own home
9. Au Pair / Nanny
10. Work-based crèche
11. Naíonra
12. Crèche / Nursery
13. Montessori school
14. Playgroup / pre-school / sessional childcare
15. Homework club
16. After-school activity-based facility
17. Special needs facility
18. Activity Camps (Sports, recreation, arts & crafts etc.)
19. Other

*Multiple responses **not** allowed*

[Q18.]

Why are you not using this type of care arrangement for your school-going children at the moment?

1. Cost \ Financial reasons
2. Waiting List
3. Transport difficulties
4. Service not available
5. Lack of age appropriate services
6. Lack of suitable hours or flexible hours
7. Lack of culturally appropriate services
8. Lack of quality programme/service
9. Lack of informal care by someone known and trusted
10. Other

Multiple responses allowed

[Q19.]

Is there any type of childcare arrangement that you would like to use for your non school-going children but which you are not using at the moment?

1. Yes
2. No

> *Note:* If respondent has previously indicated multiple options that are used for the care of the non school-going child and now indicates that they would prefer to adopt one of the same options exclusively then accept this as a response to NEEDTYP2
>
> *Example:* The respondent might mind the children themselves at home and also use a crèche, but that as an 'alternative' arrangement they would prefer to look after their children at home full-time themselves. In this case accept 'Children minded at home by me' as a response to NEEDTYP2, even though this is not strictly speaking an 'alternative' form of childcare.

[Q20.]

[Q21.]

What are the main reasons for not using this type of care arrangement for your non school-going children at the moment?

1. Cost \ Financial reasons
2. Waiting List
3. Transport difficulties
4. Service not available
5. Lack of age appropriate services
6. Lack of suitable hours or flexible hours
7. Lack of culturally appropriate services
8. Lack of quality programme/service
9. Lack of informal care by someone known and trusted
10. Other

Multiple responses allowed

Ask of all respondents to this module

In the last 12 months has a lack of childcare arrangements for your child(ren) ever....[SHOW CARD]

1. ...prevented you looking for a job?
2. ...made you turn down a job?
3. ...made you quit a job?
4. ...stopped you changing the hours you regularly work?
5. ...stopped you from taking a study or training course
6. ...made you quit a study or training course
7. ...restricted the number of hours you regularly study
8. ...made you change the hours you regularly work
9. ...made you change the hours you regularly do study or training
10. None of the above

Multiple responses allowed

Interviewer Note: 'Educational Arrangements' do not include primary education

What type of alternative arrangement would you like to use for your non school-going children?
[SHOW CARD]

1. Children minded at home by me
2. Children minded at home by partner
3. Unpaid relative (or family friend) in your own home
4. Unpaid relative (or family friend) in his/her own home
5. Paid relative (or family friend) in your own home
6. Paid relative (or family friend) in his/her own home
7. Paid childminder in your own home
8. Paid childminder in his/her own home
9. Au Pair / Nanny
10. Work-based crèche
11. Naíonra
12. Crèche / Nursery
13. Montessori school
14. Playgroup / pre-school / sessional childcare
15. Homework club
16. After-school activity-based facility
17. Special needs facility
18. Activity Camps (Sports, recreation, arts & crafts etc.)
19. Other

Multiple responses not allowed

The Department of Education and Science would like to thank all those in the Civil Service Crèche in the Department of Education and Science Campus, Dublin, who kindly consented to having their photographs taken and used in this document. The Department was kindly granted parental/guardian permission in the case of the children in the photographs aged between 0-6.

Electronic copies of the Irish Background Report and OECD Country Note are available for download from the Department of Education and Science website at www.education.ie and the OECD website at www.oecd.org/edu/earlychildhood